Dark Psychology, Body Language and Emotional Manipulation

How to Recognize the Dark Side of People and to Manipulate the Crowd to Increase Your Social Influence

Blake Reyes

TABLE OF CONTENTS

Dark Psychology & Manipulation

Body Language

Emotional Manipulation

DARK PSYCHOLOGY & MANIPULATION

Lead Your Psychological Warfare by
Discovering Advanced Secrets
to Manipulate Your Clients & Relationships
Using Emotional Intelligence, NLP and the
Art of Persuasion

Blake Reyes

INTRODUCTION

Congratulations on reading Manipulation and thank you for doing so.

There are plenty of books on this subject on the market, thanks again for choosing this one! Every effort was made to ensure it is full of as much useful information as possible, and please enjoy it!

Any wise driver will let one of his passengers take the steering wheel in his place to drive and go wherever he wants. That is what happens if we are threatened or tampered with. Someone harshly or insidiously wants one to perceive, behave, work, or love as he or she wishes. The manipulator invades and thus destroys an essential part of our lives by using techniques that paralyze us, confuse us, or prevent us from reacting. One day, you're happy and confident, and on another day, irritable, nervous, or apathetic, you might think life is so unfair. You may start crying, feel guilty or crumble, and feel depressed and lonely. But that doesn't affect anything that makes you nervous or frustrated.

For instance, when one is overworked or, on the contrary, when one is fearful of being robbed of work, it is common to encounter moments of discouragement. In the face of defeat, confrontation, disease, or an otherwise bleak condition, it is equally acceptable to lose faith or to have doubts. Sometimes, however, these symptoms often stem directly from some form of manipulation.

Some manipulations are so twisted or concealed that the victim is often unable to identify the cause. She falsely blames herself and discusses how she may be accountable for what has happened to her. Other manipulations, on the other hand, are simple, but we also realize we won't be able to fight the manipulator and eventually give in to him.

This book is intended for all those who are tired of walking on their feet, sufficient to be too kind or too nice, sufficient to be sad enough to be able to live their lives. The book is, in essence, about those sick of being abused.

CHAPTER 1

WHAT'S DARK PSYCHOLOGY?

Dark psychology can be understood as the study of the human condition based on the psychological nature of the different types of people who take advantage of others. The fact is that every human being has the potential to victimize other people or other living creatures. However, due to social norms, human consciousness, and other factors, most humans tend to contain their dark impulses and avoid acting for every impulse they have. However, there is a small percentage of the population who cannot control their darkest instincts and harm others in apparent unimaginable ways.

What kinds of traits do malicious and exploitative people have? What are the psychological impulses that lead people to act contrary to social norms and harmful to others?

With Dark Manipulation and Psychology, you will learn to know if the people in your life have bad intentions towards you. Or if new love interests that seem charming at first are likely to turn into selfish and manipulative people once you've let them into your life.

The dark triad describes the interaction of the following personality traits:

- Narcissism
- Machiavellianism
- Psychopathy

- Sadism

All of these personality traits can be found in different forms of people. The commonality is that they are all selfish and elevate their good to that of others. The three types differ mainly in their motivation. The narcissist is about admiration, the Machiavellist wants to achieve his goals, and the psychopath is about the action itself.

A certainly increased amount of this is a success factor in our society (managers). However, over-expression is devastating and has destructive effects on the environment, which even companies cannot wish for. In the meantime, the term "dark triad" is also used in the assessment and selection of executives in companies in the "toolbox."

The concept of the dark triad was coined by the Canadian psychologists DL Paulhus and KM Williams in 2002.

CHAPTER 2

THE 4 DARK PSYCHOLOGY TRAITS

People can be classified according to their personality, and the traits that compose it. Different types are differentiated by their way of acting, self-confidence, and the way they deal with others.

Just as there are different ways of being, there are also personality disorders that are dangerous and harmful. In this section, we look at the four types of personalities that science calls dark.

Narcissist

Narcissist or being narcissistic is related to narcissism. According to Greek myth, Narcissus was a beautiful young man full of pride, vanity, and callousness who despised all the maidens and others who fell in love with him.

Nemesis, the goddess of revenge, punished Narcissus. When he saw himself reflected in the water of a fountain, he fell in love with his image. He ended up consuming himself in his unsatisfied desire since he was unable to separate himself from his image, which faded every time he tried to reach out to kiss her. Narcissus, saddened by pain, commits suicide with his sword and, after dying, falls into the water and transforms into the flower that bears his name, the narcissus, a beautiful smelly but sterile flower of fruit.

Therefore, a narcissist is a person who feels excessive admiration for himself, for his physical appearance and his gifts or qualities. A narcissist par excellence is an egocentric person, and proud to the point of not being able to live a happy life. This is because he shows a sharp egoism and a disregard for the needs and feelings of others which can become perverse.

We all know quite a number of narcissists, people who stand out for having high self-esteem and little or no concern for the feelings of others since they will always take first place.

Narcissists are always thirsty for attention and show that they are superior to the rest. Perhaps at first glance, you do not realize that you are before one, but by knowing him better, you will be able to distinguish the features of this type of dark and toxic personality.

Machiavellian

Nicolas Machiavelli (1469 - 1527), political philosopher and author of The Prince, wrote, "A wise ruler must never keep the faith when doing so would be against his interests," and "a prince is never short of good reasons to break his or her promise".

In Machiavelli's opinion, honesty, and all the other virtues are dispensable if deception, betrayal, and force are more convenient. In short, people in positions of power must choose to be Machiavellian, even if that is not their usual style of leadership.

In Psychology, Machiavellianism refers to a personality type that does not choose to be but simply is a master of manipulation. The Machiavellian people do not have to read The Prince to acquire the knack for deception.

They are biased as far as temperament is concerned to be calculating, confusing, and deceitful. In essence, amoral, that other people use as steppingstones to reach their goals. From a Machiavellian perspective, if we allow ourselves to be used, we probably deserve it. PT Barnum expresses this way of thinking when he said, "There's a sucker born every minute."

The "end justifies the means"; that phrase from Nicolas Machiavelli perfectly illustrates the type of personality that bears his name. The main characteristic of Machiavellians is that they are excellent manipulators and very intelligent.

A Machiavellian knows no limits when it comes to getting what he wants and easily convinces others to act even illegally to fulfill what he or she wants, just as if they were disposable pawns in a game of chess.

A Machiavellian person is more difficult to detect than narcissists, and they are often more dangerous.

Psychopaths and Sociopaths

The most dangerous of all dark personalities, psychopathy is an important part of serial killers who are characterized by their cruelty and not only lack of empathy with the suffering of the other, but also enjoying the evil of others.

Although psychopaths and sociopaths fall under the same dark personality classification, psychopaths will sooner or later act as it is very difficult for them to control their impulses. The sociopath is more intelligent, and although he enjoys the suffering of others and causing pain, he goes more for the psychological rather than the physical side.

A sociopath can live perfectly well without committing crimes, making them more difficult to detect. In addition to dark personalities, both are considered a harmful disorder which makes them dangerous to society since there is no way to reform them, and they are born that way.

Sadism

Sadism is a word derived from Donatien Alphonse François de Sade, better known as Marquis de Sade. He is a writer and philosopher who was born in 1740 and died in 1814 and who remained in history for narrating various paraphilia and vices.

The notion of sadism, in this way, is used to name the perversion that consists of obtaining pleasure from exercising cruelty on another living being. The sadist, therefore, enjoys causing pain to others.

The usual thing is to associate sadism with the sexual: the sadist gets excited and gets pleasure from humiliating the other or generating some type of damage. Arousal is produced by humiliation and harm, and not by the sexual practice itself.

Tying the sexual victim with handcuffs, spanking, or locking them are some of the behaviors of sadism. The sadist can also resort to rape his victim.

In addition to all the above, we cannot ignore other important aspects related to sadism, such as these:

- It becomes negative paraphilia as long as it produces damage to third parties.

- According to the studies carried out in this regard, it has been shown that, after studying the brain of sadists, they have a very high sensitivity regarding what other people's pain is. Specifically, this conclusion has been reached after checking how the amygdala, which processes reactions to what emotions are, was activated in the brains of these individuals when they saw images of suffering and violence.

- Many people practice sadism with their partners because both parties agree and accept it. However, they must take certain precautions and impose certain limits since some actions can directly be very dangerous and cause serious damage to one of them, including death. We are referring to actions such as beating, raping, electric shock, torture, trying to strangle her...

- It is considered that there are a series of disorders that are associated with a certain frequency to what sadism is. We are referring to depressive disorder, antisocial disorder, narcissistic personality disorder... In some cases, we can establish that, in addition to all the above, it can also be associated with the consumption of psychoactive substances.

Beyond sexuality, sadism is understood as an act of cruelty that a person performs for his delight. A man who mistreats a dog for fun will be incurring sadism: his action generates joy from the suffering of the animal.

He who kidnaps a child, locks him in a room without light or ventilation, denies him food, and only enters the room to hit his victim, will also be developing behavior of great sadism since he does not seek anything other than to take pleasure in the abuse he exercises.

We could consider sadism to be one of the characteristics of the dark personalities that we have already named, but a sadist takes his actions much further than in other cases.

The sadist enjoys causing the greatest amount of suffering in the other and at a higher level of cruelty. Their difference from psychopaths is that sadists are not impulsive.

People with a sadistic personality seek to belong to groups or have jobs where they have power over the application of control and violence over others. A sadist is dangerous, but sadly he knows how to hide his actions as well.

It is not necessary to gather all the traits to belong to one of these groups of dark personalities since, like everything in human psychology, it is presented in different degrees and not all reach the most harmful and dangerous level.

CHAPTER 3

DO WE ALL HAVE A DARK SIDE?

If, to save one of your loved ones, you had to accept that the heart of a serial killer be grafted in him, would you accept? Before you answer, think about it... Can we say that a serial killer has "a heart"?

In all cases, from a medical and scientific point of view, this is impossible since organ donations are made anonymously, and neither the name of the donor nor the name of the recipient is given to families.

The question we should ask ourselves is rather: what makes a person coldly attack someone for the simple "pleasure" of killing?

Are we the product of evil?

According to Catharism (a religious movement which appeared in the 12th century, spread mainly in the South of France and inspired by ancient Eastern pagan beliefs based on the doctrine of Good and Evil), Man is the product of Evil.

Believers relied so much on this doctrine that they even condemned procreation because they believed that having children would only cause more Evil.

One might think that it is sordid to say that Man is the product of Evil. However, unfortunately, it is enough to look out the window, read the newspapers, or listen to the radio to see that Man is well capable of evil acts.

This, therefore, demonstrates that humanity has a predisposition to Evil and that if we allow ourselves to be guided by our instincts, the consequences would be catastrophic.

The society helps calm our aggressive instincts

Whether we like it or not, society is an entity made up of all of us. This society functions as a kind of mechanism which needs to follow rules to function.

For example, we depend on the behavior of our neighbor and his way of life. If he doesn't put the music on loud at night, then there will be no conflicts.

My colleague depends on my good humor at work. So, I don't upset his testosterone levels, and nothing trivial will affect the rest of his day. On the contrary, if the day goes wrong, he insults me, I tell others, the news spreads, and a negative atmosphere prevails at work.

And if serotonin calms the worst urges, testosterone can cause many men to commit the worst acts ever imagined, and that from a very small spark. Don't be that spark!

Fight our inner monster

It is certain that we will never be able to forget that blood flows in our veins. And that, very often, when all is well, there is always someone to play with our nerves (an insult a little too much, an attack on our physical integrity, etc.), but that doesn't mean it will always be like that.

Indeed, the balance and the good harmony of society will sometimes be altered by our fault (whether we realize it or not).

According to a recent study by the University of Beihang (China), anger is the emotion that spreads the most when it is exposed to social networks, unlike cheerful and kind SMSs.

All the more reason to continue following the example of our neighbor, but also to remember that our worst enemy guides our instinct: ourselves.

Fighting against your "inner self" is a daily task. At times, you will feel overwhelmed by this "inner self" when he shows the fangs, and brings out his anger, sarcasm, and venom.

This struggle will affect not only your relationship with others but also your desires to be happy and to live. This monster in us can be terrible. Some people don't even know it, but if it does surface one day, it will terrorize more than one.

Thus, people who know their "inner monster" must be more careful, more tolerant, calmer, and sometimes lenient enough not to wake him up and threaten the lives of innocent people in their path.

If only no one had an inner monster! However, the fact of living with him makes us aware of who we are, of our limits and our faults, and curiously of all the positive things to share.

Because even if, according to Ernest Hemingway, "It is always in innocence that real evil takes its source," Martin Luther King Jr. reminds us that, "To resolve human conflicts, we must exclude violence, and the spirit of revenge. The solution is love."

Explore the dark side to regain self-discipline

Were you hateful? Do you do things you're afraid to be thinking about? Is there a part of you that you want to do away with? Would you want to say things you hate? We do have a dark side we are afraid to face.

The cynical side is not stolen from good thoughts, sacrifices, stuff we have to do. He is marginalized, and since he is struggling for a way out, he grows in you.

Exploring the dark side will make it easier for you to take control of yourself, understand yourself, and learn about yourself.

What does your dark side feed on?

The dark side of your mind feeds on misery and self-destruction, all that you deny of yourself, and those desires that you cannot manage to materialize.

Your unmet needs produce negative emotions that fuel them. If you fail to get these needs out, these negative emotions will grow in you, and this will bring out the worst in you.

Therefore, you will think it is the real version of yourself or even that it is the only one.

Not feeding this dark part of your mind is the only way to control it.

However, there are many things you know you should not do because they are bad for you, but you do them anyway.

You know you shouldn't smoke, that you shouldn't abuse fats, that you shouldn't quarrel with your spouse or children, that you shouldn't fuel unnecessary arguments, but you do it anyway.

Your dark side is not made of good intentions, either. Either you take action and stop feeding it, or it will take control of you.

What does your dark side need?

To stop feeding your dark side, you must know what it likes the most. It feeds on negative psychological attachments. These feelings that make you cling forcefully to a previous state that creates anxiety in you.

These negative attachments keep you from feeling secure, balanced, and strong. They are expressed through rejection, humiliation, betrayal, feelings of worthlessness, and failure.

All of this negativity feeds the darkest part of your psyche, which grows with your negative feelings, thoughts, and behaviors, with the influence that toxic people have had on you and still have on you in your life.

Whenever something negative happens in your life or whenever you remember something that you do not like, your dark side gives pride of place, and it clings to this negativity as if there was no other option.

Consequently, more misery, self-destruction, and negativity arise to fuel it.

How to face the dark side?

The solution to dealing with the dark side of the mind is to train it consciously. There are things that we cannot eliminate but that we can face by familiarizing ourselves with them.

The biggest challenge is to sink into your mind and bring to light everything that is hidden there.

The dark side hides much more than unfulfilled desires, frustrated aspirations, or broken illusions. But each person is the only one who can immerse themselves and explore their dark side.

Whenever negativity arises in your life, and you feel that something dark is trying to gain power over you, it is then that you must discover why, without being ashamed.

You have to accept that there is an obscure side of your mind that is present and that it cannot go up in smoke simply because you will repress it. The repression will make him even stronger, and he will explode with more force as soon as he has the opportunity. Be brave, be honest with yourself, and try to release that negativity from yourself.

Meditation and coaching can help. Through art, you can also get the worst out of your mind, by channeling that negativity.

By knowing what your dark side is hiding, you will be able to regain control of your life and learn to manage negativity better so that it does not dominate you.

CHAPTER 4

THE DARK SIDE OF JOKER

The Joker is a film by Todd Philips. He received a golden lion in Venice, with a fabulous Joaquin Phoenix, while generating serious concerns when he left in front of the violence he could inspire. So much so that, in certain American cities, security measures have been decreed to avoid any violence.

This film shows us a clownish character who has never been so close to our lives and who highlights all the fragility of our society. In this film, it is no longer a metaphorical scenario, but a parable which is part of a raw representation of our lives and in a city, Gotham city, which no longer has anything imaginary. Gotham City only becomes the cinematic name for New York.

The joker is a clownish character who ignores all rules, transforming all organizations into a house of cards that can collapse at any moment, and plunging any society into immense insecurity.

We often make an amalgam between the character of the clown and that of the Joker, sometimes at the origin of a coulrophobia (the fear of clowns).

The clown, and in particular, the Augustus, is a theatrical character who says yes to everything to play everything. He plays with contexts to live his life in an emotional emergency and to explore his fragility. For him, a pen can be a spaceship, a gun, a car, etc. It is a philosophy of life

31

that allows him, by his posture, to free himself from the constraints to live on the margins of society. His driving force is curiosity, play, and emotion. The clown is a benevolent cabin, a four-year-old child who wants, in the end, to be loved. We laugh at him out of tenderness and not out of mockery. He does not live against anyone, and he has no claim, he is in the moment. He offers a poetic vision of life by opening other possibilities by recombining what is presented to him: Buffo or Harpo by the Marx Brothers are fine examples. Slava, one of the biggest living clowns, has a house in Seine et Marne, called the Moulin Jaune, that you could visit from time to time. In his garden, you can find cucumber trees that show the sweet poetic madness that the clown offers. The clown is a show character who only has a raison d'être within the show or as the king's jester.

The Joker is the dark side of the force. It is the antithesis of our society as black is the antithesis of white, the emptiness of the full. It can only exist because a certain society exists. Besides, in the movie Dark Knight, he says that he only exists because Batman exists. The more Batman tries to find solutions to save the world, the more the Joker exists in his shadow.

Our society connects men using rules, dogmas, laws, or morals. All these elements are stories that are told as so well written by Yuval Noah Harari in his book "Sapiens." For example, banknotes have only the value that we give them through the monetary history that we tell. In the past, this story was supported by shells, quantities of wheat, etc. For this story to work, it requires that all men believe the same story. Yuval Noah Harari shows that the stories that men tell themselves since the dawn of time are only a theater and that at any time, another theater can replace it. Likewise, in the games of mistreatment between an executioner and a slave, the two characters must exist. It is enough that one no longer wants to take on the role of the slave so that very often, the executioner no longer exists. The film "Yes but" by Yves Lavandier highlights all of these plays in particular within the families who organize our suffering.

The Joker gives himself the freedom not to believe in these stories, which makes the societal cement, and he allows himself to emancipate it all the more since the law of men has treated him badly, to express his impulses and his desires brutally. In Todd Philips' Joker story, Arthur Fleck, before becoming the Joker, was beaten, humiliated and kicked out for free by men, without doing anything to deserve it. The Joker is born from men's violence and its absurdity.

Depending on the context, in our city, the Joker is:

- A psychopath who ignores the rules in a world so complicated and empty of meaning. This world is a wonderful playground for psychopaths.
- Or a desperate person in an increasingly Kafkaesque world where nothing has any meaning and is not fair.
- Or an idiot who does not see the world from his only perspective, incapable of empathy but

capable of violence because he acts from his point of view and that if he thinks it... that means that he is right.

Do you know someone around you who can pin down at any time, and trigger violence? Are not those responsible for the killings in the USA in colleges or cinemas, Jokers?

Our society has become violent because it has lost the sense of what connects men. We are mired in incomprehensible and absurd administrative procedures. At the same time, it has gone astray in consumerism, which studies human beings and in the exploitation of men in savage capitalism for the benefit of belief in growth. Associated with this violence is a spiritual void described by the philosopher Bernard Stiegler. He says that after the Second World War, western society discarded religious spirituality and political spirituality with the retreat from communist ideas. She was unable to replace these binders with the construction of secular spirituality. In our post-modern society, we are freer but more and more alone.

We are more and more equal and, therefore, more and more replaceable. Isn't the crisis of yellow vests the emergence of little jokers who no longer want to participate in this theater? What brought them together was above all to be against, but not the construction of a common project. They never knew how to regroup in a political movement or to stand for election. Moreover, the Yellow Vests of the beginning were excluded, threatened, or even beaten. Within the same roundabout, we could find people who said that we were not helping the poor enough and others who complained that we are helping people too much.

Doesn't the political system by its violence create Jokers? What do people think of people like Trump, Hollande, Mélenchon, Marine Le Pen...? Aren't they the clowns of our political system? Jacques Chirac is dead, and one has the impression that one has forgotten the bandit that he was at the town hall of Paris. That he was at the origin of the acrobats who beat up the students in 86 and the origin of the death of Malik Oussekine. He spoke about the noise and the smell of certain French, to retain only the sympathetic dimension which sported his puppet of Guignols.

Are Daesh and Osama Bin Laden not the Jokers of our international political games?

In business, how many leaders who go from one business to another are not Jokers at the origin of mistreatment, harassment, and never exposed because they never stay long enough to be spotted?

The Joker is an anti-social psychopath who has no spirituality or morality. He is a disturbing character who shows us the fragility of our society. It is the black hole of our social universe. At any time, it can engulf us.

It is by rediscovering meaning and living together that we will best protect ourselves from it. How to do it without falling into a new religious proposal? Indeed, religion has long participated in social cohesion, and this is what the extremists are trying to replay today by offering us other hells.

The strength of Todd Philips' film is to show us that at any moment, anyone can become an uncontrollable Joker, spreading terror just as Arthur Fleck became the Joker without doing anything.

Todd Philips' film is fascinating, but it sends back the black reflection of what we are, opening the door to all dangers.

CHAPTER 5

MASKS PEOPLE WEAR

The face is not usually a very common philosophical topic. Following the Cartesian route, the rationalist tradition of disembodied thought has prevailed, pure abstraction without anchorage in the situated and concrete corporality. At least until the phenomenological and existential currents up to Marcel, Sartre and especially, Merleau-Ponty began to underline precisely that fleshiness, the idea that we are a bodily, mundane, embodied, situated, temporal consciousness. All of them spoke of the "meaning" of the body, not the face in particular. Although as expressive as the body as a whole can be (and it is), it is the face space where that expressiveness and that "meaning" are condensed in the most obvious way. It had to be another philosopher, Emmanuel Levinas, already in the 1960s and fed by these phenomenological sources, as a metaphysical and ethical category.

As valuable and fascinating as the Levinasian contribution is, this chapter takes another point of departure. On the one hand, he understands the face as what makes each human being unique, what makes him or her valuable being visible, what humanism and ethical individualism have praised. On the other hand, he understands the notion of a mask as that which hides that singularity. That which refers it to a type, to a category, to a stereotype, and that which runs the risk of being interchangeable, erasable, expendable. As Jacques Aumont summarizes, "the mask, which tends towards a constructed, social, differentiable, communicating or symbolic typology, makes it difficult to perceive the individual, innate, personal, expressive, projective, empathetic face." Seeing the other in their social masks is a frequent phenomenon, without a doubt, but seeing only the social mask or the type, regardless of the unique, personal face, is the root of any type of racist, classist, sexist, ethnic attitude, etc.: Look at a person and see a Muslim, a gypsy, see a Jew's nose, dark skin, rather than instead of a singular face.

This contrast between the individual and unique face and a generic type of face also approximates the opposition of Levinas (1999) between Infinity and Totality. Here, he advocates conceiving the face of the other as Infinite, as a singularity irreducible to concepts, in such a way that it cannot be subsumed at any time in one's idea of him. That is, by any task of objectification or thematization that makes him dissolve in some form of Totality (always bordering on totalitarianism). Levinas is aware that all the mechanisms of perception that we normally summarize under the notion of vision are conceptualized; they are an immense classification machine. In other words, we generally see faces as masks, veiled, and distorted by our cultural glasses, by the prejudices and stereotypes that serve as cognitive shortcuts to quickly typify others. They are ways of dressing the face, while the true face which, according to him, "expresses itself," "means" and "visits" us would be naked.

Now, having established these similarities, we will not follow here the development of the metaphysical ethics elaborated by Levinas. But we will focus on some aspects of the face/mask contrast, especially in a modern individualistic society, where the recognition of ourselves and the rest is made from our recognition as an individual, beyond our membership in a group, a category or a social role. In this context, the singularity of the face calls the singularity of man as an individual, so that the individual distinction makes a face value, the clearest exponent of our unique and singular being. Of course, the mechanisms of the typification, of the construction of masks, continue to work here. They would even have been reinforced in the mass society, according to some authors, which leads them to announce a "defeat of the face" that we will analyze and discuss.

For this reflection, we will start from two stories that are rarely related: the revealing etymological history that unites the notions of a person, face and mask, and the history of modern and contemporary portrait that exposes a sample of equally revealing 'faces' and 'masks.' We will end in our contemporary society, trying to compose a balance of the two faces, the dresses, and the nudes, that are offered to us within the empire of the image.

1. Face, mask, person: an etymological history

Face, mask, role, character, person... All those words are intertwined if we stick to their etymological past. Let's start with the classical Greek term for face, prosopon, which means "what is before the eyes of others." The most curious thing for us is that the same word designates, at the same time, the mask (both stage and ritual mask). That is, the Greeks lacked a specific term to differentiate the face of the mask linguistically, nor did they distinguish it iconographically (in the representations of the Greek vessels, there is no demarcation between face and mask).

To understand this indistinction of prosopon, we must bear in mind that the Greek culture is, like all traditional cultures, a culture of face to face, of exteriority, a culture of honor and shame. The individual is apprehended from the outside, by the gaze that the others direct at him. So, the face is a mirror of the soul, yes, but always for others. It does not have in itself the function of hiding; on the contrary, it is the revealer of emotions, of thoughts, of character. Despite Plato's attempts to warn about the confusions between being and appearance, the truth is that in Greek culture, this opposition is not palpable; on the contrary, appearance reveals being, it is Being. And the self-knowledge that is produced necessarily goes through that reciprocity. In essence, they are the side mirrors of others, of the like, where one sees and perceives himself with a certain identity. In fact, in the classical Greek texts, prosopon appears almost always referring to another your face or his face. The first-person, reflexive cases are exceptional.

So, the prosopon the mask is the same as the prosopon face: it is what is presented to the view of others, the visible, in front of the covered parts of the body. Prosopon is always related to looking, with what is looked at, and can, in turn, return the look. That is why, for example, they did not call the face/mask of the Gorgon that way, because crossing their gaze, according to Greek mythology, was equivalent to death. And since it could not be looked at, it only had ahead, it did not prosopon. The same was true of the face of the dead since visual reciprocity with them was no longer possible. Well, in that community of face to face, the face does not conceal, or hide anything. On the contrary, it is a translucent film that expresses, reveals, and projects an outward-oriented personality. The same happens with the mask, which is more difficult for us to understand since we associate it with concealment; for the Greeks, on the other hand, it has mainly a function of representation and identification. Why?

The mask that was worn did not hide the face that was covered. It deleted and replaced it. Under the dramatic mask, the actor's face, replaced by sight, is abolished, and his own identity, the one that revealed his face, gives way to that of the character he embodies. He is now Hécuba, Príamo, or Paris.

Similarly, the faithful who participated in a ritual masquerade had no face other than their mask, and no other personality during the time of the ceremony.

To begin to think of the face and the mask as two different realities that can even be opposed, it is first necessary to distinguish them linguistically. This is what the Romans do: they call the mask a person, and the face is called a vultus or facies. The autonomy of these two notions (which is also expressed in Roman iconography) would allow them to

41

think of them together or separately from now on, as we do. According to an old etymological tradition, the person would derive from the verb personal (that is, "to sound through something"); according to this explanation, the person would originally be the theatrical mask equipped with a special device that raised the voice of the actor. However, current etymologists prefer to root it in the Etruscan term phersu, which also meant 'mask.'

Person designates at the same time the mask and the role so that it does not indicate in the first place an individuality—whose representation would not need a mask—but a type, a timeless reality. But we found this semantic extension already in Greek, where, from s. II a. of C., prosopon comes to designate also a character (in Polibio, Plutarco, etc.). Also, prosopon begins to designate the "grammatical person": they would be something like "the faces put into play by the relation of the discourse" (the three Prosopis or persons of the discourse: me, you, him).

It is interesting to relate the notion of prosopon or person as 'character,' or 'role' with the evolution of the term character in Greek. Its initial meaning of "stamp," "mark," or "imprint" visible, acquired, between the 4th and 3rd centuries BC. C., the sense of "distinctive characteristic" and, finally, that of "moral character." According to the original sense, the character would be what is incised in the flesh or the soul in the manner of permanent writing. The 'characters' or dramatic personae find a symbolic representation in the masks of tragedy. These masks froze the expression in some emblematic configurations, recognizable even from a distance, thus creating an authentic expressive typology of the face. The rough man is depicted as having dark skin, eyes, and hair, with thick lips and warty nose; the noble-souled characters, the heroes, were generally represented with large-nosed "Greek-style" masks, etc. The playwright developed the physiognomic characterization, typifying the characters to the extreme. Each mask, as opposed to the others, emphasizing some somatic brand: "a kind of visual translation of what the encyclopedia of the time defined, on a semantic level, as a character, a passion, a vice or a virtue."

Thus, the character, the role referred to social types, not specifically to singular individuals. For a person to come to designate a new moral category, to end up meaning "every individual of the human species," many factors still have to come together: Roman law, Stoic ethics, and Christian theology have to be developed. It is the latter two that have brought us the notion of a moral person, while Roman law has left us that of a legal person.

Indeed, with Roman law, all free men of Rome become Roman citizens, all acquire a civilian person. That is, they become 'persons' capable of owning property, signing contracts, pleading, acquiring rights and contracting obligations, etc. In its fullness, only the paterfamilias will have that status. Of course, "servus non-habet personam" ("the slave has no person"), since the slave does not have ancestors and rights.

Similarly, Greek jurisconsults call aprosoponslaves, who cannot represent themselves and are 'characterized' by their masters. Roman law, on the other hand, underlines the sense of role or social role given to "person": "homo plures personas substituent" ("man sustains many people"), which meant that "persona" is, in some way, a concept superimposed on that of man, since he is capable of 'supporting' or representing different functions, of putting on different 'masks': acting now as a father, now as a merchant, now as a faithful of such religion, etc.

But the notion of a person still lacks a clear metaphysical foundation, and Christianity is going to give it to them. As Mauss insists, it is then that "the transition from the notion of person, the man clothed in a state, to the notion of man without further ado, to that of the human person" will take place. That step begins to take shape, curiously, in the context of controversies about the unity of the Holy Trinity. In the S. IV, at the Council of Nicaea, theologians argue—in Greek—about the nature of Christ, and establish that he has a double nature (divine and human), but that he only has one person, who is unique and indivisible. Now the most commonly used Greek term for 'person' was not prosopon, but hypostasis, something like 'substrate' or 'substance.' A few decades later, Saint Augustine developed the notion of person, so that it could be used to refer to both the Trinity (the "three persons") and human beings. Furthermore, the idea of a person in Saint Augustine loses the relative exteriority that continued to characterize it, to focus decisively on.

But it was especially Boethius, in the 6th century, who gave the notion of person a definition that had a great following: "persona est naturae rationalis individua substantia" ("the person is an individual substance of a rational nature"). Person "would thus become the name of all the individuals of the human species, constituted by reason. So, the term, which had nothing metaphysical in origin, enters the vocabulary of ontology and ends up signifying the ultimate principle of individuation. In essence, it is what singularizes each one of us, and what singularizes us not accidentally, but substantially, what subsists or remains beyond of the changes and transformations. The Christian tradition spreads this notion that, later, is enriched by numerous thinkers with the notes of individuality, equality, immortality, dignity, transcendence, etc. Among them, Kant stands out, who highlights the ethical sense of "person" as "an end in itself, 'who' has dignity and no price."

One of the most striking things about this etymological trajectory is that we move from an exterior and relational vision of the face/person to an interior and substantial one. As we have seen, in Greek antiquity, the prosopon, either as a face, as a mask or as a character, is something that is offered in the sight of others, which only makes sense in face to face. Also, in person, as a dramatic mask, as a character or as a role, or even in the legal entity in the vision of the first Roman law, we perceive that exteriority, that meaning only comprehensible in human intercommunication. In all these cases, these are representations and identifications that require alter egos, interlocutors, or spectators. On the other hand, in the metaphysical vision of the person as a substance (as the same word indicates, what underlies, what is below and is invariable, antithetical to our idea of the mask, as something superimposed, that hides), it is given an intrinsic value, a dignity of its own, independent of its social roles, its particular manifestations, and its masks.

In modern and contemporary times, however, many have reformulated a relational concept of the person, leaving aside its definition as "rational substance." Some of these modern trends take up the theatrical origin of a person to underline the character of human existence as Theatrum Mundi and of individuals as actors who play different roles in different situations, in the courts of justice or the rituals of society, no less than on stage. According to this perspective, our face would be a mask, or better, support for multiple masks, this is depending on the occasion, as in the sociological theory of E. Goffman, who popularizes the dramaturgical model to explain social interactions in which the self would not be more than a hanger where the dresses hang from the role she plays.

Thus, we would have gone from perceiving the masks as other faces, like the Greeks, to perceiving (in some cases) the faces as social masks. And now in the triple sense of representation, identification, and dissimulation. When we say of someone who "does not show his true face," who hides behind "a mask of hypocrisy," etc., we are not speaking as a Greek or as a member of a small community where communication is entirely face-to-face, where interiority and subjectivity have not been developed. We are speaking as modern subjects who perceive the face, at the same time, as a place of being and appearance, as a place of essence and pretense, of truth itself and artifice. The place where the soul shows and disguises itself. They wear masks, which they perceive according to those masks...

2. Portraits: the modern subject in their unique faces

Well, a brief history of modern portraiture leads us to explore, from another perspective, the complexity of the face/mask contrast that we have glimpsed in etymological history. What we generally call portraiture is the "representation of a subject" as it has developed— especially pictorially—from the 15th century to the 19th-century avant-garde. The idea that comes to mind first is that of similarity, that of mimesis: that the portrait constitutes a kind of frozen mirror, a permanent and generally improved reflection of the portrayed subject. For this reason, Peter Burke proposed this definition: "that representation of a person that his friends and relatives can recognize as his image, which includes from caricature at one end to idealization at the other."

But, in truth, a subject can be 'represented' without the exact physical resemblance being determining; whoever is presented with his name, or with a whole series of attributes or symbols corresponding to his position or his social position, already makes him 'recognizable.' In general, it is for this reason that we also speak of ancient, pre-Renaissance 'portraits' (and also of avant-garde and contemporary 'portraits'): because it is sufficient that the portrait evokes the person, even if it is not similar too. Furthermore, the essence of the portrait is not usually solely in its fidelity to the physical features of the model. In some way, he is expected to capture the interior of the model, the liveliness of his spirit, his truth. Every portrait thus aspires, in some way, to be a portrait of the soul or interiority. What is meant by interior or soul, here, is the question, because it is not the same as creating something singular (as "face") or as something typified (as "mask"), as a source of subjectivity or as the axis of social position. For this reason, the history of portraiture cannot but reflect the evolution of man's place in society, the evolution of ideas related to his value and dignity. And it is fascinating to observe how this evolution is reflected in how man represents his image, his face.

It will be, therefore, the breeding ground of humanism of the Renaissance, the transition from a theocentric vision of life to an anthropocentric one, that makes the realistic figuration of people begin to be considered important and desirable. We will have to wait for the Flemish portrait of the 15th century (starting with van Eyck and van der Weyden) and the Italian and German portrait of the 16th (Dürer, Holbein, da Vinci, Rafael, Titian) for this decisive transformation and consolidation of the genre to begin. Pay off. Until then, it is normal to represent schematic types, sanctified forms of popes and kings, without the actual physical marks of individuation. Since the Renaissance, the portrait will remain largely a portrait of the power of the privileged; He will continue to try to impress and claim the recognition of the high status of the portrayed in society. But little by little, the number of people claiming for themselves that predominant social role will begin to expand. Thus, together with the princes and members of the high clergy and nobility, from the 16th century onwards, the bourgeois were also portrayed: merchants, bankers, artisans, humanists, and artists, thus contributing to enhancing their reputation.

Until the 16th century, "the physiognomy was not yet a showcase of character, the interior of the individual human being did not yet appear, but the external image of his social identity." Until then, the usual practice was to 'portray' the social masks (the prose of the leading actors in civil and religious life); Now, little by little, the individual will appear, he will go "from the painting of the name to the painting of the self" (Martínez-Artero 82).

Indeed, it is almost commonplace—since Jacob Burckhardt already did it in The Culture of the Renaissance in Italy (1860)—to relate the emergence of portraiture at that time with the birth of individualism in the West. The existence of "galleries of illustrious men" to exalt the facts of outstanding individuals points to links between the rise of portraiture and what Burckhardt called "the modern sense of fame." It is also striking that the rise of self-portrait coincided with that of autobiography, or even that the literary portrait began to develop. That is, the narrative description of the faces of the characters, something unusual up to that time. Undoubtedly, the idea of an unrepeatable individual fits well with the increasing demands of plausibility, of the search for similarity. The life of painters Vasari's (1586) is symptomatic in this regard since he shows concern for the portraits and biographies of artists, two evident signs of the birth of individualism, of the appreciation of one's autonomy and individual freedom.

Although this individualistic society was only emerging timidly in the Renaissance, and the social role continued to be decisive (as corroborated, in turn, by multiple portraits), the truth is that this vision points to the most striking aspect developed by Western art. And especially for the portrait: its fundamental direction towards the subjective gaze and the singularizing and unique face of the portrayed subject. That this direction was not at all evident "is demonstrated by the fact that this has not happened in the other figurative traditions matured on this planet. Neither in Chinese, lyrical, and naturalistic painting. Nor in Byzantine, hieratic, transcendent, and spiritualist painting. Not in the Islamic, abstract, and irreverent. Not in the Indian, plastic, and decorative. Not in the African, synthetic, and in its formalistic way." According to Caroli, that approach of western figurative painting to individual psychology would constitute its main "originality."

The search for similarity that is an indication of this developing awareness of one's singularity did not exclude, in any case, a more or less high degree of idealization. As he explained, at the end of the 16th century, Lomazzo, in his painting treatise, "the painter, in the portrait, must always emphasize the dignity and greatness of the person and repress the imperfection of nature." Thus, many of the works of the Italian Renaissance—think of those of Botticelli, for example—as well as of the French painting of the time, looked like images of statues, rather than of flesh and blood beings: sharp figures, with smooth surfaces, wrinkle-free, perfectly silhouetted. In Flemish painting, which continues the line opened by Van Eyck, on the other hand, that is less common. Influenced, undoubtedly, due to the Protestant Reformation, the portrait began to function as a mirror that reflected the truth without beautifying touches; the figures begin to expose themselves to a clean face, often with all their ugliness. This is especially clear in the German, Flemish, and Dutch Mannerist and Baroque portraits.

Thus, psychological deepening reaches a more than remarkable virtuosity in baroque portraiture, with artists such as Velázquez, Rembrandt, Franz Hals, Rubens, or Goya. The portrait becomes more stark and realistic, often without idealization. Also, the list of people portrayed will be increasing, since although the portraits of royalty and bourgeois portraits commissioned are the main ones, some painters will start to notice the others, in the miserable, the mentally disabled, the humble. Note that until then they had not appeared reflected in the artistic works. But "as it had already happened with the painting of the mad, elderly, blind, crippled and physically handicapped in general who had invaded the art of Brueghel and Bosco, the Renaissance images of the poor did not constitute true individual portraits, but rather showed almost caricatural human types, charged in addition to moral connotations." They were the representation of vice and unreason rather than that of a specific dispossessed. But, already at the beginning of the 17th century, Annibale Carracci, Caravaggio, Ribera, Murillo, and other artists made what appear to be true portraits of humble figures such as a water carrier or a street egg fryer. However, yes, they were still anonymous figures, their names did not matter. In the 18th century, painters like Traversi, Chardin, or Goya also portrayed other humble figures, not as mere funny characters or as representatives of any profession, but as individuals with their faces. The neoclassical and romantic portraits (David, Ingres, Delacroix), however, once again gave greater idealization to the characters, to the detriment of the realism achieved in the previous stages. Velázquez painted the dwarves and jesters of the court, endowing them with considerable dignity.

With the avant-garde begins the decline of what until then had been understood as a portrait. From 1900, mimesis, the resemblance of the artistic portrait with the one portrayed is no longer a defining criterion. So in these cases, we can only continue to speak of portraits in an approximate sense, by evocation. Therefore, there is talk of the decline of the portrait genre. Now, we must be clear that we are speaking from an artistic point of view since from a sociological point of view, one cannot speak of failure, but the absolute triumph of the portrait after the invention of photography and the subsequent techniques of visual reproduction. It cannot be denied that quantitatively speaking, this is the contemporary, the true golden age of portraiture. So much that, we can speak of the "triumph-defeat", "of the contemporary portrait": the portrait as a mere document overwhelmingly triumphs; portrait as art suffers a defeat or, at least, an overwhelming transformation.

Photography, invented by Niepce in 1824, and perfected by Daguerre, came into the public domain from 1839. By then the commissioned pictorial portrait had already reached, since the second half of the 18th century, an unprecedented extension. The demand to have your image, the awareness of your uniqueness, will only grow dramatically in increasingly larger layers of society through the photographic technique, a more comfortable, economical, and exact way of accessing reproduction. The invention of photography coincides, moreover, with an industrial revolution that profoundly modifies local belongings, provokes the rural exodus, accentuates urbanization, and arouses in more and more people the feeling of their individuality. It is significant. Seeing oneself, therefore, becomes a constant, almost banal fact. And more with photography, which supposes, even more, this "advent of myself as another," in the words of Roland Barthes: "[t] he curious that the disorder (of civilization) that this new act announces has not been thought of." Without a doubt, already at the end of the XIX century, we are in the process of democratizing individualism.

Precisely, owning your image, a singularizing portrait, ceases to be a distinctive sign, a privilege of a few. The opportunity to have a face that provides anyone with a photographic portrait irritates more than one, beginning with Baudelaire, who—in 1859—writes: "[a] filthy society rushes like a single Narcissus to contemplate his trivial image on the metal. A few years earlier, in 1850, Melville had already expressed his deep displeasure: "the portrait, instead of immortalizing the genius as it did before, will do little more than show a fool to the taste of fashion. And when everyone disposes of his portrait, the true distinction will undoubtedly consist of having none."

Melville, undoubtedly, failed to understand what was coming: the absolute impossibility in a world like ours of staying aniconic, of withdrawing from having multiple portraits and images of ourselves. Sooner rather than later, in the second half of the 19th century, various proposals began to be considered to establish an identification document with a photograph of the face. At the Universal Exposition of 1867, in Paris, they were already used as access letters. Later, the police authorities and the state administration would soon develop the idea. In essence, each individual should be identified using an identification letter with his full name and a photograph of his face. A photograph from the front, with the most neutral expression possible, without a smile or gesture of any kind. Exactly like the photo of the National Identity Document that every five or ten years, we must renew, face resting on a light background. Made mechanically, often without human mediation (in a practical photo booth), we tend to call it a "passport photo" since we are no longer even aware that we are making a portrait. A portrait that long ago became mandatory as an identifying document.

Painting could hardly rival the hyperrealism that photography produced. It is clear that what was once interpreted as stiff competition, was also liberating for the plastic arts. The obsession with mimesis, with perfect resemblance, decreased—that was what photography was for; the artist was free to explore abstract pathways, beyond the formal imitation of nature. This, as it could not be otherwise, greatly affected the most symbolic of genres: the portrait.

3. The "defeat of the face"?

Thus, begins with the avant-gardes—and especially with cubism—a process of disfigurement, of progressive loss of the degree of similarity that scandalized the spectators of its time. Suddenly, the portrayed subject tends to blur, to merge with the other elements of the environment. Without meatiness, the faces flatten out, become uniform. For Galienne and Pierre Francastel, it is no longer possible to speak of portraiture, given that—following the path inaugurated by Cézanne—artists consider subjects as fragments of reality among other fragments:

It is a portrait when an artist simply uses the features of a face to introduce them into a composition that in his eyes has another purpose. But only when, in his spirit, the real purpose of the work done is to interest us by the figure of the model by itself. Now, at no time does a Matisse or a Picasso try to link us to the personality of their model. They only insert him into the complex network of his imaginary activities.

In other words:

Fauves and Cubists use man as they do with a bottle or a guitar, as a simple accident of the sensible, without granting any action to the individual character of this object. Nor to the possibility that it embodies something different from themselves.

However, it is not only in portraits, but in representations of heads and faces in general, where this disfigurement occurs, to such an extent that there are those, like Jacques Aumont, who speak of a "defeat of the face" that would be appreciated evidently in avant-garde painting. And which is later extended to all parts of the image society: from the cinema to the press, from advertising to television. This "defeat" would be expressed in factors such as the following:

Return of the type, of the generic: the individual only interests insofar as he belongs to a class or a group; the representation of the face excludes the expression or only includes it if it strengthens the type, the trans individual. The extent of roughness: [...] reaches everything, potentially—animals, masks, landscapes, parts of the face. The disintegration of the face, rejection of its unity: parts of the face cut out, glued, returned to the surface of the image. Infinite magnification, monstrosity of the size, or sometimes, on the contrary, lilliputization. All kinds of damages, erasures, tears.

Factors, all of them, that would abound in the same direction: "that of an abandonment of the reference to the face as an expressive concentrate of humanity. And even, in most cases, that of deliberate destruction of that reference.

All these movements of disfigurement, of decomposition, are perceived, indeed, in contemporary painting: exploded faces (by the cubism of Braque or Picasso); scattered faces (scattered all over the canvas, Duchamp; and more, with the collage technique); twisted faces (faces like rubber; or bitten, gnawed on the inside..., Francis Bacon); crossed out faces (scraped, as with wounds..., Atlan, Dubuffet, Lam); unfocused faces (frequent in the 70s in paintings made from photographs..., Gerhard Richter); enlarged faces (Warhol and pop art, Chuck Close...), etc.

We could easily increase the list since there are very many cases in which the subjectivity of the portrayed individual is diluted, turned into one more of an anonymous mass. As there are numerous portraits in which the face resembles a mask.

Consider the famous portrait of Gertrude Stein, painted by Picasso in 1906: his face is like a wood carving, smooth and impersonal without any accident. Even clearer in Matisse's 'portrait' of Ivonne Landsberg, strikingly similar to an African mask. Something similar occurs in portraits painted by Modigliani or Giacometti, for example. These "portraits" are hardly distinguishable from the other paintings of anonymous and depersonalized faces that appear in the paintings of avant-garde artists. Malevitch, for example, approaches the art of icons: his flat, geometric, austere pictures, present frontal characters, a kind of mannequins or robots, immobile, timeless, with empty faces and erased features. Sometimes he replaces the features of their faces with the hammer and sickle, other times with the Christian cross. Like the Chirico mannequins, those egg-shaped heads, which cannot look at, nor be distinguished by unique features, have no individualizing signs, they are just pawns of the mass, expressionless machines.

Many other artistic portraits of the twentieth century, driven by German expressionism (think of the portraits of Kirchner, Beckman, or Otto Dix), lose the calm of the factions at rest, as until then had been customary, and add the cry, the disfigurement conscious, violence. In addition to this, it is not often a single portrait (portrait-summary or portrait-biography) of the model, but a series of them, often following a process of metamorphosis. The classical genre of portraiture was based on the idea that the identity of an individual was fundamentally defined and more or less invariable so that the portraitist only had to capture it on the canvas, copying his features, the expression of his character. The artist of the 20th century, on the other hand, has often repeatedly portrayed the same person, each time with a different identity, refractory to the idea that only one of them is the 'true' one. In this sense, some conceive the genre of modern portraiture as "a sample of masks—as, perhaps, all portraits to a certain extent—but differently insofar as it is openly and consciously."

Also, Warhol's 'portraits' are more like a mask or a surface without substance, without any psychological background. As numerous critics have pointed out, rather than making portraits, Warhol fabricated icons transforming the identity of his characters—and himself—into a frozen and depersonalized image through the manipulation of photography. With that brilliant use of superficiality, he is considered the perfect illustrator of show society, the initiator of postmodern aesthetics that today floods advertising in all its forms everywhere.

In recent decades there has been talking of a boost in portraiture, especially after the revitalization of the English figurative school, with Hockney, Freud, and Bacon. Undoubtedly, a renewed attempt to unravel man is perceived in them. Lucian Freud, for example, develops the tendency (rare in the classical portrait era) to portray his characters (and himself) completely nude, making the whole body, and not just the face, a significant psychological canvas. Francis Bacon also focuses obsessively on the human bodies he 'portrays': beings always isolated, helpless, unstable, whose bodily and facial limits are unfinished, blurred, or rather twisted, outlined, deformed. It is in many of his works of contorted, mutilated bodies, with broken or half-erased faces, which express—and create in the viewer— considerable existential anguish. Cortés affirms: "[n] o there is no identity, only pain, animal rebellion, threatened mortal flesh" and he adds: "what Bacon tries to capture is the psyche of the subject, his determined efforts to get to know him and to define himself in an image that spreads and disperses as a response to the myth of the subject's unity.

The "myth of the unity of the subject": this is precisely what seems to have been blown to pieces in the contemporary era. Pedro Azara interprets that setback of the traditional portrait (which captured that whole subject so serenely and recognizably) as a consequence of the death (disappearance or concealment) of God, so often proclaimed since the 19th century. If we were made in his image and likeness, and now it no longer exists, it is that we no longer have a model, an image to resemble and according to which to compose our integrity. The disappearance of God also entails the loss of faith in the unity of being. So only appearances would remain: "the contemporary artist is content with masks because the model no longer exists (outside of the mask game)." This fact would not stop revealing the condition of the current man:

The image, which in ancient times had the purpose of rescuing the soul from death and oblivion, giving them back an imperishable body, has ended up being the exposition of the fleeting and terminal condition of contemporary man.

But it is in the multiform society of the image where the most fundamental manifestations of the "defeat of the face" would be appreciated, according to Jacques Aumont. The symptoms of this 'defeat' that we have seen in pictorial art, or those that Aumont himself analyzes in the recent history of cinema, would only be reflections of the more general decomposition of the face in the extra-artistic circulation of images. His thesis is that "representation has extremely affected his most beloved object": "by dint of being the target of gazes, the face is disfigured." If in the early days of the naturalistic representation of the face, it obeyed a humanistic impulse to dignify man (at least the one portrayed), the main effect of all this would be, therefore, the preeminence of the type of the generic face removed from its individuality. A process that began in the early days of the technical reproduction of the face, with the beginning of photography as a documentary medium that leaves the multiple faces that it depicts anonymous or, moreover, contributes to catalogs, typologies, supporting the administrative and police eagerness: "[t] he faces must be identical, not to the subject, but its definition. It is no longer the window of the soul, but a poster, a slogan, a label".

The largest means of diffusion of faces today, television, which constantly accompanies us with its talking busts and close-ups, and where we see millions of faces, near and far, nominated or unnamed, parades, produces an effect of massification, saturation. And, of course, being the basic pillar of the image society, it is full of advertising, direct—more usual—indirect, which refers to some typology, to a succession of stereotypical features and gestures. The faces of the advertising are faces that represent an ideal of the consumer/spectator, and that they are generally of an exalted perfection, fruit of the computer retouching. Bottomless perfection, like the mannequin in a shop window. And it is that in the face of the advertising, the portrait we will hardly find the soul. Rather, we will only be left with the suspicion that there is nothing underneath that beautiful facade. These stylized advertising portraits are nothing more than mock portraits, brand masks that they promote.

In short, has this overexploitation of the image and its technical reproduction means become today a factor of trivialization, depriving the face of the meaning and value that its first humanistic representations seemed to confer on it? Does the hypertrophy of the face or its representation suppose its loss, its silence, its dissolution in the mass?

4. Individualism and mass society: faces and masks

We have seen it in the brief tours of the etymological history and the history of the portrait. For a long time, the gregarious conformation of social groups did not raise concern in their contemporaries for their faces; the singularity was not valued, the feeling of autonomy or personal freedom was not associated with the social definition of the individual. It is in modernity when there is a sharper awareness of man's individuality, a 'feeling of self' that accompanies—and is enhanced by—the diffusion of the mirror and the portrait in which the singular similarity of the model is sought. The face is beginning to be valued as an element of individuation and an exponent of human dignity, in parallel with the rise of individualism in privileged social classes.

As the anthropologist and sociologist David Le Breton emphasizes:

The promotion of the individual on the scene of history is contemporary with the acute feeling that he has a body and the dignity of a face that reveals before everyone's eyes at the same time his humanity and his dissimilarity.

There is no doubt that—Le Breton continues—"the more importance society gives to individuality, the more the value of the face will increase [since, ultimately, the dignity of the individual implies that of the face]." In all this process, it seems clear, therefore, that the singularity of the face calls for the singularity of man as a person.

The visualization, objectification, and externalization of one's face and that of others is positive to promote that self-awareness. At the end of the 19th century, the proliferation of useful artifacts for this purpose (mirror, photography, pictorial portrait), coincided in the West with the industrialization, urbanization and growing uprooting of holistic societies, which extended to large layers of the population. That awareness of one's individuality. It was this same process that led to the mass society, and eminently urban society, with a multiplied population.

The first great thinkers of this modern technological metropolis—like Simmel, Spengler, Kracauer, Jünger, or Benjamin, however already warned about the dissolution of the modern individual in the massification and gregariousness of big cities. All of them alluded in one way or another to the neutralization of the face in the anonymity of the mass; they spoke of the masks that would populate that metropolitan universe, deprived of individual expressiveness. And it is that the development of medicine, hygiene, education, the migration of the population, contributed more and more to the homogenization of physical types and to erase in the constitution of the citizen middle classes the social origins inscribed on their faces. The identity of origin is blurred, the faces, the clothes, the gaits begin to homogenize, to become anonymous. The reflex mechanisms of imitation and collective emulation of behavior, as well as gestures and facial expressiveness, promote a massive resemblance.

The homogenization and typification of the forms would come hand in hand, of course, to standardization and neutralization of the characters, to a depersonalization of the individual. In several of the cited authors, the mass-man, cannon fodder of the totalitarianism of both signs, is already foreshadowed. The very dissolution or alienation of the face in much of 20th-century art—which we have reviewed—can also be understood as an attempt to capture that social reality: the face of crowds, an empty, interchangeable, anonymous stain. Or erased, devoid of singularity.

In that sense, all those thinkers already announced, in some way, the "defeat of the face" that we read in Jacques Aumont. That technician mass society and, later, that image and consumer society, would have privileged the technical-objective-conceptual gaze that transforms quality into quantity, the face into the number, into a stereotype; in short, in a mask. Role theories to explain our social interactions also start from this principle: they announce that in those interactions, we deal with masks— classes of masks, stereotypes, like those personae Roman—more than with singular, unique faces. The mask determines who I deal with and what my responses should be; that is, social learning would consist largely of assimilating the meanings of each tip or mask and displaying the associated responses.

Now, the affirmation that our social interaction is a relation of the masks already had its most radical prophet in Nietzsche. For him, the logic of the mask leads to the annihilation of the face: there is no longer an interiority to hide. It speaks of the multiplicity of masks that we wear so that the subject would be nothing but their masks, without behind, underneath, within each one of them there is an I, a character, an individual, but only another and another mask, up to Infinity. It would be, therefore, the realm of pure appearance devoid of essence.

But, if this were the case, the very idea of a mask would lose its meaning, since the idea of artificially concealing, hiding, or covering something remains implicit in it: a natural, authentic, substantial face against the variability of the mask. That is, the interior/exterior, essence/appearance dichotomies would no longer make sense as such. And this would suppose a metaphysical revolt that, however much one may think in the philosophical field, exceeds our common life.

In front of the spokesmen of the "defeat of the face," who affirm things such as that "the long historical period of full characters and real faces has passed, absorbed by the ageless history of empty masks and faces virtual, I am inclined to think that contemporary, urban, media and mass society offers both the opportunity to dignify and typify the face. That is to say, the contemporary society of the image reproduces to the end the two faces of which we spoke before: to a great extent, of course, the social mask, the typology, the assignment of individuals to some groups, according to stereotypes; but also the individual face, the one that was the protagonist of the classic portrait, the one to whom all the depths of the soul dance in the face, and the valuable singularity of their emotions and thoughts. The media preponderance of the first face may not be enough to talk about his "defeat," as Aumont does, nor to maintain that all interaction is a relationship between masks; no, at least, as long as the humanist causes that the other face continues to battle, while we continue to remember or enhance the meaning and value of that face.

CHAPTER 6

PSYCHOLOGICAL WARFARE

Psychological Warfare is used to influence the opinion, feelings, attitude, and behavior of the enemy. Be they people, allied and neutral nations, or the masses under the control of the enemy. So that they support the objectives and achievements of the mission entrusted by the one who employs it.

The Psychological War tries to change the mentality of the masses that support the enemy forces through propaganda systems.

Concept

Psychological warfare, or war without rifles, is the planned use of propaganda and psychological action aimed at directing behavior, in pursuit of objectives of social, political, or military control, without resorting to the use of weapons.

The concept of war of nerves is synonymous with the war of Zappa, terminology used by San Martín, one of the creators of modern psychological warfare.

Description

Psychological warfare consists of scaring the enemy to reduce their chances of success in combat. Psychological warfare seeks, on the one hand, to paralyze the adversary, to defeat him before he even enters to fight, and, on the other hand, to win the "minds and hearts" of the people he does not intend to demolish.

Experts on the matter believe that war is not won only in the trenches, or from the air with refined and sophisticated automated weapon systems. But it can be won, also, in the minds of people, both from their side and from the enemy.

Psychological Operations

Psychological Operations, also known by its acronym (OPSIC), is a term that replaced that of psychological warfare in 1957, (although currently used simultaneously). It has planned actions to transmit information and selective signals to foreign audiences and influence their emotions, motivations, reasoning and finally the behavior of governments, organizations, groups, and individuals.

It is the set of persuasive measures in times of peace or war that are designed to influence the attitudes, opinions, and behavior of the opposing forces, be they civilian or military, to achieve national objectives.

The purpose of psychological operations is aimed at inducing or reinforcing in foreign audiences the attitudes and behaviors favorable to the objectives from which they originated.

Psychological warfare and psychological operations have also been known under other terms, such as political warfare, to "win minds and hearts."

The term psychological warfare is used to "define any action that is practiced primarily by psychological methods to evoke a planned psychological reaction for other people."

Various techniques are used to carry it out, and it is aimed at influencing the value system, belief system, emotions, reasoning, or public behavior.

This is used to elicit confessions or affirm beneficial beliefs and actions to the person who has a particular intent. They are also paired with covert operations and false flag tactics.

This is often used to break enemy morale using techniques that help weaken state troops.

The targets can be governments, organizations, groups, and individuals, and not just soldiers. Civilians from foreign countries may also be the targets, with the use of new technologies and the media, to cause some effect on the government of that country.

Psychological warfare procedures

Among the various procedures, methods, and tactics used are:

1) The Letters

They are written in personal form or by pseudonyms, having as content facts and incidents manufactured to align, scandalize, create conflicts, and arouse suspicions within the adversary to seek a psychological transformation.

It is one of the best means of Psychological Warfare, due to its economic simplicity and the major effects it causes.

2) The Slogans

They are short words or phrases that are a vivid and powerful statement to express ideas, inspire the psychological requirements of the masses, and to seek the psychological transformation of adverse organizations. They must have the following characteristics:

- a) Current validity responding to the situation.
- b) It must tend towards the strengthening of the National Policy.
- c) Satisfy the wishes of the people; for example, the slogan of the French Revolution "Liberty or Death."
- d) It must stimulate and encourage; for example: "I'd rather die fighting than..." or "I have sacred duties...".
- e) They must attack the main target.

3) The Rumors

They are unfounded words that circulate in society, and that, applied in the Psychological War, have functions to discourage, confuse, and alter order within the opponent.

They take advantage of the psychological factors of the people, such as curiosity, suspicion, desire, horror, and hatred.

Nowadays

Currently, the "power of the media" is often a recurring theme, as they install debate topics, ideas about the "good and the bad," define presidential elections and impose certain consumptions.

However, very little is said about psychological warfare. Below, we present a brief historical review that is essential to understand how and why psychological warfare strategies continue to be applied today, which seem to continue the Cold War in the region.

In general, psychological warfare is understood as propaganda and deception through the media.

However, it is something much broader, considering the practices implemented since its institutionalization (early Cold War) until today. It includes and combines development assistance strategies (economic pressure and extortion), handling of information, propaganda, cultural and educational programs, student exchange, training of leaders and security, military intervention, and generally low intensity.

It is a war that combines political, economic, cultural, and military aspects. People's psychological factors, such as curiosity, suspicion, desire, horror, and hatred, are exploited.

Influential aspects for its application:

- Appropriate opportunities to spread rumors.
- It takes into account when major changes or disorders occur in the adverse ranks of the

organization, or possibilities of its occurrence arise.

- When there is discontent or confusion in the masses controlled by the adversaries.
- When their leaders have been captured or attacked, ideological disorientation reigning in their cadres.
- When they are in disorderly retreat or when the opponent is cornered.

Principles for creating rumors:

- Adapting to the desire or mental state of the target:

- Attack the opponent's weaknesses based on his mental state.
- Exaggerate minor facts and vice versa.
- They must be based on important, strange, and curious aspects that concern everyone.
- Using infiltrators to spread the rumors, so that their effects are greater.

Example of Psychological Warfare

One of the paradigmatic cases of this war is the one directed against the governments of Hugo Chávez and Nicolás Maduro in Venezuela. Although it seems simple and repeated, oil is undoubtedly the axis of this conflict, since it is a fundamental resource for the reproduction of the United States' military-industrial complex.

The Bible refers to various events that occurred in antiquity, and among them, the case of Gideon stands out.

This biblical character excluded 25,000 soldiers from the 40,000 he had to select to join his army. This happened because his men confessed, after a series of interrogations, that they were afraid of the fight. Thus, he made a psychological selection.

In the writings of the Chinese strategist Sun Tzu Sun, vestiges of psychological warfare can be found, as he set out to subjugate his enemy "without firing a shot."

Another example can be found in the famous boast of Genghis Khan (the Mongol general Temujin), who weakened the enemy's combative will by spreading rumors about the strength and ferocity of his army. His planning was simple, outstanding, and effective.

The concept of war of nerves is synonymous with the war of Zappa, which was the terminology used by San Martín (I), one of the creators of modern psychological warfare. San Martín, in Peru, exclusively managed the psychological factor. In this way, he was able to get to Lima without firing a single shot and with the loss of very few men, recorded in isolated and extremely minor combats.

During World War I, psychological operations became formal. Almost all the countries involved in the war used some form of propaganda in their strategies and tactics, and most of them organized specialized military units in that activity.

Propaganda activities began to be known as "psychological operations" or Psychological Warfare during World War II.

Application by the United States

As it is known, it was in the Korean War (1950 - 1953), where for the first time, the US in an orderly and planned manner used the Psychological War as part of the warlike actions in the military conflict.

It was a few years before that the US Armed Forces (1949) developed their first regulation for the conduct of psychological operations (OP).

To carry out the PO in Korea, an apparatus and a structure were created with the necessary units. In 1951, the US Department of Defense created a Psychological Warfare Directorate, also organizing the system for preparing cadres and specialists for the new structure created. For the year 1952, the Psychological Warfare Center was located in Fort Bragg (State of North Carolina).

At the end of the Korean War, the US Armed Forces unified the GP apparatus with that of the Special Forces, leaving the Psychological Operations (OP) as part of the Special Operations (OE).

As of this moment, there has been no attempted coup d'état, military intervention, "humanitarian" intervention, or US intervention, in which the Special Operations and Psychological Warfare Forces have not been involved.

Relationship with Informative War

In recent times the term Information Warfare has been positioning itself in the slang of analysts, who in one way or another study and investigate these processes. It is no secret to anyone that after the collapse of the socialist camp and the repositioning of parties and left movements in the world, the language of war prevails in the international arena. Yugoslavia, Afghanistan, Iraq, Sudan, Rwanda, Somalia, Libya, Haiti, [[Honduras], Bosnia-Herzegovina and currently Syria, Iran, North Korea, Venezuela and the never forgotten Cuba are examples of this.

Beyond the military context

This proposal is not exclusive to military confrontations, as it is also present in other types of situations. There are wars of this nature between couples undergoing separation, between companies vying for the same niche or between mass communication.

How to Enter Your Clients' Mind

Human behavior does not very much. This is why salespeople and marketing teams have been using psychology as a tool to get more customers, creating loyalty in them, and ultimately their most precious goal: sales. It is not necessary to give examples, and it is enough to pay a little attention to online advertisements, on television, in magazines, on the street, etc. If they use psychology, it is basically because it works.

Therefore, these techniques can also be applied to social networks. Let's see here some of the most successful strategies:

1. Giving gifts

Giving gifts to users generates a kind of commitment to correspond later with the company.

When you are given a gift, the first two thoughts that probably come to mind are: say thank you and "in return, I have to do something for this person."

The gifts you offer need not be extravagant or expensive. Here are some examples of attractive gifts that are easy to give and will encourage your users to become customers:

- A discount or extra money on next purchase in exchange for subscribing to your mailing list.
- An extension of an offer for a few days, in exchange for sharing images of the product or service received on social networks.
- A low-cost gift item included in a purchase order.

- A free electronic book.

2. Don't give too many options

If you give people too many options, they can feel overwhelmed.

Decision making is a stressful process and can harm a person's mood; The result may be that your potential customer "bounces" and leaves before making a purchase. Instead, creating a limited number of options makes choices easier to make. There may be cases where offering only a single option is the best thing to do.

3. Become an expert

Before consumers shop, they seek advice and opinions from others they feel they can trust. This could mean that they are going to check web pages to read people's opinions about products and services. Therefore, they will visit forums, sites, and social networks to investigate. Fortunately, you can also become their source of information. Create a blog with interesting articles and lots of useful content about your products and services and related topics that can add knowledge to your customers.

4. Add emotion to the equation

Every time you enter Facebook, you will see at least one video or meme that appeals to emotion or makes you feel passionate about something. This is because emotional content has a big impact. It is attractive, and people tend to like and share this type of post.

Does it mean that sharing self-improvement videos and pets in funny situations will increase your website traffic or that sales will go up? No, not necessarily; However, what should be clear is the importance of the emotional impact of your content.

5. Make your users feel part of your company

Social media marketing is about building relationships. Your goal is to create an online social circle that spans all social media platforms so that people want to become a part of that circle, and then make them feel valued when they arrive.

This can be done with simple actions like posting a thank you message when you are followed on Twitter or responding to comments on Facebook. You can even take this a step further by finding followers who are providing you with a great deal of engagement and reaching out to them as a hobby and sharing your content. This can not only build brand loyalty, it could even lead to them becoming ambassadors for your brand.

5 Techniques to Read People

Cold reading is an analytical and communication tool between individuals increasingly used in professional communication. It makes it possible to target the needs of a person quickly, to communicate effectively. It makes it possible to recover information on an individual by observing his reactions and an imprecise line of questioning to target his needs or his shortcomings quickly.

It is used by sellers, interrogators, psychologists, politicians, hypnotists, magicians, seers, mentalists, palmists, astrologers, sects, and scammers. Knowing your techniques well is an effective way to better communicate with your loved ones, but also a way to protect yourself from manipulation better.

1. Watch the signals of body language

Research has shown that words make up only 7% of how we communicate, while body language (55%) and tone of voice (30%) make up the rest.

Reading non-verbal language is divided into three main categories:

Observe the posture: When you read the posture of people, ask yourself the question: Do they have their heads held high, self-confidence? Or are they walking indecisively or curled up, a sign of low self-esteem? Do they strut around with a swollen chest, a sign of a big ego?

Observe the physical movements: Are they leaning towards us or not? In general, we lean towards those we love, and we move away from those we do not love. Do they cross their legs and arms? This often suggests a defensive attitude, anger, or self-protection. In what direction are the feet pointing? In general, the feet point towards the person with whom they are most comfortable. Are the hands hidden? When people put their hands under their knees, in their pockets or behind their back, it suggests that they are hiding something.

Observe the facial expression: Emotions can be engraved on our faces. The deep wrinkles in the face suggest excessive worry or thinking. Crow's feet are the smile lines of joy. Pursed lips signal anger, contempt, or bitterness. A tight jaw and gnashing of teeth are signs of tension.

To go further and become a real pro of nonverbal language, I highly recommend the training *The Basics of Nonverbal Communication* by Annabelle Boyer, an expert in non-verbal language and human behavior.

2. Pay attention to the appearance

We can learn a lot about people's personalities by simply looking at their appearance. Do they wear a power suit and well-waxed shoes, dressed for success, indicating ambition? Jeans and a T-shirt, indicating that they are comfortable with relaxation? A tight top with a neckline, indicating the desire to seduce? A pendant such as a cross or a Buddha indicating spiritual values?

3. Watch your breath

"I feel like I can't breathe, like I'm sinking."

How does he breathe? If someone is breathing from the chest, it means they are relaxed. If his breathing is shallow, then he is tense. If you want to know someone's mental state, watch their breath.

If his breathing is choppy, he will be more likely to be nervous, which means there is something he doesn't want you to know. The reason may be shyness, anxiety, or that he is hiding something from you. If someone is breathing from their stomach, then you know that their mental state is calm, which generally means that they are sincere.

4. Trust your intuition

Intuition is what your gut feels, not what your head says. It is non-verbal information that you perceive through sensations, rather than your logic. Listen to what your instincts tell you, especially during the first meetings.

Here are three techniques to better understand your intuition:

Your visceral reactions: Visceral reactions occur before you have had time to think and manifest yourself quickly since it is a primary biological reaction. They tell you whether you are comfortable or not, and they are your internal truth barometer, which lets you know if you can trust people.

Goosebumps: Goosebumps are a wonderful part of intuition that makes us understand that we are in resonance with the people who touch us, inspire us, or tell us something that touches a sensitive chord. Goosebumps also occur when you experience deja-vu, a recognition that you have known someone before, even if you have never met them.

Intuitive empathy: Sometimes, you can feel the physical symptoms and emotions of the people in your body, which is an intense form of empathy. Does my back hurt when it didn't hurt before? Am I depressed or upset after an uneventful meeting?

5. Perceive the emotional energy

Emotions are an amazing expression of our energy and the "vibe" we give off. We record them with our intuition. Having people you feel good with improves your mood and vitality. Other people are exhausting, you have low energy, and you instinctively want to get away.

Here are four techniques for reading emotional energy:

Feel the presence of people: It is the global energy that we emit, which does not necessarily correspond to words or behaviors. It is the emotional atmosphere that surrounds us like a cloud of rain or the sun. Do they have a friendly presence that attracts you? Where do you get goosebumps, making you back off?

Notice the feeling of a handshake, a hug, and a touch: We share our emotional energy through physical contact, much like an electric current. Ask yourself: is a handshake or hug warm, comfortable, confident? Or is it off-putting, so you want to retire?

Listen to the tone of the voice: The tone and volume of our voice can speak volumes about our emotions. Sound frequencies create vibrations. When you read people, notice how the tone of their voice affects you. Ask yourself: Is the tone of their voice soothing? Or is it abrasive, snarling, or whiny?

Look at people's eyes: Our eyes transmit powerful energy. Just as the brain has an electromagnetic signal that extends beyond the body, studies indicate that the eyes also project it. Take the time to observe people's eyes. Are they attentive? Sexy? Quiet? Bad guys? Angry?

CHAPTER 7

BEHAVIORAL AND CHARACTER TRAITS OF MANIPULATORS

Shake Your Confidence

Self-confidence means being sure of our worth, capacity and strength, regardless of the situation we are in. Someone who is self-confident has a good sense of self-worth and self-awareness expressing calmness, serenity, and self-confidence. Trust in oneself is also related to possessing some expertise and abilities, whether learned or innate.

Although possessing aptitude in a particular field will help increase self-esteem, self-confidence is not a prerequisite. Someone will get positive self-esteem without any pressure.

How to bolster self-confidence: Conditioning

The first step to create a sense of self-confidence is conditioning. It is extrinsic, that is, an outward strategy, in which action is taken to inspire trust in oneself. This is the most common approach within the culture of self-help, and also the best way to produce results. For example, an exercise in self-confidence is based on making an optimistic phrase, believing you already have a certain height, positively speaking and behaving, etc.

Here are few examples of how to use training to:

- Improve self-esteem: clothing: dress elegantly,

have a good look and a healthy presentation.

- Body language: walking and speaking have a purpose, be cool and composed, hold your head straight, maintain a good attitude and smile.
- Motivational techniques: positive thinking, visualizing positive outcomes/scenarios, concentrate on strengths rather than flaws.

These actions are useful because they can provide a confidence boost almost immediately after taking them. However, the effects are seldom lasting; that is, you need to remind yourself to do them repeatedly. Otherwise, the results will dissipate over time.

Tips to shake your confidence

The second is to work on the issues that make you feel low in self-confidence. This is the most practical approach to shake your confidence.

Acquisition of symbols of value

Self-confidence is often linked to possessing certain knowledge, abilities, and skills. There is a lack of trust in many people because they believe they lack a certain skill. For example, if you don't feel confident about your role in a job, it may be because you lack the information and knowledge necessary to perform well. People with a high level of competence in a certain area often develop great self-confidence in that area as a result.

Competence can always be developed through reading and practice. For example, if you play sports and are preparing for a competition, you should train every day.

Whether it's a presentation or public speaking, continually practice in front of different audiences to develop your skills. Eventually, you will find yourself so competent in that area that you will feel naturally confident in it.

In addition to the competition, there are other symbols of value, of which the most common are:

- Attributes such as the level of attractiveness, popularity, grace...
- Material possessions such as the amount of wealth you own, cars, property, luxury brands, etc.
- Status symbols such as academic qualifications, achievements, job.
- Depending on the value symbol that is relevant to you, you can purchase it to increase self-confidence. For example, throughout life, different people pursue different things to increase their sense of self-esteem. Some people strive to be more attractive and popular. Some people try to acquire material possessions, such as making more money and buying material goods. Others seek to obtain status symbols and titles.

The problem with acquiring symbols of value to shake your confidence is that the increase in self-confidence only lasts as long as the symbols are valid. If they lose their relevance as a symbol of value, self-confidence will change accordingly.

Therefore, to increase your self-confidence permanently and in the long term, there is another option.

Projecting the Blame

The unconscious guilt that is deeply in our subconscious is not guilt that comes from any personal history, that you feel guilty for something you have done, but it is guilt without reason. It is a feeling of deep emptiness present in all conditions. This deep-rooted guilt makes us judge absolutely everything that happens, including ourselves as the protagonist of the story. This guilt comes from the belief in separation, and this belief in guilt always asks for punishment.

Punishment represents different ways to attack myself unconsciously. The ego uses other people and myself through illness, feeling unwell, etc. in my own body to prove that I have sinned.

Take a moment to reflect on your life and make a list of some ways the ego uses your body, or others to prove your guilt.

Any painful sensation that we experience in the body include anxiety, confusion, weight gain, devaluation, low self-esteem, illness, scarcity, physical or emotional pain, depression, conflict, anger, etc. We can stop judging them and learn to look at them. Realize that any painful symptoms we experience are a form of punishment and a consequence, and the true cause is our unforgiven belief in sin. Sin begets guilt, and guilt demands punishment.

For example, if I hold an unconscious belief that overeating is bad, I am unconsciously asking for punishment for it, and I will unconsciously punish myself by gaining weight.

Another example, if I believe that someone has hurt me and I see that wound as a sin, a judgment on that person, I unconsciously ask for revenge for the sin that I think has been committed. Therefore, I will suffer a punishment directed by the ego, which is the one who guides us when we believe in sin. I will suffer the punishment in the form of illness, physical pain, or any other symptom. The solution is not in remedying the symptom, but in giving us what the cause is, and the cause is always my unforgiven belief in sin. This symptom will be an opportunity to become aware and realize where it comes from.

We would be cured very quickly of any symptom if we recognized that none of these errors is a sin. It is simply a wrong perception, committed by the lack of faith that we have.

Can you inquire, what would Love do? How would Love respond to these errors? What would the voice of Love tell you?

Love forgives all errors, but for this, we have to keep in mind that they are not sins, but errors. The error of perception, I have perceived from the ego, and I want to see it from Love. The vision of Love is the true vision, and any other is just a perception, a mistake.

If your purpose is to heal the unconscious guilt, you use all the situations, people, scenarios, around you that generate conflict, to realize that you are using them to attack yourself. We must begin to recognize the "sins" we have made real, the events where we believe we are victims.

There is no healing until this is done, we have to reverse cause and effect. The symptom, or the effect I experience on my body and my environment is just that, an effect, and the true cause is in my mind, which is misperceiving.

The punishment applied for believing in scarcity is usually more scarcity, and so on. This is how the ego has us trapped in its circle of sin, guilt, and fear. And this circle ends when we deliver all these errors to our inner guide, to Love, for its reinterpretation.

Every feeling of discomfort, pain, dissatisfaction, however subtle, becomes conscious. I open myself to feel it, and I recognize that there is nothing external that is producing that, but that the cause is unconscious guilt. I make an act of surrender, to be able to see it in another way, and if you do this process truly, the miracle happens, the healing. I stop feeling that way, under the same circumstance. My liberation is greater every time, experiencing deep enjoyment every time—more time in my life.

You can do an exercise to identify where the areas of your unconscious beliefs reside in sin and guilt:

1. Make a list of all the people or events that you see as a sin, a judgment, or something that deserves punishment. You can also use historical or social events, those that irritate you the most.

2. Observe in your life story, who have you not completely forgiven? Where you refuse to look from the gaze of Love

and feel resentment for that situation or person. Write everything that comes to mind.

3. All these situations or people that you have not completely forgiven symbolize unconscious guilt. You see them as sins, and as long as you continue to have that perception, sin requires punishment.

Remember that all those "unforgiven" scenarios and people are not out there but inside our minds. As long as you don't change all the wrong perceptions, giving them to the voice of Understanding, and Love, so that you reinterpret it and see Love and innocence, they will demand and get you to punish yourself.

Play the Victim

People who suffer because life hits them require all the respect and space to elaborate on their suffering. Talking about a traumatic situation with another human being who listens compassionately causes the pain to shrink until, little by little, it becomes a permanent scar on the heart that allows life to continue. However, it is different from the one anticipated before the damage. Curiously, those people from whom authentic suffering springs tend to complain little they even take refuge in silence and try to rise under the cover of the enormous capacity for recovery of the human being. However, there are other types of individuals who use their misfortunes (real or imagined) to complain, feel sorry, or make you feel guilty. It is victimhood, a behavior that constitutes a real temptation for human beings because it has been repeated throughout the history of humanity (think of some rulers).

Look for Another Side

Coping is a concept used in psychology to refer to the set of strategies that a subject uses to deal with stressful events that occur in the environment or internal demands themselves. Some coping modalities are active and effective. Others are dysfunctional, and there is a risk of further damage.

Coping focused on changing reality can be harmful when the facts cannot be changed: we cannot always resolve a loss, some diseases, and even less death.

The Dramatic Triangle of Handling

For the psychologist Stephen Karpman, in human relationships we can fall—unconsciously sometimes and very deliberately others—into what he called 'The Dramatic Triangle.' This is a manipulation strategy in which (groups, institutions, and even, nations) these three roles are shared:

1. The victim: Is not responsible for his misfortunes, seeking that others do for him what he should do for himself. To achieve his goal, he wants to be the center of attention and uses sentimentality, grief, and emotional blackmail. His traumatic event becomes his calling card.

2. The persecutor: He is always the victim of others whom he blames for his ill-fortune so that the image of himself is always safe, he has no problem and is right in everything he says and does. His tool is accusation and reproach until he makes you feel guilty (he is willing to look for your fault so as not to see his own) and afraid of a new accusation.

3. The savior: Usually the well-meaning person who felt sorry for the victim's laments and overwhelmed if he does not do what the persecutor asks him to do. In return, he obtains self-assessment because by helping, he assumes that he is the best.

Victim

Marta has the role of savior in the family. Ana's husband has asked for a loan to pay his sister the 14,000 euros that he owes. It oscillated between feeling the need to do everything for Ana as she has always done and the anger of having to go into debt. The pressure from her mother and her friends (who do not pay the loan) has been decisive: "Poor thing, she is having a terrible time; she often fears her husband. How can you not help your sister?" They said. Society plays a key 'persecuting' role in the development of victimhood that favors abuse and compassion fatigue. Professor Danielle Giglioli, in his essay "Criticism of the victim," indicates that victimhood has been installed in our culture as a form of manipulation. We are not what we do but what we have suffered. "The victim is the new hero of our time," he says.

Presenting yourself as the affected, with sentimental tones included, is well seen (just turn on the television). In Ana's case, the first blow is inflicted on her by her husband. She provides the second with her ineffective response, the third by the culture of 'victimization' that needs 'poor little ones' to rescue to feel better by converting the world to a place where you can only be a victim or a villain. Marta (Ana's sister) is the collateral martyr who has to pay happily for helping and should not be regretted.

Tell Distorted or Half-Truths

In our day to day, we usually lie or tell half-truths in many of our conversations. Why do we do it? What are its consequences? And finally, what should we expect?

There is no worse coward than the one who makes constant use of half-truths. Because whoever combines truth with falsehood, sooner or later, evidences the complete lie. Tricks camouflaged with good manners are damaging and exhausting. Also, they tend to float, just like whole lies.

Unamuno said that there is no good fool. That everyone, in their way, knows how to conspire and deploy effective tricks to catch us off guard. Now, if there is something that abounds in our society, it is not exactly the fools or the naive. The incomplete lie or the half-truth is the most familiar strategy that we see in almost all our contexts, especially in the spheres of politics.

The value of truth

Making use of headless truths or falsehoods with many short legs gives those who use them the feeling that they are doing nothing wrong. That he comes out unscathed from the responsibility, he has with the other. It seems that default pity discharges responsibilities. It's like someone saying, "I love you so much, but I need time." Or "I appreciate how you work, and we value all your effort, but we have to do without your contract for a few months."

The truth, although it hurts, is something that we all prefer and that we need at the same time. It is the only way we can move forward and join forces to deploy the appropriate psychological strategies with which to turn the page. We need to put aside the lack of certainty, and above all, that emotional instability that supposes not knowing. And finally, unmask the false illusions.

The bitter taste of half-truths

Oddly enough, the subject of lies and their psychological analysis is fairly recent. Freud barely touched on the subject. Until then, it was an aspect that remained in the hands of ethics and even theology and its relationship with morality. However, starting in the 1980s, social psychologists began to take an interest in and study the topic of deception in depth. Also, all the interesting phenomenology associated with it. All to confirm something that Nietzsche himself already said at the time: "lying is a condition of life."

We know that it can seem devastating because even though we are socialized from a very young age, in need to always tell the truth, little by little and from the age of 4, we realize that resorting to lies often involves getting certain benefits. Now, something that, in turn, becomes clear to us very early is that a direct falsehood and without real aroma is rarely profitable in the long term.

Research on lies or half-truths

On the other hand, as Professor Robert Feldman of the University of Massachusetts School of Psychology showed us, many of our most everyday conversations are riddled with those same incomplete truths. However, 98% of them are harmless, not harmful, and even functional (such as saying to a person with whom we do not have much confidence "that we are fine, pulling with this and that," when in fact, we are passing a complicated comment).

However, the remaining 2% do show that half-camouflaged truth, that perverse strategy where the half-truth fallacy executes an express deception by omission. There, also, the person tries to escape unscathed by justifying himself with the idea that since his lie is not complete, there is no offense.

CHAPTER 8

PSYCHOLOGICAL MANIPULATION TECHNIQUES

We are in the areas we most visit. It can be your supervisor, your neighbor upstairs, a coworker, a client, a near or distant relative, or some other. Think of people who know those methods of deception completely, and who use them to annoy us.

These people are not easy to spot even when they are among us. The features and traits of their personality are not clear. None wears an alarm bell on their forehead that they are a narcissist or a sociopath. So how do we get away from them?

How do I?

Those kinds of individuals feed on others' suffering. It's not, then, because you're poorer, more fragile, or different, but you're just another prey for them. Another total.

In certain cases, in which we are involved, we all have felt remorse or distrust. And the worst thing is that without learning, we sense it: not how, nor why. Yet the situation is that the consequences are splashing us out, weakening our confidence, complicating our lives, and our insecurities. Why do they do it without us knowing it?

Search for manipulators?

There are several forms of dishonest people in general: sociopaths, narcissists, liars, the so-called zombies in psychology. So, finding them is more a realistic matter than abstract. And you'll be quicker to predict if you've ever been a survivor of them.

However, it should be assumed that dishonest people's goals are very simple, persuasive and that they follow a certain template. Any of them include:

Nullify your will power: They seek to sow doubt and remain under your protection.

Destroy your self-esteem: Get rid of everything you do or have done. They are not constructive, and they only try to focus on defects.

Passive-aggressive revenge: They punish you with their ignorance. When you need them, they leave you out; so, it is enough that you ask them something so that they give you a sit-down or they don't even speak to you again.

Misrepresent reality: They enjoy confusing people and creating discussions and misunderstandings of others. Having generated a dispute, they stay on the sidelines, having fun with other's disputes.

Learn How to Avoid Their Manipulation Techniques

The consequences of manipulation can generate a very deep mark on each of us. Therefore, it seems necessary that we know which manipulation techniques are used most frequently. The point is to learn to anticipate by ourselves and not to be their puppets.

These people often laugh at our opinions, hold us accountable, or make us feel guilty. They subtly attack, question us, delay what they are not interested in, feel sorry for, deny truths... Everything necessary to control the situation. But, what manipulation techniques do they use to achieve this?

- **Gaslighting**

Known as the "gaslight," it is one of the most insidious. "That has never happened," "You've imagined it," or "Are you crazy?" They are some of the words they use to manipulate and confuse your sense of truth, which would make you believe something has not happened.

Barton and Whitehead (1969) defined "gaslighting" as "the intentional pursuit of making a person appear insane and profiting from him." It instills in the victims an extreme sense of anguish and confusion, to such an extent that they stop trusting themselves, their memory, perception, or judgment.

In an investigation by Galán and Figeroa (2017), they describe making "gaslight" with denial of the damage caused, the elaboration of lies, offering false information, and disqualifying the feelings towards the victim. It is also a method to confuse the partner, manipulate, blame, and downplay the experiences, and thus destroy the victim through his mental health.

The attacker's communication to the victim is hostile through silences, complaints, damaging jokes and humiliations, threats, etc. The consequences on the victim, according to the authors, can be several:

- **Guilty feeling**

- **Disorientation**
- **Panic**
- **Anger**
- **Duel**
- **Low self-esteem**
- **Lack of autonomy**
- **Emotional dependence**
- **Alcohol consumption**
- **Even suicide**
- **Projection**

The manipulator passes his negative traits to someone else, or shifts blame for his behaviors. The narcissists and psychopaths use this, claiming that the evil that surrounds them is not their fault, but yours.

- **Nonsense conversations**

Ten minutes of conversation. That is the time that you surely take to leave the talk. The manipulators say nonsense, illogical explanations, smoke screens, past events...

They just mess around. They make monologues and try to wrap you up with their repetition. Advice? Cut early. And if you can leave after 5 minutes, the better. Your mind will thank you.

- **Generalizations and disqualifications**

They make ambiguous, general comments. They can seem intelligent, but they are lazy. Their conclusions are too general; their goal is to dismiss you and destroy your opinions.

For example, "You always want to be right," "Everything bothers you," "You never agree." Keep calm. You can pull irony, with a simple "Thank you," or by ignoring him with a resounding, "I think you're a little upset, we'll talk later."

- **The absurd**

Remember that they seek to undermine your morale and make you rethink what you believe in. They may put things in your mouth you didn't know, they'll make you believe they have the superpower to "read your mind." But no, they're all tricks. Simulated claudication will support you. You tell him he's right to believe that, but you're always holding on to your stance. You can also respond with a "voucher" or with laconic phrases to their blackmail.

The main thing is that you take away from their hands your self-esteem. They think that is what they want to throw on the ground to control you. Once they have weakened you, the task for them is much easier.

No greater contempt does not appreciate it.

- **Kindness Costume**

"Yes, but...". If you just bought a house, they will tell you what a shame it is you still don't have one on the beach; If you have become more elegant than ever, they will point out that other earrings would have been better for you... If you have completed an impeccable report, they will notice that the staple is not properly fixed.

But that should not affect you, and you should know what

you are worth! Your achievements and your virtues are worth more than their manipulation techniques. Don't give them credibility. Hang out with people who spend more time stressing what's right and cheering you on; the ones that flatter you when they have to and issue constructive, not destructive criticism.

Resist his attack of rage

When you oppose a manipulator, it is normal for his anger to increase within a few seconds, especially if you don't play along: his tolerance for frustration is usually not very high. It is possible that he begins to speak outrageously and even insults you and refers to you in derogatory and pejorative terms. It is the result of their mistrust.

These are the most subtle and frequent manipulation techniques these people use to humiliate you. Master your emotions and keep a cool head: the only way to escape control. If you don't succumb, they'll get tired and end up looking for another victim. Life away from toxic people is much better.

CHAPTER 9

THE ROLE OF DEFENCE

Assertiveness is a characteristic of our way of being that allows us to express our emotions freely and without altering ourselves. It allows us to defend our rights, tastes, and interests, directly, simply, and appropriately, without assaulting others and without consenting to being attacked.

Being assertive means that you have a healthy relationship with yourself (self-esteem) and with the people around you. That is, an assertive person has a natural balance that allows him to socialize in a fluid and healthy way, without leaning towards passivity or aggressiveness, thinking, acting and communicating appropriately and adaptively.

The most assertive people feel more sure of themselves. That is why healthy self-esteem plays an important role to have appropriate behaviors in interpersonal communication; without making a value judgment or showing passivity or aggressiveness towards the other person.

All people, no matter their personality traits, can use Assertiveness to improve their relationships with the people around them and themselves because Assertiveness is a skill that can be learned and modified.

Where can we locate the form of assertive interpersonal behavior?

Assertive communication is somewhere in the middle of 3 other forms of communication:

Aggressive communication: This style of communication occurs when we are not able to respect the ideas or actions of others. There is no empathy or we do not take into account the feelings of the other.

Passive communication: It is a style in which the person does not defend his interests, allows third parties to decide for him, or does not comment on his true feelings and does not express a disagreement. People with passive communication are little conflictive, but it has the disadvantage that they can feel frustrated or resentful at some point.

Passive-aggressive communication: A person who communicates passive-aggressively does not put himself or the other in the foreground but communicates poorly or in a confused manner. He often uses excuses and has little personal ambition.

Assertive style: When communication is assertive, it means that our interests or points of view are just as important as someone else's. One learns from the other person, and both people end up satisfied. It is the ideal communication and behavior, relationships benefit, and the interlocutors respect themselves and those around them.

Examples of assertiveness

A child is playing alone; another child approaches, and they end up playing together, sharing their toys without any alteration, enjoying the moment.

A person comes up smoking and asks if the smell of tobacco bothers us. By telling him we don't like tobacco, he understands it and walks away.

Assertive Communication Techniques or how to work on assertiveness

One of the first attempts by behavioral clinicians to improve patients' social skills is focused on an extensive set of procedures and skills, generally called assertive training. Assertiveness training was a method to help people overcome anxiety aroused by interpersonal encounters.

The explanation of assertive training was presented as follows:

- When anxiety inhibits the behaviors required in interpersonal relationships, the person is almost inevitably at a disadvantage when he is face to face with other people... His unexpressed impulse continues to reverberate within him and that can cause somatic symptoms, including pathological changes and a wide variety of clinical problems, such as social anxiety.

- It has been used in the treatment of diseases such as social dysfunction, alcoholism and depression. In the first clinical work on assertive training, the expression of irritation, resentment and feelings of anger was emphasized in a socially appropriate way. Anxiety would gradually be inhibited since it was assumed to be incompatible with the assertive expression of feelings. In assertive training, operational aspects were also considered, that is, acts of assertive interpersonal capacity were programmed that agreed with favorable consequences in the person's natural social environment, thus being reinforced.

- More recently, however, assertive training has expanded to include the expression of positive feelings, such as the ability to convey praise, affection, and approval.

Some skills to train assertiveness:

It is important to identify what you feel through self-observation. Do you feel anxiety, tension, sweat? In this case it is important to learn self-control techniques that help us relax, such as muscle relaxation, mindfulness, etc.

- Social skills techniques.
- Understand what thinking errors are.
- Understand the different levels of communication and learn communication skills.
- Know what the defense mechanisms are.
- Learn cognitive flexibility and work possible blocks.
- Assertive response techniques.
- Having adequate non-verbal communication.
- Impulse control.

Why is being assertive so important

Some people with interpersonal behavior deficits never seem to have learned appropriate social skills. Because of these deficits, the person has great difficulty in obtaining the types of social reinforcement required. In the absence of an appropriate social interpretation, different forms of deviant behavior are reinforced, including illusory language, periods of crying, and antisocial behavior, which is maintained by the attention that they invariably arouse from others.

Causes of assertiveness deficit and the importance of self-esteem

Several researchers argue that assertiveness has a direct relationship with self-esteem.

Self-esteem is the feeling of appreciation or rejection that accompanies the global assessment that we make of ourselves. This self-assessment is based on our perception of specific qualities, such as the ability to relate to others, physical appearance, character traits, etc.

People who do not consider themselves valuable usually choose not to actively defend their rights, creating a vicious circle by undermining their self-esteem again when their rights are not respected.

Other reasons for the assertiveness deficit would be the influence of certain social and labor stereotypes. In some highly hierarchical cultures or organizations, submission is established as the accepted behavior in certain roles and genres.

The emotional state also influences the response that can be given at a specific moment. A high-stress load can cause excessively aggressive or passive behavior, sometimes generating greater anxiety due to the rejection that the response itself causes in others.

It was also discovered that assertiveness has to do with the degree of maturity of each individual. As well as the emotional and intrinsic factors of personality, people whose self-esteem is high tend to develop a higher degree of assertiveness. The differences between assertive people and those who do not develop this ability lie in the lack of character, as well as ideologies, lack of confidence in their abilities or, that they lack clear objectives when communicating.

Assertive behavior can be trained and, in this way, increase the number of situations in which we will have an assertive response.

What is an assertive response?

The assertive response is a tool that makes it easier to carry on smarter conversations without bullying, offending, or humiliating anyone, creating empathy with the speaker. Your knowledge can be very useful for conflict resolution.

Being assertive in a conversation allows us to verbally engage intelligently without verbal aggressiveness when defending a position on something. The assertive response makes it easy to find the balance between aggressiveness and passivity in an argument.

The term "assertive behavior" is used broadly to cover all socially acceptable expressions in an appropriate way of personal rights and feelings.

Dialogue with assertive responses or assertive communication

What are the main assertive response techniques to successfully tackle an argument?

The way to have a conversation or discussion with another person depends on our personality and the purpose of the conversation. When we have discrepancies in opinions during a conversation, it can cause psychological and physical discomfort. By being skillful in using assertiveness responses, we are more agile in expressing our thoughts, desires, and feelings, we maintain our well-being and even strengthen our self-esteem.

Here are some of the resources to respond assertively that may be helpful in a discussion or under pressure from others:

Fogbank. Agree on the possibility of what the other says. It is effective when they criticize us. The "fog bank" is useful to avoid entering into a discussion about who has the last word or not. We let the words enter this cloud as if we haven't heard anything.

Example: - You have gained a lot of weight. - Maybe I have to start taking care of myself.

Negative assertion. Clearly say something in me that I do not like or that something is bad according to the opinions or attack of the interlocutor. We react to fair criticism without too many excuses or justifications.

Example: - You are late. - It's true, sorry.

Self-disclosure. Assertively disclose personal information.

Example: - But how can you eat that? - Because I like it.

Broken record. Repeat the request persistently and calmly. It is very useful when we meet a very persistent person. In this case, it works to repeat the request over and over again in a calm way, as if it were a mantra, to reach our goal.

Example: - We can go out tonight - I don't feel like it - It makes for a nice night - I don't feel like it - etc.

Assertive agreement. Admit that I have made a mistake but separating it from being a good or bad person. It is useful in situations where the person is right to be angry, but we do not agree with the way to tell us.

Example: - I've been waiting for you. - Yes, I forgot about the date we had to eat. I am usually more responsible.

Assertive question. Directly ask the details that have led to criticism or attack on me. We do not question what they have told us, and we use the "assertive question" to understand the attack without denying, defending ourselves, counterattacking, justifying, etc. The assertive question helps us understand why they are criticizing.

Example: - I understand that you do not like the way I acted the other night in the meeting. What bothered you? What is it in my way of speaking that you dislike?

Deviation. Shift the discussion towards the analysis of what happens between my interlocutor and me, leaving aside the topic of it.

Example: - We are moving past the question, and we will end up talking about past things.

Simulated claudication. Giving ground, giving part of the reason to the interlocutor, but without actually giving it up. You have to agree with the other person's argument but without agreeing to change your position.

Example: - You may be right, surely it could be more generous. Maybe I shouldn't be so tough, but...

Ignore. This technique is recommended when the interlocutor is wrong, and you can be nervous, upset, angry, etc. In this situation, it is better to ignore the reason why the interlocutor seems to be angry and to postpone the discussion until he has calmed down. Empathy is recommended at this time.

Example: - I see that you are very angry, so we better talk about it at another time.

Breakdown of the process. Respond to criticism or provocations with a single word or brief phrases.

Example: - Yes... No... Maybe...

Assertive irony. It is about responding ironically or positively to hostile provocation or criticism.

Example: - You are boastful... - Okay, thanks.

Assertive postponement. When we find ourselves upset or angry, it is simply a matter of postponing the response to the "attack" until we feel calm and able to respond to it appropriately.

Example: - Yes, it is a very interesting topic, but we will discuss it later. I do not want to talk about that right now. (Because I'm wrong)

Thanks to being skillful in using assertive responses, we can express ourselves freely and clearly, respecting ourselves and respecting the rights of our interlocutors.

The assertive response can be a very valuable tool for:

- Company managers,
- Public persons,
- Teachers,
- Family relationships, etc.

Being assertive is essential to our quality of life; Through the ability of assertive communication, we can successfully manage interpersonal relationships, achieve tranquility and personal satisfaction, and create a good environment.

CHAPTER 10

THE POWER OF EMOTIONAL INTELLIGENCE

Most researchers in psychology consider emotional intelligence as the most important ability to succeed in life. Studies have shown that, for example, activities related to high IQ are only useful in 20% of everyday situations. On the other hand, emotional intelligence is a type of broader capacity that includes both internal and social understanding, making it essential for such fundamental factors as choosing the right partner or the ideal job.

Here we review the main elements that have been found important in the process to acquire and develop emotional intelligence. This quality is not innate, but can be developed, and helps us for a large number of routine questions, from knowing how to solve problems, until we understand each other.

What Is Emotional Intelligence?

Emotional Intelligence per se is a concept that is quite recent in the study of human behavior; It was only in the 20th century, mainly in the second half, that efforts began to try to define its nature, trying to make a different classification to cognitive intelligence.

It was from 1995 that the work called Emotional Intelligence by Daniel Goleman managed to spread the term, from a compilation of scientific research that allowed to organize and begin to define its characteristics better.

In general, Emotional Intelligence is considered as the set of behaviors and forms of knowledge that allow us to assimilate and respond in a useful way. Both towards our own emotions, as well as about impulses from the outside, which allows us to develop the better way in a social environment, and thus achieve a more efficient way of achieving objectives that allow the individual to feel happy and satisfied.

Although Emotional Intelligence has a large component of subjectivity and is difficult to measure, various scientific experiments have been developed to understand better and define its essence, based not only on human behavior but also on the neurological processes that are carried out.

Various theorists also agree that emotional intelligence does not lead to responses that have to be good or bad, but rather that they can generate positive or negative consequences. For example, a traffic light in a person who does not properly use emotional intelligence can result in an accident, which is notoriously a response with mostly negative results, compared to that person who acted in moderation, and avoids a further incident. Big and meaningless.

Emotional Intelligence is another type of intelligence

Through multiple scientific and social experiments, it has been possible to differentiate emotional intelligence from other types of intelligence, particularly linked to cognitive abilities. The most widely accepted definition in this field is that of Howard Gardner, who lists intelligence such as musical, spatial-visual, mathematical logic, linguistic verbal, and kinesthetic body, which refer more to intelligence that denotes a certain type of physical ability.

In this same widely accepted definition of intelligence, other types are also included, such as interpersonal and intrapersonal intelligence. These are more related to the psychological skills of both internal and external understanding, respectively.

It is these two classifications also that Goleman takes up and mentions as the main types of Emotional Intelligence, and which refer to the ability to regulate human relationships, as well as understanding, valuation, and internal development.

Main Elements of Emotional Intelligence

In the analysis of Emotional Intelligence, not only does the internal and external focus influence, as we have mentioned, but these are also combined with two essential behaviors: interpretation, which is how we assimilate the perceptions and knowledge acquired, and the response, which is the result of the analysis performed. In the conjunction of each of these perspectives, four main elements are generated, which we analyze below.

- **Emotional self-awareness**

This is the ability to understand not only what we are feeling, but also the reasons for having those emotions or feelings. It is essentially about the ability to understand yourself, value yourself, appreciate yourself, which also involves the series of acquired values and paradigms.

This element is particularly essential for such basic and important questions as knowing how to express our feelings to other people because this is where the motivations and beliefs that govern our way of thinking can be clearly understood.

- **Emotional self-control**

This approach essentially refers to the ability to regulate our emotions, that is, the internal emotional response. This type of emotional intelligence is important, for example, to contain and assimilate feelings of sadness, frustration, or anger, to name a few examples.

It should be noted that through scientific research such as that of Joseph LeDoux—also mentioned in Goleman's masterpiece—it was possible to identify an important neurological factor in this process of self-control. It normally works as follows: the Emotional reasoning process usually begins in the thalamus, which is where the impulses from sensory organs such as the eyes or ears come from. Then they are passed to the neocortex, which is the area of the brain where these data are recorded and analyzed. Next they are sent to the lobes prefrontal where the stimuli are organized and try to be understood, making a detailed analysis of the context, background and situation, to then send the final signal to the limbic system. This is the one that will generate the consequent response; however, it is not in all cases that thoughts flow with this same efficiency.

LeDoux discovered that, especially in situations where impulsive and fast acting was performed, the neurological pathway took a kind of shortcut. And instead of sending impulses from the thalamus to the neocortex, it diverted them to the amygdala, where a response occurred. Almost instinctively from the most vivid memories of the moment and sending it directly to the limbic system; that is, without going through the prefrontal lobes or the neocortex, and thus avoiding the main analysis processes to resolve a situation.

The researchers point out that this reaction is understandable, particularly from a human evolutionary condition originating from ancient times, where it was important to have a capacity to respond quickly to possible and constant threats. This being, in reality, a natural protection system. However, specialists consider that this type of reaction could be somewhat discordant in our times since a greater proportion of reasoned and non-impulsive responses is required.

This is where their emotional intelligence can work, especially people with neurosis problems or who rely too much on spontaneous impulses. Because from deeper reasoning and based on broader judgment, they can make more accurate decisions.

- **Empathy**

Empathy is essentially the ability to understand other people's vision and thoughts; sometimes it is confused with listening and paying attention to others, although it is not just about this. But the ability to see things from a third-party perspective, which can allow us to understand other people's perspectives better, and in this way to be able to develop a more efficient social exercise.

This ability represents what the individual feels about others, which is also usually a type of emotional intelligence important to have a greater tolerance and understanding towards the outside. In the same way, it can help us to resolve a wide variety of conflicts. For example, family fights, since in this way you can adopt a broader understanding of things, allowing solutions to be found, also considering other people's needs; after all, man does not stop being a social being, which is why this becomes an important factor for better social development.

- **Social skills**

And if empathy represents the conception of others, social skills become the answer, the consequence, or in other words, our reaction to the exterior in the face of these internally defined paradigms and judgments.

This element of emotional intelligence allows us to develop adequately, also according to the main conventions and norms of healthy coexistence, and of course, also according to the context of the individual. Here the social capacity is shown if you have developed emotional intelligence, or in contrast, you can also adopt sociopathic behaviors.

And while the primary focus of emotional intelligence is based on these four newly exposed elements, some also add to adaptability and self-motivation as two other important factors within intrapersonal intelligence.

Habits of People with High Emotional Intelligence

After multiple studies with high academic rigor, it has also been possible to identify certain characteristic behaviors that are usually present in people with a developed emotional intelligence:

- **Extroverts**

One of the characteristics that distinguish people with developed emotional intelligence is their ability to express their emotions and ways of thinking with great ease; that is, they are quite extroverted.

This ability becomes even more marked in women since an energetic character can be developed, where the woman is not afraid to make spontaneous reactions with great security either.

- **Sociable**

The outward qualities of a person with high emotional intelligence are also important abilities to cope with great ease in a social environment. Generally speaking, they do not find it difficult to strike up conversations with strangers, and they have a great capacity to adapt to different environments and situations.

- **With trust**

Another characteristic quality is trust, which has two main meanings; since on the one hand, they have a greater capacity to be able to trust people—of course, those who, in their opinion, meet the requirements of a trustworthy person.

And on the other hand, this idea also refers to self-confidence; since emotional intelligence not only allows us to interpret our characteristics, conditions, and qualities. But also to assimilate them, value them, and of course, take advantage of them with a higher level of security.

- **Ethical vision**

It has also been shown that people with this type of intelligence tend to have a higher level of social commitment, since they seek to put into practice the moral and established values, as much as possible in aspects of daily life.

In the case of men, for example, it is usually exemplified in practice through the determination in environmentalist, political, humanitarian positions. Or those that in the person's opinion are appropriate and are also part of the common good of that which we are also part of.

- **Leadership**

Some of the important skills of people who develop their emotional intelligence are those related to the ability to convince, and of course, also to manipulate other people.

These types of behaviors are characteristic qualities of people with a broad sense of leadership, which of course, has a strong basis in the trust they have acquired, but in this case, it is precisely the response expressed in behaviors with outstanding abilities and leadership.

- **Kind and loving**

Another outstanding skill mentioned in the different bibliographies on emotional intelligence is the ability to express feelings more fluidly and directly. This is reflected through behaviors such as affection and love.

People who develop this ability also tend to have a stable emotional life. They are not only able to find a better partner, more related to the expectations and desires of the individual, but as a consequence they are also more consistent and respectful of relationships. This allows you to have greater stability in this regard.

This is particularly noticeable in the female sex, and is also related to the ability to have a full sex life; unlike those who only develop their IQ, and those who usually have greater problems such as anxiety or difficulty in fully enjoying their sex life.

- **Joyful people**

And as a consequence of all these abilities, people with advanced emotional intelligence also tend to have a higher degree of satisfaction in general. Which is why they tend to maintain an appearance not only outgoing but also cheerful, sometimes joking and generally with a much more positive outlook.

The importance of emotional intelligence as a factor to regulate, assimilate and dilute negative issues is an important capability. It allows us to maintain a positive posture towards life, which is why visibly happier people are generally generated. This also means a noticeable behavioral difference compared to those who only develop their IQ and those who tend to maintain a colder, more balanced, and less expressive posture.

Emotional Intelligence in working life

One of the important points where emotional intelligence can be put into practice is in terms of working life. Of course, starting with the choice of our profession or trade, for which an exhaustive analysis of both skills and expectations must be carried out.

This type of intelligence is also essential to develop within a job, particularly in cases where teamwork is required. The ability to adapt, as well as leadership skills, can be factors of success for the individual with this type of intelligence developed.

This is important to measure since according to reference works on the subject, it has been documented that the development of the IQ, interferes only in a fifth of the factors that determine the success of a person. This explains why individuals who are obsessed with having a perfect grade during their academic development, neglect essential factors of emotional intelligence, which often ends up obstructing the professional development of the individual.

And although to achieve success, there are also factors such as social status, and even luck, it is currently considered that emotional intelligence also plays a crucial factor. It is involved with a greater variety of essential success factors, particularly in comparison to cognitive intelligence.

Emotional Intelligence can be developed

The most reputable researchers on the subject also agree that emotional intelligence is not only innate, but also has a great capacity to be learned and developed. This is part of the process that is normally known as maturation, and which essentially means the human capacity to be able to make decisions based on a broader criterion and analysis. In contrast, as many factors as possible are taken into consideration, thus seeking to reach more successful solutions.

This type of intelligence is developed mainly and with greater emphasis from own experiences; hence famous sayings such as "no one is cheating on someone else's head," for example, although in reality, the human being also can learn from external or third-party experiences. Still, you have to have a high level of empathy to be able to assimilate this kind of knowledge. To incorporate it within the framework of judgments that are part of the neural process in the neocortex, that is, in the chain formed by values and paradigms.

What is an Emotional Intelligence test?

This type of test seeks to measure in some way the level of development of this type of intelligence, although mainly based on certain specific elements. In this case, unlike IQ, there is no fully agreed scientific procedure here to design an exact evaluation of this type. Mainly because more subjective factors are involved and, therefore, they are more difficult to measure or assess, since you never have such clear answers.

In IQ tests, for example, there is full scientific certainty of obtaining the volume of a three-dimensional geometric body according to the number and size of its edges; but on the other hand, in emotional intelligence, it is not possible to determine with the same precision which is the correct or incorrect answer. Much has to do with the interpretation and even the same concept and value framework of each person or region.

In this sense, the tests of emotional intelligence are rather informal experiments to know certain tendencies about specific situations or elements; without having, to date, a formula to give a precise qualification to the development of this type of intelligence.

Busting the Myths About Emotional Intelligence

MYTH 1. The most emotionally intelligent people tend to be more likable and outgoing.

It is very typical that when we create in our minds the image of an emotionally intelligent person, we think of someone very kind, popular and with many friends. Or if we know someone like that, we label them as emotionally intelligent.

However, introversion-extroversion is a different dimension of the person, which has nothing to do with emotional intelligence.

A person can be very introverted and have a high degree of EI, and a very extroverted can have very low EQ. The first, the introvert, may have high knowledge of her emotional world and know how to manage it for the benefit of the goals she wants to achieve in life (e.g., managing her anxiety before an exam or in a discussion where you have to be assertive). The second, the extrovert, may not have that knowledge and ability (e.g., being blocked before the exam or not daring to attend, or speaking and speaking a lot in a discussion but not acting assertively, instead of saying things clearly and in a respectful manner).

MYTH 2. People with a high degree of Emotional Intelligence are very emotional people.

It is common to misinterpret emotional intelligence in which it is understood as the ability to express, not save, emotions. For this reason, those who are very emotionally expressive, who "do not keep their emotions," are labeled with a higher EQ. This is another clear myth about emotional intelligence.

Although the recognition and expression of one's emotions are indeed part of EI, taking only this part as the key element can lead us to misunderstandings. Emotional intelligence has to do with a series of abilities such as "accurately perceiving, valuing and expressing emotions; the ability to access and generate feelings that facilitate punishment; the ability to understand emotions and emotional intelligence, and the ability to control emotions that foster emotional and mental development" (Mayer and Salovey).

According to Mayer and Salovey (parents of EI), emotional intelligence would consist of four major skills related to emotions:

1. Perception-expression.

2. Thought facilitation.

3. Understanding and analysis.

4. Reflexive regulation.

Therefore, a very emotionally expressive person may have the first skill (and sometimes not even that) but may not have the other three. For example, when faced with the challenge of starting a new job, you can be very conscious and expressive about how you feel (perhaps fear, insecurity, anxiety...). But not knowing how to use your emotions to facilitate positive thoughts (skill 2). Nor to understand more deeply that fear and insecurity and its relation with what one thinks and says, nor the reason why these sudden changes of emotions come to one, from fear to joy, followed by insecurity and anguish, etc. (skill 3). Nor being able to regulate those emotions that block you by taking perspective and not letting them block or condition you too much in your first interactions at work (skill 4).

MYTH 3. Women, in general, have more emotional intelligence than men.

The third of the myths about emotional intelligence is also widespread. This belief is very common. Part of one of the most widespread gender stereotypes: women are more emotional and men more rational. According to Natalio Extremera, one of the great experts in EI, "the scientific evidence on the subject is controversial and, globally, gender differences in emotional intelligence are small and depend on many factors such as age, educational level, specific training or culture."

The important thing, from Extremera's perspective (which follows the line of work of Salovey and Mayer), is that each person knows their emotional intelligence profile. They know their strengths and weaknesses in each of the four dimensions of EI, and seek to improve progressively.

Therefore, it is not a question of having more or less EI than someone else, which, although it is measured with some tests, is still difficult to calibrate and compare. I'm going to give an example of two people. One could be defined—never exempt from subjectivity—as having less EI than the other. But whom is very aware of his strengths and weaknesses and has a clear improvement attitude. And on the other hand, the other that, having much more emotional skills—and scoring better on tests—is not aware of his improvement points (he has blind spots that he does not recognize). Possibly, although on paper the tests the first would have a lower level of EI. We could almost qualify it as more EI due to the growth potential he reflects and because self-knowledge itself is closely related to present EI and future potential.

CHAPTER 11

WHY DO YOU NEED EMOTIONAL INTELLIGENCE IN YOUR BUSINESS?

If you are a manager, director or boss, you should read this chapter about emotional intelligence. It will help you improve your leadership.

In a world of business which promotes and admires a hypercompetitive culture and in which the achievement of objectives seems an end that justifies all means, talk about emotional intelligence seems somewhat misplaced.

However, for Leonardo N'Haux, president of Qualtop Group, a company that seeks to maximize organizational capabilities through processes of innovation and agility, these skills are absolutely necessary to travel through the corporate corridors, the World Economic Forum reports.

For his part, the psychologist and writer Daniel Goleman, affirms emotional intelligence is the ability to motivate ourselves. The ability to persevere despite frustrations, to control impulses, to regulate our own moods, and to empathize and trust in the others.

Here are three corporate examples where emotional intelligence can help you:

1. Negotiation

In any negotiation situation you have, your emotional skills serve you to connect better with your interlocutor. In a negotiation, what you are looking for is a result that the two of you will be happy with. That is the best result that you can have from a negotiation and, in that sense, emotional skills can help you a lot.

2. Construction of work teams

In the construction of work teams you have to look for needs that are complementary and achieve a synergy such that everyone feels they are going for the same goal and commit themselves. In this sense, being able to communicate this and reach people's emotions, that is, emotionally convince them that it is worth the effort, the challenge, is key to that.

3. Conflict resolution

You have to understand that people, in general, do not fight for pleasure. In general, there is an emotional clash between needs, and between different positions. Such that, when you analyze it from the emotional components of the problem and manage to transmit it to the people who are intervening in the conflict, you help a lot of things to be unleashed in a much more agile way and for the benefit of all.

Why Is Emotional Intelligence Important in The Workplace?

The inability to understand and deal with human emotions is an unfortunate trend in western society. This trend has spread to many areas of life, especially the workplace. Emotions often stay on the doorstep when you start working and this has devastating effects not only for companies, but also on employees (from assistant to CEO). Because we are emotional people.

Every day we make emotionally charged decisions. We believe Plan A is better than Plan B, and sometimes we make decisions based on our visceral emotions or feelings. As much as we try to base decision making on rational methods, emotions influence. Understanding the origin and source of these emotions will help us make better decisions. Also, when we work as a team, we will be more in tune with each other.

With globalization, emotional intelligence is more important than ever. In an environment where teams are intercultural, multi-generational and global, the complexity of the interactions of emotions and the way they are expressed increases.

Emotional intelligence in the workplace comes down to understanding, expressing and managing good relationships, and problem solving under pressure.

Applications of emotional intelligence in the company

Since the initial research was published in 1990, innovative organizations have begun testing how to integrate Emotional Intelligence into training and hiring for a competitive advantage. It is becoming increasingly clear that these skills are the foundation of high-performance organizations.

Multiple emotional intelligence implementation strategies have been used in the company, particularly in leadership and culture development, and for selection and retention.

Emotional intelligence skills are measurable and can be learned and improved through training. The most effective implementation strategies seek to integrate emotional intelligence into the organizational culture.

Benefits of applying emotional intelligence to the organization

Benefits and good results have been demonstrated in many areas of the organization:

- Increased sales performance through recruiting and training emotionally smarter salespeople.
- Better customer service by hiring customer service agents with higher emotional intelligence ratings.
- Superior leadership performance, developing and recruiting executives with high Emotional Intelligence.
- Better team performance, with higher productivity and profit growth.
- Using emotional intelligence in training and organizational change initiatives reduces costs associated with turnover, absenteeism, and poor performance.

Results of applying emotional intelligence in business

Research has provided clear data that emotionally intelligent leaders are more successful. Studies in large companies show these results:

- At PepsiCo, executives selected for emotional intelligence skills generated 10% more productivity.

- Sellers with a high emotional intelligence index at L'Oreal brought in $2.5 million more in sales.
- An emotional intelligence initiative at Sheraton helped increase market share by 24%.

Emotionally Intelligent People Handle Pressure Better

Pressure has to do with Stress, with what is happening, and with the demand that we have. But beyond that, stress is the inability that people show to deal effectively with a stressor. This means that stress does not affect all people in the same way, it depends a lot on our ability to handle situations. Therefore, emotional intelligence has become the key competence if we are to understand why some people are successful, and others are not in an increasingly competitive environment.

There are two key elements that we must consider if we are talking about high organizational performance.

The first element is self-management the ability we have to manage ourselves. Self-knowledge the ability to know how we are and how stressors are affecting us. When a person knows how to recognize their emotions and knows what is happening inside them, they have a greater ability to direct what is happening to them adequately. So, we take a break and realize when we are going out of our boxes, see how it affects us and become aware of how situations can overtake us. Then we know how to act, how to go out and take a break knowing that is not the best time to resolve the issue. That is to be aware of yourself.

Self-management is the ability we have to channel our emotional energy to more productive levels. To levels that take us to better control of what is happening to us. How do we channel those emotions? Through thoughts, the way we are interpreting them, and the situations that happen to us. So the drama that happens to us as human beings is not because of the situations that happen outside, but rather because of the way we interpret them in our mental universe. Channeling the correct thoughts can adequately direct the emotions to be able to motivate them. That element of self-motivation, so linked to self-regulation, is capable of transforming and changing the emotional level that we have at that moment. So instead of diving into depression, thinking about all the debts, why not direct your thoughts to more creative places and say things such as: "This situation is a challenge that I have to meet, what I can do right now to get ahead of this situation." Channeling energy correctly is what is going to make you resolve the situation or not, but this is a skill that you have to develop. Generate discipline so that you do not fall prey to your emotions, but that thoughts are capable of guiding your emotions.

The other component is the ability to manage the relationships we have with others; work, home, friends, etc. This is essential. We have to learn to recognize the emotions of others. You achieve this through a great tool called empathy. What we have heard many times is that we must put ourselves in the shoes of others, but also put them on and walk about 5 km with them to understand what it feels like. This means realizing what is happening in the mental universe of people, how emotions are affecting them, what worries them, or what motivates them. If I can detect those mechanisms that trigger your emotions and I have the knowledge to be able to properly direct your emotions in search of the results that we are all looking for, that is called influence.

After managing emotions comes another important point—social skills. This refers to how I manage relationships with other people so that I can generate results, synergy, and collaboration to direct ourselves towards a common goal. The social skills that are very important to develop include effective communication, assertiveness, and negotiation. These are the skills that allow me to work in a team to achieve results. I'm only going to do that with the right language, the right arguments, the right whys so that people can join the common goal.

If you are a leader who has a vision, but you do not know how to share or transmit it to the emotional world of people, no matter how capable or intelligent you are, or how much experience you have, you will not be able to go very far. Yes, your technical skills are very important, no one denies that knowledge will be decisive for success, but unfortunately, it is not the most important thing. The ability you have to manage your emotions and manage the emotions of others, to manage to direct your efforts towards a shared objective, that is what generates great results. Daniel Goleman, in 1995, said it clearly: "Emotional competence is twice as important as technical competence when it comes to explaining top management performance."

Emotionally Intelligent People Are Better Decision-Makers

"Colder, more rational people make better decisions."

"I was wrong because I got carried away by my emotions."

"Psychopaths are evolved beings because their emotions do not influence them."

Such statements are topics that I keep listening to and reading, and they are not true. We cannot criminalize our emotional side, which makes us human, intuitive, sensitive, and creative when it comes to solving our conflicts.

Emotions influence us every day, and it is inevitable. Therefore, it is essential to enhance our emotional intelligence, because, in this way, we will be able to recognize both our feelings and those of others to value successful decisions, avoiding impulsiveness and risk. Emotions are signs of our inner world, we cannot ignore them, but yes, through self-awareness, 'select' constructive emotions and discard those that block us. The challenge is learning to use emotions effectively.

Science supports it; a 2013 study by the University of Toronto concluded that we are prey to emotional influence all the time and that emotionally intelligent people don't remove all emotions from their decision-making, they just ignore the emotions that have nothing to do with the decision and take into account those that are relevant.

"People often decide influenced by emotions that have nothing to do with the decisions they are making," explained Stéphane Côté, co-author of the study. Therefore, those with higher levels of emotional intelligence can make better decisions. However, those who have less emotional intelligence but become aware of what they are feeling and manage to separate it from the choice they must make can also block the emotions of others that influence their decisions.

Côté suggests that if the person feels anxiety or other emotion before making a decision, pause instead of taking it immediately. "You have to pay attention only to the feelings that are relevant to the decisions that are made," the researchers stressed. Also, they clarify that we must not only pay attention to the negative emotions that a person may experience but also to the positive ones, which can also condition us erroneously.

Five Ways Emotional Intelligence Helps You Make Decisions

According to the psychiatry faculty of the National Autonomous University of Mexico (UNAM), emotional intelligence is "the ability to perceive your feelings and those of others, distinguish between them and use that information to guide thought and conduct of oneself." Learn to manage your emotions:

1. **Identify.** Emotions are signs that show our inner and social world to those around us. Knowing how to identify them helps us maintain a better ability to communicate with others.
2. **Use.** The proper use of emotions helps us guide our thoughts to solve the problems that arise.
3. **Understand.** Each of our emotions has different causes that, if we learn to detect, we can understand why we react in a certain way at a specific time.
4. **Drive.** It intelligently incorporates emotions in the way of solving problems, which helps us know how to manage our behavior.
5. **Control.** Emotional intelligence goes beyond the ability to control a bad mood. It plays a very important role in the quality of life since by putting the above points into practice, people can learn to use emotions effectively.

According to research carried out by the Dr. Rafael Belloso Chacín University (URBE), in Venezuela, 83% of the people evaluated who put this technique into practice, learned to regulate their emotions. This benefited their self-knowledge and control of them.

The use of emotional intelligence helps to create awareness about our actions by contemplating the importance of our emotions and the impact they generate on our behavior and way of life.

People with High EQ Handle Conflicts Better

It is important to know how to handle conflict because they have become part and parcel of our everyday lives. In this section, I will attempt to demystify how this can be carried out properly.

It is possible to achieve peace of mind. I cannot promise you that it will be easy, however. This is because when emotions run high, things tend to go out of hand. But if you are willing to make an effort and put your mind to it, you can achieve anything you want to. On a lot of occasions, I have found out that the past plays a very big role in determining how you will react to pressure.

If you had been burned badly in the past, the actual thought of it occurring once again would send you jumping high to the mountains. You can try to avoid it for some time, but you are just delaying the inevitable. You will have to face the music in the end.

So, what can you do to handle conflict?

The first step is Just Breathe; you must learn the art of thinking before you act to calm yourself. In your mind, right now, I know you must be saying that it looks too simple an exercise to make a major difference. My advice to that is that you do not criticize an idea that you have not yet tried. If it is that simple, then you should have no problem setting aside a few minutes every day for it. Just look for someplace that is quiet and slowly take a breath in and out.

Clear your mind of negative thoughts because they just drain your energy. This is an art that takes some time to be perfect because you will constantly be tempted to think about what you need to do. To try to help these occurrences from happening, remind yourself that it takes only 5 minutes of your time to do it. When you get upset, or someone makes you angry, find a safe place, and count to 10 right away. This has been proven to be of great help and prevents you from saying things in the heat of the moment that you would later regret to have said.

Secondly, take action. Problems are not solved purely by thinking about them. Some action has to accompany it to make things happen. As soon as you have calmed your nerves, you must be willing to show that you have gotten past the fight and are looking for ways to remedy the situation. Think of possible solutions if it is something that keeps coming up.

Get some advice from your well-meaning friends. Should you need to confront a person about a certain issue, make sure that you do it with a clear mind. Avoid letting the situation turn violent. Be wary of the words that you use when you are dealing with your partner. Try to see where they are coming from as you tell them why you are hurt. It is good always to remember that if you plant kindness as a seed, you will harvest kindness in return.

Show Some Kindness; this is another method of showing your loved one that you are a good person despite the conflict. You may be asking yourself how this is related to your problems, but I assure you that when your loved one sees that you are attempting to be nice, you will feel more complete because they will acknowledge it. If you focus on the good side of a person, you will soon realize that your situation is not as bad as you thought it was and that other people are facing worse challenges.

It will help you realize that every couple has their fair share of challenges, and your relationship is not an exception to the rule. I have no better way of fueling your hope than to let you know that if you are willing to be better than the rest, you will be able to make a change for the better.

CHAPTER 12

THE ART OF PERSUASION

Within advertising, politics, and in general, any other area of daily life, persuasion is a skill that we must develop.

Many speak of it and recognize it as a weapon, probably if it is, but a weapon is within everyone's reach, and that is why I recognize persuasion as an art.

But why is persuasion an art that we should all develop?

I will give you an example that cannot fail:

The famous and scary job interviews... We all have to face them at some time in our lives.

Have you ever thought about why you didn't get to keep the position?

The first option may be that your profile was not what they were looking for. Your knowledge and skills were not necessary; in that case, you cannot do anything, but when the job description and you seem to be the same person, everything indicates that you will get the job. But when that doesn't happen, what went wrong?

Perhaps your speech was not good enough to persuade the interviewer and make him see that you are the piece that the company lacks.

Now, have you seen how persuasion is something that we all must learn?

But to continue talking about the subject, it is necessary

that we first define what persuasion is, since it is also a concept that has different opinions and perceptions.

Aristotle is considered the father of Rhetoric, and he was the first to speak of persuasion. Rhetoric is nothing more and nothing less than the technique and art of speaking; remember that in Greek society oral trials and speeches predominated, which were perfected thanks to it.

So, persuasion is supported by good intention. It must be trustworthy and transparent and promote a positive benefit or impact; it does not manipulate as it is almost always thought.

It should be noted that in most cases, by not generalizing, the result is impacted by our beliefs and culture; however, persuasion can seek a good for both parties and not only for one, as our selfishness generally does.

Aristotle spoke to us about the existence of 3 pillars on which persuasion is based:

Pillars of persuasion

- **Ethos:** These arguments are of an affective and moral order and can be seen in the sender of the message. They appeal to the authority and credibility of who issues the speech, here the relationship with their audience is defined.
- **Pathos:** The pathos arguments are effective and are more related to the receiver of the message. We can remember that what changes people and causes a change in actions are emotions and not facts.

- **Logos:** Here, more reference is made to discourse itself. The arguments must be solid, appealing to the reason and intelligence of the audience. This is where the balance is found between emotional and analytical discourse.

In this way and leaving aside all these theoretical parts, let's talk about how persuasion influences advertising.

For this, we can approach persuasion from different angles and perspectives, such as consumer behavior, social influence, and design.

Surely when you think about advertising, the first thing that comes to your mind is manipulation and subliminal messages. But let me tell you that not everything works like this. Within the consumer, there are already certain patterns and beliefs that make them act in some way. The only thing that persuasion does is take advantage of these areas and accentuate the obvious.

What are the needs of consumers?

These personalities change from time to time, even daily, but we go a little further, to social influence.

When people belong to a group, new needs arise. Think about what were the needs that were created when you entered your current job?

For example, when people are promoted, they may no longer be able to get there by public transport, so they need to buy a car; maybe you also had to buy new clothes.

All these needs arise from a sense of belonging.

So here persuasion has pretty much won everything.

The need is already created and arriving at the store means that you must buy something, you only have to choose one option.

This is what we call consumer behavior; another example of this could be when you need to buy a new cell phone.

How is the purchase decision made?

Let us take the example of Apple; within its range of products it has three types of phones: cheap, medium and expensive.

When you get to the store, the seller shows you the first option, and you think "It is very expensive."

And then the second option is the cheapest...

But when you know its price, this comes to mind: "It is cheaper, surely it has some error."

Finally, the third option is the most expensive, and you know that you definitely cannot buy it, so you end up buying the first option, which was the medium.

This purchase is closely linked to the beliefs we have as a society, and we always think that if it is cheap, then it is not so good.

Here is part of what you take advantage of when creating a sales strategy, but that does not mean that "brands want to sell you the most expensive."

Regarding the persuasive design, the information must be presented clearly and pleasantly, without being so pretentious. Also, depending on what you want to show, different technical and visual resources must be used, all to make the user feel comfortable, and you can have a good memory of the experience you had. This is where we put into practice the pillars of Aristotle, and you must manage emotions, arguments, and give confidence to the public you are addressing. The goal is achieved when you generate a memory in the consumer's mind.

Remember that persuasion is not only used by speakers or politicians in their speeches; this is a skill that we all must develop to achieve things and the common good.

Do you remember Emma Watson's speech at the UN?

It is persuasive! And she advocates not only for an objective or benefit for her but for that of the world.

For work, a raise, at school, with your partner and with your family... persuasion is everywhere, put it into practice!

If you start creating persuasive designs, your brand will surely be more successful in terms of positioning it in the minds of consumers.

The History of Persuasion

Do you know what they have in common; a speech by Barack Obama, an announcement by Chanel, a gamification campaign for the VW Polo, and a press release by Repsol? The answer is found in work written more than 2,300 years ago! Its title is The Rhetoric and the author, Aristotle. This treaty establishes the foundations of corporate advertising, political, institutional, emotional, and journalistic communication.

Through this section, I will try to discover how the theoretical precepts and the methodology exposed in The Rhetoric are applied daily and in a multidisciplinary way in the areas of professional communication. The conceptual basis of the work revolves around the command of the word and discourse—discursiveness—as instruments to exercise persuasive communication. Along with these elements are the arguments or reasoning that will be presented to the public to convince them by appealing to their feelings and emotions. Likewise, Aristotle determines and analyzes the protagonists of this process: sender, receiver, message, and channel or medium. The issue is you must project an image of credibility, authority, and moderation that facilitates the acceptance of your messages by the interlocutor. As for the recipient, it will be essential to know their approximate age and social status. In this way, the contents will be adapted to the particularities of the audience. A persuasive message is characterized by a simple style but elaborate, not conveying the feeling of artificiality. The vocabulary will be clear and intelligible for all audiences. And the use of 'linguistic' resources that attract the attention of the interlocutor will be pertinent. Aristotle defines the structure of the messages in preamble, proposition, and epilogue. The preamble will capture the attention of the public to present the topic that will be addressed later. In the proposition, all the argumentative and narrative forces of the exhibition will be overturned. The epilogue will contain a synopsis to summarize and consolidate the transmitted message. The message will appeal to the rational and emotional component that predisposes the interlocutor in a sense desired by the sender. Finally, it specifies that the message and its structures will always be adapted to the channel or medium through which it is transmitted.

As a result, this section constitutes a look at the past that takes us back to the original concepts of communication. This appeal is relevant in the prevailing digital environment in which we are located. In fact, at present, we use the infinite number of technological supports and channels that are within our reach. Thus, we are present in traditional social networks (Facebook, Twitter, Instagram, Pinterest, YouTube, etc.) and other emerging ones (Periscope, Meerkat). And we are up to date with private messaging systems like Telegram and innovative applications like Snapchat. Of course, we know the trends in the creation of branded content (storytelling, scroll telling, etc.) And we try to approach the public through personalized, gamified, and quality themes, thus developing the cross-cutting nature of the information. But, simultaneously, we must not forget that the means technological support is not the end but must be a tool in the exercise of our profession. And we must remember the assertion of the classical thinkers: 'the oldest is the most modern.' Past and present shake hands, since the final objective to guide, influence the interlocutor's will using persuasive stimuli and appealing to his emotions continues to be the same twenty-three centuries later.

Persuasion 101

The Latin word "persuasĭo" came to our language as persuasion, the procedure, and the result of persuading. That Latin word, in turn, derives from a cultism, the verb "persuadere," which is made up of two elements: the prefix "per-," which means "completely," and the verb "suadere," which is synonymous to "advise."

This action (persuade) consists of convincing a person of something, using different motives, or appealing to different techniques.

For example: "First we are going to bet on persuasion: if we do not succeed, we will use force," "It does not serve to impose things with violence, it is essential to achieve persuasion," "Hours and hours of the talk were necessary for the persuasion of my parents, but finally I got permission, and I will be able to travel."

Persuasion is accomplished through influence. The intention is that a subject modifies his way of thinking or his behaviors, for which it is necessary to influence him through his feelings or by supplying him with certain information that, until now, he did not know.

Persuasion can be said to be the opposite of coercion or imposition. While persuasion is accomplished by suggesting things, coercion and imposition are accomplished by force. This means that a person, when persuaded, will act as the other intends but on his own, without fear of a violent or repressive reaction.

Several factors contribute to persuasion. The common

thing is usually to appeal to the commitment of the people, convincing them that what is proposed to them is the right thing. The position of the person trying to persuade another is also relevant. If the individual in question is an authority or is popular, his views are likely to have more persuasive power than the views of others. That is why many political parties bet on bringing celebrities as candidates in election processes.

To persuade someone, it must be taken into account that there are various methods, the most significant of which are the following:

- **Emotional.** Within this group, techniques such as seduction, pity, faith, tradition are used...

- **Rational.** In this case, recourse is made to proof, rhetoric, the establishment of arguments or logic, among others.

- **Polemics**. Such as torture, mind control, and even brainwashing.

Nor can we overlook the existence of a well-known novel that chooses to be titled with the term in question. We are referring to Jane Austen's "Persuasion" (1816) (1775 - 1817), known for other works such as "Pride and Prejudice" (1813) or "Sense and Sensibility" (1811).

Specifically, "Persuasion" is the last book the English author wrote. It involves a protagonist Anne, a woman who suffered, due to social norms, a hard blow to love when she had to reject the man she was in love with, simply because she did not come from a wealthy family. That circumstance meant that she watched the years go by on her own. However, everything changes when she meets that man again, who is now a highly recognized and also enriched captain.

Discover When You Are the Target

Are you the puppet of others? Learn the three steps to cut the threads that bind you to those who try to handle you...

I don't understand how it happens, but every time I meet my sister, I lose. When Lidia wants me to do something for her, she always succeeds! Again, I don't know how it happens, but does the situation unfold in a way that leaves me no choice but to do what she wants?

This is Francis' complaint; Lidia, his older sister, is a teacher in the art of manipulation. And Francis is not alone; his sister's name can be substituted for a son, a husband, a mother-in-law, a colleague, or even a best friend. And there are people who, to get away with it, handle others as if they were puppets.

The manipulators, those skilled "puppeteers," know how to handle the strings of those who fall into their orbit to achieve their goals. Some do it consciously because their plan is coldly calculated; others act like this because it is the only way they know to get away with it. But everyone, without exception, can continue to work that way because they have a great partner. Guess who? The person who lets himself be manipulated. In many cases, she is not a victim, but a volunteer in that frustrating game. In other words: manipulation happens and persists because the manipulated allows it to happen.

Review your case. Perhaps you give in out of grief, out of a sense of obligation, because you fear offending that person or keeping the peace. Many times you feel that the circumstances have conspired in a way that leaves you no choice but, once again, to dance to the music you are playing (the most typical case is the vendor who warns you to act now! because the "wonderful" offer ends in five minutes). You end up feeling frustrated, irritated, exhausted, and full of resentment. The truth is that your relationships with these "puppeteers" are not the best. Also, how much time, money, resources, and peace of mind have you lost in the hands of the manipulators!

But is there a light at the end of this tunnel? The good news is that while you are responsible for what happens, in the same way, you can take control of your life and cut the threads that tie you to the manipulator. Here are three steps to achieve it.

1. Recognize the Game

Some victims of manipulation feel uncomfortable after dealing with one of these specimens but cannot identify exactly why. As Francis says, "I don't know how, but my sister always gets me to do what she wants."

That is why the first step to cut the threads that tie you to the manipulator is to recognize what their game is. In other words: discover what weapons he uses to wield you. Do they employ the penalty? "I have not had as good luck in life as you." Maybe they control you with guilt feelings. "If you don't help me, my children your nephews! Will go bankrupt." Or he presents you with the fait accompli, believing that "it is better to ask for forgiveness than to ask permission." Example: "I took the liberty of taking this from your home." You must know their strategies so that you are prepared and not taken by surprise. "I discovered that my sister's tactic is to use the penalty." Does she play the unhappy, plagued by bad luck? "And I always fall," admits Francis. Once you recognize this person's modus operandi, take the next step.

2. Discover Your «Buttons»

Manipulators have an effective secret: they use the appropriate tactics for each person because they know which one works with each individual. With one is the feeling of guilt, while with another it is a pain; with some, it is vanity (the manipulator pretends to be incompetent to be rescued, making the rescuer feel important - without realizing that he has been used) or even fear of divorce, dismissal, abandonment or ruin.

What is your Achilles heel? Discover the «buttons» that you have, and that press you to operate as if you were a robot. When you determine that you always fall out of grief, vanity, or because you don't know how to act when you are presented with a fait accompli, stop. Discuss why you have that particular "button" and what your fear is if you don't budge. Are they realistic? Or are you allowing yourself to be influenced by the "puppeteer"? Is it fair to yourself that you feel influenced by the "puppeteer? And that you think like this? How does it affect you or harm you? And what effect does it have on your relationship with that person? Do you want to keep the threads that bind you to the «puppeteer»? If you want to cut them and be free, continue to the next step.

3. Modify Your Behavior

Now that you know what tactics these people use to manipulate you and you recognize why you fall into the trap; you should modify your behavior.

- Recognize tampering

- Don't be rushed. Take all the time you need to assess the situation and determine how you want to respond.

- Mentally prepare yourself for everything you will feel in those moments: grief, fear, guilt, and anxiety. Let those feelings flood you and pass, like a wave that envelops you and then drifts away. Remember: the "puppeteer" uses them precisely because they are effective. Accept the possibility that some people will stray from you or that some relationships will radically change. But if you are clear that nothing based on manipulation is positive, you will be at peace with that possibility.

- Express your preference or your position with kindness, but with total firmness. If the person insists, be consistent, since it is you who will teach others how they can be with you, simply by the treatment you allow. Be prepared to repeat the same thing a thousand times, and for the "puppeteer" to find other tactics to handle you. Again: be consistent. The moment you stop accepting manipulation, the person will understand that their tactics do not work for you - and you will be free.

When You Should Seek Help

Sometimes the situation reaches levels that you cannot handle using the same tactics that would work in normal situations. If you are dealing with an unstable person, physically abusing you, threatening suicide, or acting "crazy," take that situation very seriously and seek help urgently. Both you and others affected must be safe from a dangerous situation.

Behavioral Traits of Manipulation

If you still do not know how to identify a manipulative person, certain tips can help you. These types of people usually have some characteristics that make them evident, so you must know what they are.

The dangerous thing about manipulative people is that they do not usually have any kind of scruples. When they detect a potential victim, they immediately search for their vulnerabilities to exploit them and take advantage of them through emotional manipulation.

This is done gradually; gradually enveloping people with words and acts of pretended empathy, which are only tools they use to achieve their nefarious purposes.

Although we are aware of the damage that a manipulator can bring to our lives, it is not an easy task to identify them and detect if we are facing any of them.

Fortunately, some fairly clear indications give them away, and to which we must remain vigilant, to avoid falling into their networks and to escape in time from their bad influences.

Traits that reveal a manipulative person

These are the most common behavioral traits that manipulative people present:

1. They are skilled speakers

Manipulators effectively handle the gift of speech.

They spin everything with great skill and always at their convenience, managing to dupe their victim through the distortion of ideas and their emotional exploitation.

All their activity is focused on mastering the situation and obtaining benefits or some type of performance; it always consists of their victims.

To do this, they purposely create a power imbalance; that allows them to exploit the other person without this fact being evident to their victim.

2. They are never satisfied

The manipulative person is not easily satiated and is always asking and squeezing incessantly.

His behavior has more to do with the satisfaction of his ego, through which he achieves the total manipulation of his victim.

This makes him feel that he has absolute control over her and that he can exploit her at his whim until he reaches the limit, demanding more and more until he achieves the emotional breakdown.

3. Impersonating a victim

This is the preferred role that is often played flawlessly by the manipulator.

It is a kind of emotional blackmail in which the manipulator turns out to be the victim and you the victimizer.

They proclaim that their situation is due to the bad behavior of other people and that they are the target of their injustices.

With this behavior, they manage to awaken people's sense of pity.

4. Present a picture of being needy

The manipulators present themselves as a weak person of spirit, who urgently requires support and is dependent on others.

But behind that lamb mask is a manipulative wolf, who exploits your good feelings until you feel responsible for his person; this is just a tactic to know how you act.

5. Lies easily

He has an extraordinary capability to lie, without being revealed by any gesture or the tone of his voice. He is a myth maniac with all the letters.

The level is such that in some cases, he becomes convinced of his lies, which makes them even more credible.

That is the reason why he turns to his victim at all stages of the manipulation process until he reaches his goals.

Lacking scruples, he tries to make one believe that his lies are not important and that they were not told with malicious intent, when these are evident.

Details you should not miss

For a manipulator to exist, there must also be a manipulated victim. If you allow a manipulator to recreate his tricks on you, he will have the fertile ground to launch his nets.

Manipulators completely devalue their victims, so it is necessary to avoid living with them at all costs.

CHAPTER 13

HOW TO RECOGNIZE DOUBLE-FACED PEOPLE

Double-faced people have both a private and a public face. Depending on the situation, they use different masks to harness opportunism to their banner. They pretend to be what they are not, to take advantage of it. In general, to receive social approval, or to place themselves above others. Did you know that Hypocritical people are sometimes called double-faced people?

Relationships are always challenging with a fake person since we're never sure what they think or feel. They certainly have no doubts about exploiting us to achieve their goals.

Hypocritical People: Definition.

Hypocrisy is confusion in what is being said and what is being done, or between what one thinks and feels and what is being portrayed. It is a way to hide or suppress true desires, thoughts, and emotions and instead, adapt to environmental expectations.

The word hypocrisy derives from an ancient Greek word, hupokrisis, which means "step." In that sense, a hypocrite, or hupokrités, was merely an actress, someone on stage pretending to be someone else.

But perhaps the best description of hypocrisy comes from American politician Adlai E. Stevenson, who said: "A hypocrite is the sort of individual who would cut a redwood, set up a stage, and then make a speech about nature preservation."

We all indeed experience a crucial tension as social beings between our interests and the interests of others. The desires cannot always coincide with those of others. To solve this conflict without renouncing our "I," and without causing undue social tension, we are developing different, more, or less assertive strategies that allow us to combine public and private interests.

There are individuals, however, who have not developed such techniques but tend to hide what they think or feel. It is not about people who are dependent or submissive, but they resort to hypocrisy as a tactic to achieve their goals. At the same time, it is a maladaptive tactic in the long run as it produces a deep dissonance between actions and feelings, values, and ideas.

How do you unmask the wrong person? Here are Double-faced people's top five behaviors:

1. They are happy to see someone punished. Their "high" moral norm causes them to point the accusing finger at someone, and it is not uncommon for them to humiliate or disqualify someone even in public. It's a retaliation tactic in which they seek to concentrate attention on the other's perceived mistakes, failures, or flaws so that those around them don't know their differences and hypocrisy.

2. They have an aura of moral arrogance. Double-faced people appear to be halfway between narcissism and moral dominance. We are also victims of the Dunning-

Kruger effect, and the level of arrogance will make us feel low-level, inexperienced when we communicate with them, or we may just assume that we are not good enough.

3. They never get the rules. There are laws and regulations, but they apply only to others. Hypocrites assume that they are above the law because they have an inherent sense of justice and morality and are not obligated to obey it.

4. The blame is never theirs, and they always have an excuse. Double-faced people typically do not notice their conflicts and errors, even though they are really clear. Such people do not apologize or accept their guilt, and they are continually resorting to excuses. Circumstances are always mitigating for them, and mistakes never belong.

5. Do what I'm saying and not what I am doing. This may be the maxim that guides hypocrites. Their acts rarely align with the underlying beliefs of their expression or attitudes. This is because their primary incentive is to look nice and make the best of it for others.

The three tactics Double-faced and Fake people use

1. Moral double standards. It refers to hypocritical individuals who invoke irreproachable motivations on an ongoing basis but who do not personally behave according to those moral laws. For example, a person may continually speak about the importance of helping others, but they look the other way when the time comes to reach out to those who need support. Or a person who praises ideals such as honesty and the importance of telling the truth, but then his wife becomes unfaithful.

2. Equal moral principles. This applies to false people who are soft when it comes to self-judgment but apply a strict moral norm to others. For example, if a driver doesn't stop when he gets to a crosswalk, the pedestrian will be really upset, but when this pedestrian is behind the wheel and doing the same, he will use reasons to justify why he did not stop. He's the one who can see the speck in another's eye but not the log in his own eye.

3. Moral frailty. There are individuals who, due to cognitive dissonance, contradict their own attitudes. For instance, a person may talk about the importance of going to vote, but he doesn't go to the polls on voting day. In this scenario, what fails is self-control. The individual believes what he says, but he doesn't have enough courage when it comes to putting it into action. However, he doesn't want to admit it publicly and continues to offer moral lessons.

How are we so double-faced?

You probably know more than one Double-faced person in your world. And you're probably still wondering how you could seem unaware of the tension between his words and his act. The theory for this phenomenon comes from psychologist Patricia Linville who worked at Yale University, and the word "self-complexity" was coined in the mid-1980s. Their theory is that the less complex the "I" cognitive representation is, the more severe the variations in the mood and attitudes of the individual would become.

In other words, some people seem to view themselves from a very narrow viewpoint. For example, they define themselves by the positions they perform, so they think they're a "self-sacrificing mother" or a "good boss." The issue is that having such a restricted self-definition makes us mentally more dysfunctional and prevents us from coping with the contradictions inherent in ourselves.

We will take a look at an experiment performed at the University of Miami to understand this phenomenon better. Psychologists asked college students to determine the value of research competencies. They were then asked to recall all the occasions they had ignored the report, intending to unmask the potential hypocrisy behind the initial responses.

Interestingly, students who had less self-complexity at that time were more likely to change their initial opinions; that is, they rectified suggesting that learning was not so necessary after all.

This could clarify why some people are saying one thing and doing another. Their remarks come from a completely different portrayal of the "me" in certain situations acting on the "me." In practice, double-faced people are only trying to keep the identity simple, and they have built up immunity by separating their words from their actions.

For example, in the case of politicians, it is normal for them to hold a conversation related to their "political self," while doing something diametrically opposite in their "job" or "family" life. They try to preserve their separate "selves" in this way, so they cannot combine them.

Such reports indicate that many people have double-faced faces without knowing it. In reality, they sometimes fail to understand and hide behind excuses when we bring them face to face with their contradictions.

Not everyone lives in this "hypocritical ignorance" society. Some learn to manipulate hypocrisy, particularly when they understand that it is neither practical nor beneficial to pursue those ideas. Such people have no trouble announcing something and doing the opposite only because they think it's more convenient. Yet neither do they publicly accept their hypocrisy because it is too humiliating and would be a major blow to their "I," which is why they argue that circumstances have changed them.

How do Double-faced men trouble us so much?

The response comes from research conducted at Yale University or at least part thereof. Psychologists have discovered that what most disturbs us about Double-faced is not the incoherence between their words and their acts, but rather that their moral proclamations are misleading and tend to appear as more upright people than they are.

We don't like hypocrites in reality, because they trick us. Also, it has been shown that we tend to accept and support moral claims or that to justify the actions implies a certain degree of generalization. For example, if a person leaves a project, we prefer the reason, "There is no point in spending more energy" than "I don't want to spend more energy." And when we come across the truth, we feel more disappointed and discouraged.

That means we are also contributing to the hypocrisy that persists on a social level, in a way. In reality, we might have acted in a Double-faced manner, even in other circumstances, to try to give us a better picture of ourselves.

How to deal with Double-faced people?

Being truthful and recognizing that many inconsistencies coexist within each of us is the best way to combat hypocrisy. In certain circumstances, we can all act hypocritically, but there is an important line between the level of social and tolerable hypocrisy and the intolerable hypocrisy which pretends to offer moral lessons. We don't have to meet other people's expectations, nor do we have to become morals preachers. We just have to live and let live.

Hear him out. While a Double-faced person's first response to criticism is to become angry, the smart thing to do is to calm down and listen. His words may well stem from genuine concern for us. And we have to learn to distinguish the grain from the chaff, and we will consider it if the idea is worth it. If it is not, then we should still disregard it.

Don't beat him up. It is typically futile to explicitly accuse a Double-faced person of not practicing what he preaches because it will produce a defensive reaction. Oddly enough, that person will respond by counterattacking, falling into an argument that makes no sense to figure out who is the less hypocritical of both. Therefore, no matter how much his words annoy you, do not lose composure, and do not strike him. Remember that you are influenced by who makes you mad.

Don't feel bad about it. The hypocritical person would probably make you feel bad for not being good enough. When you are aware of the reasons for your actions, it is important that you retain perspective and do not feel guilty. Remember that it can only damage you, to which you add undue importance, after all.

Conversation explains. In certain cases, double-faced people go around the bush, spreading a general and ambiguous argument in which everyone is guilty and immoral, but in particular, they do not point the accusing finger at anybody. If you think, in his voice, he refers to you, ask him if he is. It's just enough to ask for a clarification of his vocabulary to put a stop to his attitude.

Mark your boundaries. If the hypocrite crosses your red lines, then feel free to mark them. You should let him know you are not going to tolerate moral discourses or undeserved rebukes that make you feel bad. Speak quietly and with certainty. If the Double-faced person realizes that his discourse does not make an impression on you, he will leave you alone sooner rather than later.

CHAPTER 14

DARK PERSUASION METHODS

In Aristotle's Rhetoric, logos is the most prominent type of rhetoric. It refers to logical reasoning, to our attempt to make use of the intellect.

When we present our arguments, whether oral or written, we try to be persuasive. Just before accepting our claims, the public must consider our point of view. That is what rhetoric is; that others adopt our point of view.

So, who better to explain the rhetoric than Aristotle? Plato's student studies focused on rhetoric. For this reason, Aristotle's rhetoric consists of three categories: pathos, ethos, and logos.

In Aristotle's rhetoric, pathos, ethos, and logos are the three fundamental pillars. Today, these three categories are considered different ways of convincing an audience about a particular topic, belief, or conclusion. Let's delve into the topic below.

Aristotle's pathos

Pathos means 'suffering and experience.' In Aristotle's rhetoric, this carries over to the speaker or writer's ability to evoke emotions and feelings in his audience. The pathos is associated with emotion, appeals to empathize with the audience, and spark your imagination.

Essentially, pathos is seeking empathy with the audience. When used, the argument's values, beliefs, and understanding are engaged and communicated to the audience through a story. Thus, according to studies such as those carried out at Nijmegen University in Norway by doctors Frans Derkse and Jozien Bensing, empathy is key to improving not only communication but the connection between people from an emotional point of view.

The pathos is used when the arguments to be presented are controversial. Since these arguments are often lacking in logic, success will reside in the ability to empathize with the audience.

In a case for constitutionally banning abortion, for instance, the descriptive language may be used to depict babies and the promise of a fresh beginning to elicit sorrow and fear on the part of the public.

Aristotle's ethos

The second category, ethos, means character and comes from the word ethnos, which means moral and showing moral personality. For speakers and writers, the ethos is shaped by its credibility and similarity to the audience. As an authority on the subject, the speaker must be trustworthy and respected.

It is not enough to allow rational justification for the arguments to be successful. To appear trustworthy, information has to be delivered accurately, as well.

Ethos is especially important in generating popular interest, according to Aristotle's rhetoric. The message sound and style would be crucial to that.

Furthermore, the character is also going to be influenced by the speaker's reputation, which is independent of the message.

For example, speaking to an audience as an equal, rather than as passive characters, increases the likelihood that people will engage in actively listening to arguments.

Aristotle's logos

Logos means word, speech, or reason. Convincingly, the logos is the rationale behind claims by the author. The logos refer to every effort and logical arguments to speak to the intellect. Thus, logical reasoning presents two forms: deductive and inductive.

Deductive reasoning argues that, "If A is true, and B is true, the intersection of A and B must also be true."

For example, the logos argument of "women like oranges" would be "women like fruits" and "oranges are fruits."

Inductive reasoning also uses premises, but the conclusion is only an expectation and may not necessarily be true because of its subjective nature. For example, the phrases "Peter likes comedy" and "This movie is a comedy" can reasonably conclude that "Peter will like this movie."

Aristotle's rhetoric

In Aristotle's rhetoric, logos was his favorite argumentative technique. However, on a day-to-day basis, everyday arguments depend more on pathos and ethos. The combination of all three is used to make rehearsals more persuasive and central to the discussion team's strategy.

The people who master them have the ability to convince others to perform a certain action or to buy a product or service. Even so, in modernity, the pathos seems to have a greater influence. Populist discourses, which seek to excite rather than provide logical arguments, seem to be catching on more easily.

The same is true for fake news. Many may lack logic, but, despite their strong capacity to empathize, the public embraces them. Being aware of these three techniques in Aristotle's rhetoric will help us to understand certain arguments that are intended to convince us even by fallacies.

CHAPTER 15

NEURO-LINGUISTIC PROGRAMMING

It is easy for the concept of Neuro-linguistic Programming to generate confusion. What is it based on? When does it apply? Here are some key ideas to know what NLP is.

What is Neuro-linguistic Programming?

Steve Bavister and Amanda Vickers (2014) define Neuro-linguistic Programming as a communication model that focuses on identifying and using thought models that influence a person's behavior as a way to improve the quality and effectiveness of life.

One problem with NLP is the nature of its name, since, when the term "Neuro-linguistic Programming" is mentioned to people who have never heard of it, the reaction is usually a bit negative. On the other hand, the name could suggest that we are dealing with empirical techniques derived from neuroscience, but no evidence confirms their efficacy.

Stephen Briers (2012) says that NLP is not a coherent treatment, but "a hodgepodge of different techniques without a very clear theoretical basis." This author maintains that the maxim of Neuro-linguistic Programming is narcissistic, egocentric, and dissociated from the notions of responsibility.

Also, he states that "sometimes we have to accept and mourn the death of our dreams, not only occasionally dismiss them as inconsequential. The re-framing of NLP puts us in the role of a widower avoiding the pain of mourning by jumping into a relationship with a younger woman, not stopping to say a proper goodbye to his dead wife."

What does the Neuro-linguistic Programming model focus on?

The world is experienced through five senses: sight, hearing, touch, smell, and taste. Much information comes to us continuously; consciously and unconsciously, we eliminate what we do not want to pay attention to. We are told that the remaining information is based on our past experiences, values, and beliefs. What we end up with is incomplete and inaccurate, since some of the general information has been removed, and the rest has been generalized or distorted.

What is NLP based on?

The most important thing to have a vision of what Neuro-Linguistic Programming is, is to know that it is based on four fundamental aspects, which are known as the "four pillars," according to Steve Bavister and Amanda Vickers (2014).

1. Results

To achieve something, we talk about objectives; in NLP, the term of results is used. If there is a prior concentration on what you want to achieve, there will be a guide that will guide all of that person's available resources toward achieving a goal.

2. Sensory acuity

Sensory acuity refers to the ability to observe or detect small details to be aware of what is happening around us. People vary greatly in realizing what they see, hear, or feel. Some people are dedicated to observing their environment more, while others are more focused on their own emotions and thoughts.

3. Flexibility in behavior

When you start to know what your results are and use your sensory acuity to observe what is happening, the information you obtain allows you to make adjustments in your behavior, if necessary. If the actions you perform don't take you in the direction you want, then you should obviously try to go another way or try something different. However, many people lack that flexibility in behavior and insist on doing the same thing over and over again.

4. Rapport

The rapport could be considered as that component that unites people. Most of the time, it happens naturally, automatically, instinctively. Some people we meet seem to share our life perspective, while there are other people we don't connect with. The capacity for rapport with other people must be improved to obtain more effective relationships.

The presuppositions of Neuro-linguistic Programming

Salvador Carrión (2008), refers that a presupposition is something we take for granted without any proof. It tells us that Neuro-linguistic Programming does not intend that the presuppositions are true, although there is quite palpable evidence to support many of them. I have tried to search for the "evidence" that supports these assumptions, but I have only found an explanation for each of them.

Life, mind, and body are one system

The mind and body are considered as a single system; each was directly influencing the other. For example, what happens inside your body affects your thoughts and will affect the people around you.

You can't stop communicating

The message we are trying to convey is not always the one that others receive. Therefore, from Neuro-linguistic Programming, it tells us that we must be aware of the reactions of others to see if our message has been successful. This can lead to serious difficulties when preparing a message, since focusing on reactions or being alert to possible consequences is not something that will add quality to communication.

Beneath each behavior, there is a positive intention

In addiction or bad behavior, there is always a positive intention. Therefore finding the root of that problem and externalizing the positive intention, you can go from smoking for 15 years to not having that need.

If what you're doing doesn't work, do something else

If you try a way to approach a problem and don't get the results you expected, try something different and keep varying your behavior until you get the answer you were looking for.

If one person can do something, everyone can learn to do it

There is, in NLP, the process of modeling excellence. If you want an article published, for example, you could look at someone who is brilliant at writing and imitate the way they do it. In this way, you will be immersing yourself in the knowledge of great value.

Criticism of New Language Programming

Roderique-Davies (2009) states that using the word "neuro" in NLP is "effectively fraudulent since NLP does not explain the neural level, and it could be argued that its use is falsely fed on the notion of scientific credibility."

On the other hand, Devilly (2005) maintains that the so-called "power therapies" gain popularity because they are promoted, like other pseudoscience's, using a set of tactics of social influence. These include making extraordinary claims such as "a one-session cure for any traumatic memory." These types of strategies are incredibly disproportionate and play with the health of many people who place their trust in professionals with supposed preparation and ethics when carrying out their activity.

The few effective tools or more or less proven theories of Neuro-linguistic Programming, do not belong exclusively to it, and what is new has not been empirically proven. What's more, what's new about it, either seems very simplistic or contradicts what science says.

Verbal vs. Non-Verbal Communication

NLP uses both verbal and non-verbal language. Rapport can be established both through the verbal language as the non-verbal. The meaning of communication is the verbal and non-verbal response we receive. By understanding the power of non-verbal language, we can realize that rather than investing in word management, it is much better to invest in the control of our internal states and to make our verbal language consistent with non-verbal language.

The interlocutor's unconscious psyche will capture the discrepancy between verbal and non-verbal language. Observing the non-verbal language of others is very interesting. NLP supporters, by way of example, argue that through aspects of nonverbal language such as eye movement, we can discover if someone is cheating.

For this, you must take into consideration, apart from your sensitive state, the other person's channel, the connection, the verbal language (not just words), and your non-verbal language. This is a tool to have a better understanding of what people do essentially through the language and observation of their non-verbal language.

Neuro-linguistic programming is the science that takes care to study the mental patterns of each person.

The moment a person cheats, their non-verbal language runs counter to their words, if we are careful to capture their non-verbal language. Calibrating a person means knowing, through their non-verbal and verbal language, their internal state. That is, their state of mind and taking it into account in the communication process.

This form of internal representation is reflected in the way of meditating, the verbal and non-verbal language used, the movement of the eyes, the physiology, the genre of breathing, the timbre of the voice, etc. Words can disguise thoughts and feelings, but the body does not so that in the case of dissonance between verbal and non-verbal language, one is going to have to adhere to what is communicated by the body. We already know that NLP is the science of how language, verbal, and non-verbal, affects the neurological system.

However, the best way to notice our partner's lies is to observe non-verbal language. The non-verbal language alone is not an impact tool, but is an addition.

Verbal (words spun with logic and cohesion).

Non-Verbal (gestures, postures, movements, tone, etc.).

For example, for a politician speaking, it is not so essential precisely what is stated, but rather the emphasis he places through gestures and changes in voice modulation.

Learn to notice inconsistencies between verbal language and the anatomical can be very useful for you. Words and verbal language are largely a selective summary of what is going on in our heads. What we know by persuasion is an NLP model that affirms to us that through the superficial structure, which is a verbal and non-verbal language, we can get to know the deep structure, that is, the internal representations of our interlocutor.

NLP To Influence

You are constantly influencing others. Maybe that surprises you, but it's true. Here's why.

Language does not allow us to embrace and express all of reality at once. Choosing your words is necessary to exclude others. Choosing your words also means limiting the immense wealth of your thoughts. What you communicate thus necessarily orientates in one direction or another. Therefore, communication is inseparable from influence.

That is why in NLP, it is said that it is impossible not to influence. Without you being necessarily aware of it, each of your words, each of your actions is capable of having an impact on others (by frightening them, destabilizing them, or by convincing them, inspiring them, motivating them).

It remains to be seen which way you want to influence.

Influencing others does not mean manipulating others. It is entirely possible to broaden your sphere of influence with ethics. You exercise manipulation when you turn fully to your personal goal without taking into consideration the interests of the individuals involved. This might surprise you, but you are unconsciously constantly influencing others, especially when you choose your words to communicate and exclude others. What you express necessarily leads to some meaning. So, you can't talk about influence without talking about communication. In NLP, it is said that it is impossible to perform acts or speak without impacting on something or a person. But all your gestures and your words are not necessarily emitted with a conscience. You can learn to convince, to be the source of inspiration for those around you, to motivate your colleagues to influence with NLP. Read on to find out how.

Methods to influence with NLP

Now that you know the difference between manipulating and influencing NLP, you will be able to ethically impact the behavior of others without focusing solely on your cause. It remains to be seen for what purpose you wish to do this. Below you will find a set of methods to apply daily. These will also allow you to make good use of your sales, seduction, or persuasion skills.

Influencing with NLP and foot in the door

The "foot in the door" method consists, first of all, of asking for a small service that no one can refuse, then demanding a more important one.

Example: You ask your neighbor to empty your mailbox during your absence. This person accepts, then before leaving, you also ask him to water your plants, he cannot refuse you after accepting the first service.

Influencing with NLP or the door in the nose

Unlike the foot-in-the-door technique, the door in the nose is asking a person for a service that they cannot do. The influencer knows this, but behind this request, he will propose something much more acceptable.

Example: You are influenced by the "door in your nose" when your boss asks you to work this weekend. He knows that you will refuse this request and has planned something else. He then suggests that you work more than 8 hours next Monday. It will be impossible for you to have to say "no" again.

Influencing with NLP and priming

"Priming" is not a technique of influence, but rather of manipulation. It should not be used if your goal is not to manipulate others. One feels the lie by playing on the incompleteness of the information.

Example: You have seen on the Internet that a store offers cheap clothing. When you arrive, the vendors tell you that these items are sold out, when in reality they only wanted you to come to spend more money than you expected when you saw something that you liked. These inexpensive clothes never existed.

Foot to mouth technique

The foot-in-the-mouth technique uses formulas of interrogative politeness to obtain positive responses until the end of the conversation.

Example: To get a positive response from a healthy person,

you will ask them, "How are you?" » « "Do you like the weather?" » And so on until asking him, « "Would you like to go there and eat some good ice cream?"

Influencing with NLP or fear-relief

The fear-relief system consists of causing great anxiety by indirectly making threats. Then the person who tries to influence will change his tone after a while by the presence of an associate. The person who has suffered the fear will suddenly relieve it. This relief will instinctively push him to submit to expectations. Doesn't that remind you of your couple's arguments?

The "forearm touch" method

This technique may surprise you, but you can try it to find out. It turns out that touching a person's forearm without provoking them while avoiding that person's gaze allows you to obtain what you expect from this individual very easily.

The participation

Even the smallest participation allows you to get what you want. Commit as long as possible because it will change the image that others had of you. Little effort can be enough to impact many things.

Emotionally classify people

When you rank someone for what they do well, you will touch their heart. Tell him that he is orderly when you see his room well cleaned and furnished. Unconsciously, he will spend more hours cleaning this space in the future.

Support your statement with well-chosen words; for example, "it shows that you like taking care of people."

NLP Techniques You Must Master

We have heard of them, but what are NLP techniques? Indeed, we cannot speak of Neuro-linguistic Programming as a science, which is why it has received some criticism. But it is considered a "model," that is, a set of techniques and theories focused on understanding behaviors and orienting the human being towards self-knowledge and the achievement of objectives.

But better, let's first analyze its acronyms carefully:

On the one hand, we have the word "programming," which refers to the intention to reprogram psychological behaviors, beliefs, and processes. The concept "neuro" leads us to the idea that all behavior is based on a series of neurological processes. And finally, "linguistics" responds to the concept that all these neurological processes are expressed through a specific verbal and body language.

NLP is a set of models, skills, and techniques to think and act effectively in the world. The purpose of NLP is to be useful, increase options, and improve quality of life.

-John Grinder-

NLP principles And Techniques, You Must Master

That dimensional triad that we mentioned has the initial objective of understanding our internal processes to reprogram the way we communicate and express ourselves, to change beliefs, and to make us feel safe to achieve our success. Quite a challenge, right? But let's get to know, in a brief way, some more of its aspects and NLP techniques.

1. Communication

NLP tells us that the way we communicate and the words we use define our reality and the way we understand the world. A personal perspective that sometimes does not coincide with that of our interlocutors.

In addition to this, people have two types of communication: internal (what we think and feel within ourselves) and external (where in addition to the words that we express aloud, gestures, postures and gestures are united).

2. How to process information

We differentiate ourselves in our way of "capturing" information. Some people are guided more by the visual, others by the auditory route, others by the sensations... Stop for a moment on this idea: How do you remember things the most, with words or images?

Try to remember a moment from your past; how does that memory come to mind? Observe how you analyze and capture the information around you, if you are, for example, more visual or auditory.

3. The anchor

A way to achieve objectives or overcome certain problems would be based on this concept, already used by behavioral psychology and one of the basic NLP techniques.

Let's imagine a situation that causes us a lot of anguish and anxiety; public speaking, for example. One way to deal with this reality would be to "anchor" a pleasant, relaxed, and positive moment of our memory and associate it using visualization and breathing techniques with the "stressful situation."

A walk on the beach when we were children, a sunset with our partner, relaxing music... all this should help us "weaken that fear" and reprogram new realities where harmony prevails. In this way, gradually, we "anchor" ourselves in a calm and pleasant situation to face an event that is stressful for us.

4. The time

Time is of particular importance for each person, but you must know how to manage yourself appropriately. In the past, our memories and emotions come together, a trunk from which good things can sometimes be taken to redirect the "now."

Because it is in the present where sensory experiences prevail, in which truly important events take place and where we must invest all our efforts given a good future. Therefore, working in the present is essential in NLP to sow the future that we would like to have.

The future does not yet exist; hence it must be established as that point where our desires are nailed to push our present. Our now.

5. Ecology of systems

We all have a system of beliefs and determined values built throughout our lives, and they are the motors that guide our neurological axes. "We are what we believe," and beliefs are the conceptions of our world, which promote action and behavior.

Sometimes these beliefs are so ingrained in our being that we do not even realize if they are beneficial for us or not. We may be hurting ourselves without knowing it... Hence, NLP delves into our ecology of systems to make us aware and reorganize these structures more beneficially and optimally.

These are then, in broad strokes, the basic pillars on which this approach to the human mind is based. Neuro-linguistic Programming, where the way we interpret our reality and organize the information prevails: the senses, the language, the time, words, memories, beliefs... are those leaves that make up the tree of our life.

NLP techniques help to vary or focus differently on some of these parts to direct our lives towards certain goals.

CHAPTER 16

BODY LANGUAGE 101

Body language: Body movements and learned or somatogenic gestures, non-oral, visual, auditory, or tactile perception, alone or about the linguistic and paralinguistic structure and the communicative situation. It may also be defined as the specific term used for modes of communication that include body movements and gestures, rather than (or beside) sounds, verbal language, or other types of communication. Body movements that bring special meanings to the spoken word during a communicative event can sometimes have an intention or not. These movements are studied by kinesics.

Developing

Sometimes a text is used instead of a word or a sentence, or something is drawn with the hands to complement what is said orally. For example, the signal of what is said goes between quotation marks which are made with the index and middle fingers of both hands. For example: To indicate late arrival, the clock is tapped. It belongs to the category of paralanguages, which describe all forms of non-verbal human communication. This includes the most subtle and unconscious movements, including winking and slight eyebrow movements. Also, body language can include the use of facial expressions and posture.

Paralanguage (including body language) has been extensively studied in social psychology. In everyday discourse and popular psychology, the term is often applied to body language considered involuntary. However, the difference between what is considered voluntary and involuntary body language is often controversial. For example, a smile can be triggered consciously or unconsciously.

Body posture

Body posture is the posture of the body or its parts about a reference system, either the orientation of an element of the body with another element or with the body as a whole, or its relationship with another person.

Within the body language, one talks about open or closed postures. The first ones are those postures where there are no barriers such as arms or legs between one interlocutor and others, otherwise in closed postures, where for example, crossed arms are used to isolate or protect the body (unconsciously in many cases). Furthermore, it is important to consider the ideal positions to speak according to the case, for example:

- In competitive situations: face to face.
- To help or cooperate: next door.
- To chat: at a right angle.

Head posture

- Side to side movements: denial.
- Up and down movements: assent.
- Above: neutral or evaluation.
- Laterally tilted: interest.

- Tilt down: disapproval, negative attitude.

Arms pose

- Standard crossing: defensive posture, can also mean insecurity.
- Crossing them while keeping your fists closed indicates a sign of defense and hostility.
- Crossing your arms holding your arms is a sign of restriction.

Leg pose

- Standard crossing: defensive attitude.
- Cross in 4 ("in Indian"): Competition, discussion.
- Cross while standing: Discomfort, tension.
- Cross the ankles: Used to conceal a negative attitude.

Important considerations

If you lean too much towards the other person, you will be invading their personal space. And this should not be done when there is still not much confidence, you will appear too aggressive.

Arms crossed are a sign. Keeping your arms crossed is a sign of withdrawal; it means that the person does not want to be intimate, that they do not feel confident, or that they are not completely well.

A shrunken posture means boredom.

Maintaining a relaxed position with slightly open arms and legs demonstrates self-confidence and security.

Getting closer than you should or a rigid body can demonstrate aggressiveness.

Showing yourself upright is the best thing for when you want to demonstrate security, courage, and importance in what you do.

Hands on the waist: defiance, aggressiveness.

Thumbs on the waist or pockets: manhood.

Finger-pointing: challenge.

The gestures

A gesture is a form of non-verbal communication executed with some part of the body and produced by the movement of the joints and muscles of the arms, hands, and head.

The language of gestures allows a variety of feelings and thoughts to be expressed, from contempt and hostility to approval and affection. Virtually all people use gestures and body language in addition to words when they speak. There are ethnic groups and certain communication languages that use many more gestures than the average. Certain types of gestures can be considered culturally acceptable or not, depending on the place and context in which they are performed. Five categories of gestures are distinguished, proposed by Paul Ekman and Wallace Friesen:

- **Emblematic gestures or emblems:** They are signals emitted intentionally and that everyone knows their meaning. (thumb raised)

- **Illustrative gestures:** Gestures that accompany verbal communication to clarify or emphasize what is said, to impersonate a word in a difficult situation, etc. They are used intentionally. These gestures are very useful in speeches and when speaking in public.
- **Regulatory gestures of interaction:** With them, communication is synchronized or regulated, and the channel does not disappear. They are used to take over in conversation, to start and end the interaction, to give way to speak... (shake hands).
- **Gestures that express emotional states or displays of affection:** This type of gesture reflects the emotional state of the person and is the emotional result of the moment. As an example, we can mention gestures that express anxiety or tension, grimaces of pain, triumph, joy, etc.
- **Adaptation or adapting gestures:** These are gestures that are used to manage emotions that are not wanted to be expressed. Here you can distinguish signs directed at oneself (such as pinching oneself), directed towards objects (pen, pencil, cigar, etc.) and those directed towards other people (such as protecting another person). Adapters can also be unconscious. Very clear examples are biting a fingernail or sucking a finger, very common in young children.

Facial expression

With facial expression, many moods and emotions are expressed. It is used to regulate interaction and to reinforce or emphasize the content of the message addressed to the recipient. The facial expression is used to express the mood, indicate attention, show disgust, joke, blame, reinforce verbal communication, etc. Paul Ekman developed a method to decipher facial expressions while working with Wallace Friesen and Silvan Tomkins. It is a kind of atlas of the face that is called FAST (Facial Affect Scoring Technique). FAST classifies images using photographs (not verbal descriptions) and dividing the face into three areas: the forehead and eyebrows, the eyes, and the rest of the face, that is, the nose, cheeks, mouth, and chin.

The look

The gaze is studied separately for its importance, although it is part of facial expression. The gaze fulfills a series of functions:

- The regulation of the communicative act.
- Source of information.
- Express emotions.
- Communicate the nature of interpersonal relationships.

The study of the gaze contemplates different aspects, among the most important of which we can mention: the dilation of the pupils, eye contact, the act of blinking, and the way of looking:

- The dilation of the pupils indicates interest and attractiveness, and they dilate when something interesting is seen.
- The number of times you blink per minute is related to calm and nervousness. If you blink a lot, it is a symbol of nervousness and restlessness, and the less you blink, the calmer you will be.
- Eye contact consists of the gaze that one person directs to the gaze of the other. Here we must mention the frequency with which we look at the other person and the maintenance of eye contact.
- The way of looking is one of the most relevant behaviors to distinguish high-status, dominant, and powerful people from low-status people who are not powerful.

The smile

Although the smile is included or can be included in the facial expression, it deserves to be explained in detail. It is used to express happiness, joy, or sympathy. The smile can even be used to make situations more bearable. It can have a therapeutic effect on pessimistic or depressed people.

- **Simple smile:** With this type of smile, an insecure, doubtful message of lack of confidence is transmitted. It should be avoided if you want to give an impression of firmness and confidence.
- **Simple smile of high intensity:** This smile occurs with a more pronounced separation of the corners of the mouth, and this rises more. A small part of

the upper teeth can be seen. It transmits confidence and heat.

- **Upper Smile:** The upper lip retracts so that almost all or all of the teeth can be seen. A message of some satisfaction is transmitted by seeing someone.
- **Superior smile of high intensity:** It opens the mouth more, and the teeth are seen more. A light closure of the eyes usually accompanies it. Apart from conveying happiness, it is often used to say a happy question or to represent a funny surprise. It is often used deceptively; for this reason, care must be taken.
- **Wide smile:** It is one in which the gaze narrows slightly. The upper and lower teeth are fully exposed. This type of smile expresses the highest intensity of joy, happiness, and pleasure.
- **Laughter:** It is the one that goes beyond the broad one. It is the most contagious and occurs in a group of people.

Make Body Language Your Superpower

It is common for tension to invade us in situations of pressure, such as taking exams, speaking in public, job interviews, etc. But did you know that you can easily manipulate your body chemistry to feel safer and more powerful? Studies indicate that you can achieve this simply by practicing certain changes in your body posture before undergoing stressful situations.

It is already known that our postures and gestures, often unconscious, communicate and allow others to have an idea of how we are or how we feel; this is called the body or non-verbal language.

Experts in the field of psychology and communication have devoted countless studies to understanding the effects of body language when looking for persuasive communication or a positive projection towards others. Still, Amy Cuddy, a specialist in social psychology at Princeton University, highlights that our body language not only influences how others see us but can determine how we feel (literally).

Cuddy explains that although the smile is the physical way in which we demonstrate the feeling of happiness, studies show that we can consciously provoke the same feeling of happiness by holding a pencil between our teeth and smiling for a few seconds. This means that not only does our mind dominate our body, but we can also use our body to manipulate our mental state.

According to these same studies, powerful people tend to have more positive, confident, and risky attitudes than non-powerful and insecure people, and this is reflected in their body language. While a secure person shows openness, the insecure person hides his body more in rigid and collected postures. Biologically we can find similar differences between the power poles, where the powerful have high levels of testosterone (hormone of domination) and low levels of cortisol (stress hormone). At the same time, insecure people show low levels of testosterone and high levels of cortisol.

Based on this relationship between our chemistry and our body language, Cuddy carried out several experiments to check whether taking different positions can affect our internal chemistry and, with this, consciously change how we feel.

The experiments consisted of taking different types of postures for 2 minutes and then taking saliva samples, gambling, and answering questions to determine the level of power/confidence one felt after adopting the two types of posture.

Results in individuals who adopted "High Power" positions:

- They decided to bet: 80%
- Testosterone level: 20% increase
- Cortisol level: Decrease by 25%

Results in individuals who adopted "Low Power" positions:

- They decided to bet: 60%
- Testosterone level: Decrease by 10%
- Cortisol level: 15% increase

The experiment showed amazing results, noting that with just 2 minutes of practicing the different postures, the internal chemistry of the body changed in significant percentages. This determined how individuals felt about themselves and influencing their attitude and decision-making.

A second experiment, which involved people practicing the same postures before a job interview, verified the positive effects of adopting "High Power" postures. This is because those who practiced these postures were more confident and assertive during their interviews, favoring their selection by 85%.

CHAPTER 17

HYPNOSIS 101

ANYONE can quickly and easily learn the techniques necessary to become a hypnotist. In any case, to become a good hypnotist, it is necessary to be upright, honest, and to dedicate oneself to this activity for humanitarian purposes. In the case of having all these qualities, the only thing you need is to memorize the techniques and then practice, practice, and more practice to continue learning every time you practice hypnosis. After practicing and learning a lot, you can consider yourself a hypnotist.

What Is Hypnosis?

Hypnosis is akin to the state of daydreaming, in which the conscious mind becomes quiet or passive. Through his practice, the hypnotist suggests the powerful subconscious mind of the subject.

Let's quickly and slightly technically examine how the brain works. Its activity is carried out in measurable frequency cycles that correspond to certain types of activity.

In 1929 Hans Berger used an EEG (electroencephalogram) system to discover that the brain produced normal waves in a sequence of 8 to 12 cycles per second (cps) while a person's eyes were closed. He called these waves alpha waves. Later, other types of brain waves were discovered, which were called theta, beta, and delta. These brain waves correspond to various mental functions, including hypnosis and psychic experience. Experts agree on the classification of these waves and their target but disagree regarding the exact limits of each wave type. An expert can define an alpha wave between 8 and 12 cps, while another can affirm that it is between 7 and 14 cps, and so on. The following four paragraphs provide a consensus regarding these brain waves.

Delta. For delta, the frequency spectrum of brain activation varies from 0 to around four cps. It is unconscious. There is not much knowledge about the delta range.

Theta. Theta frequency range is from about 4 to 7 cps. Theta is part of the subconscious range, and sometimes hypnosis takes place in this area. It seems that all our emotional experiences are registered in this wave. Theta is that special state that opens the door of consciousness beyond hypnosis to the world of psychic phenomena. Psychic experience generally takes place in theta.

Alpha. The alpha frequency range is approximately 7 to 14 cps. Alpha is generally considered to be the subconscious zone. In one's dream, the daytime reverie, and practically all the hypnosis take place. Meditation and also the psychic experience occur mainly in alpha (although in the state of meditation occasionally theta is reached). Alpha is a very important region when it comes to hypnosis.

Beta. It is the conscious area of the mind with frequency ranges from 14 cps. Beta is where our reasoning takes place and conducts most of our occupations when we are awake. Almost all our activity is carried out mainly at about

20 cps. At approximately 60 cps, a person is in a state of acute hysteria. Above 60 cps, I don't know what could happen, but I suspect it wouldn't be pleasant at all.

When we go to sleep, our brain automatically descends from the beta to the alpha range and then, for brief periods, switches to theta and delta. Most of the dream takes place in alpha. Hypnosis abuses this natural phenomenon: it induces brain function to descend to the alpha level without the hypnotized person resting. The subconscious mind is open to the advice in alpha.

The conscious mind does not readily accept the suggestion. It is useful to reason and think, and also to put into action everything you know. The subconscious consciousness, though, is like an obedient slave. He does not think or understand; he reacts only to what is being said to him. In this lies the importance and strength of hypnosis, as it causes the message to be conveyed directly to the subconscious that embraces it and transforms it into fact. Also, the subconscious mind is reminding the conscious mind that there is and needs to be progress on new knowledge. The conscious mind is inclined to behave according to its contents, so it believes and behaves accordingly with the new knowledge. Though nobody understands why hypnosis is successful, and the subconscious mind is responding.

Suggestions

For now, you just need to know that it is extremely important that they are positive, constructive, and provide benefits. This is because the subconscious mind ignores the difference between a positive and a negative suggestion. The subconscious mind simply accepts what is offered to it and then acts accordingly.

Words used during the recommendation process ought to be very alert. A man used a filthy term composed of four letters hundreds of times a day, and it has a close meaning to defecating. He gradually told his subconscious he had to defecate, and constant diarrhea resulted. Words are very powerful, and the subconscious mind embraces them.

Myths

There are too many mistakes regarding hypnosis, many of which have been spread by movies that deal with people turned into zombies by an extremely powerful person who exclaims: "Look me in the eye!" This may be interesting, but it is mere fiction and has nothing to do with the truth. Below we will expose some of the most common myths and explain them:

A hypnotist has magical powers. This is false. A hypnotist is an ordinary human being who has prepared himself to use the power of suggestion to bring about certain desired results for the hypnotized person.

A hypnotist possesses supernatural abilities. That is completely wrong. A hypnotist is an average human being who has trained himself to use the power of persuasion to achieve the desirable effects for the hypnotized person.

A hypnotized person may do things against his or her will. Untrue. Second, they can't hypnotize someone against their will. That the subject wants to agree is necessary. Third, no hypnotized person will be compelled to do things they wouldn't do in a normal state. The subject may accept or refuse any suggested order during hypnosis. When what the hypnotist suggests disturbs the subject, the subject would be able to exit the hypnotic state in all likelihood.

Only weak-minded people will be hypnotized. Actually, the reverse is the case. The smarter a person is, the easier it is to hypnotize them. It is completely difficult to perform hypnosis in some instances of intellectual illness. Practically someone wanting to be hypnotized will be hypnotized. Due to mental disabilities or other causes outside our knowledge, about 1 percent of the population cannot be hypnotized.

An individual being hypnotized is in a trance or unconscious. False. A subject under hypnosis is awake and conscious: extremely conscious. What happens is that he has simply focused his attention on where the hypnotist has indicated and has abstracted himself from everything else.

Anyone can remain in a hypnotic state forever. This is completely false. Even assuming that the hypnotist died after hypnotizing the subject, the subject would easily leave the hypnotic state, either falling into a brief sleep and then waking up normally or opening their eyes by not listening for a while to the hypnotist's voice.

To obtain positive results, a state of deep hypnosis is required. It is not true. Any level of hypnosis can offer good results.

Hypnotic state

Anyone undergoing hypnosis is very aware of where they are and what is happening. The subject listens to everything that happens while immersed in a state similar to daytime sleep, deeply relaxed. Often the body is numb or unaware of having a body.

Autohypnosis

It is possible to self-hypnotize. Many people do it daily to give themselves constructive orders. It is much easier to self-hypnotize if you have already had the experience of being hypnotized by someone else and have been instructed to do so. Through this chapter, you will learn to hypnotize other people, but with the same instructions, you will learn to self-hypnotize yourself. If you work with someone who hypnotizes you, you will accelerate the learning process of self-hypnosis.

CHAPTER 18

HYPNOTHERAPY

So far, hypnotherapy has only achieved a few scientifically recognized successes, but it can still be used as an alternative healing method in many areas. Although conventional medicine is still skeptical, there are many people who firmly believe in the effectiveness of hypnosis. We will tell you how hypnotherapy works, whether it can actually work small miracles and how much such therapy costs.

Hypnotherapy: This is how the therapy works

Hypnosis takes advantage of the state of consciousness of the trance. In the trance, our selective thinking is switched off, which makes it possible to make suggestions to the patient.

Our subconscious is addressed during the trance. The subconscious stores all habits and is also our long-term memory. Reflexes, our breathing and the autonomic nervous system are controlled unconsciously. Our consciousness, on the other hand, is responsible for short-term memory, decisions and our will. The reason why good resolutions fail so often: our habits are stronger than our will!

There are various initiation techniques to achieve the trance state:

- In classic hypnotherapy, direct instructions are passed on to the patient; this can be achieved with the help of verbal suggestions, fictional stories, acoustic signals, imaginary images or physical sensations (warmth, heaviness).

- Indirect hypnotherapy based on the Ericksonian model uses subliminal instructions. This maintains the feeling of control for the patient and the change in consciousness occurs unexpectedly.
- Nonverbal trance induction is often combined with verbal. During mesmerizing, the state of trance is initiated by energy transfer, i.e. by sweeping along without touching the arms or legs. If the patient fixes a certain point in the room or on the face of the hypnotist, one speaks of fixation.

Flash hypnosis is not advisable; this state of trance only lasts briefly and is only used for entertainment in show hypnosis.

By repeating sequences of sentences and numbers or images, the hypnotist enables the trance to be deepened. The aim is to promote the greatest possible relaxation and to start troubleshooting in this state.

At the end of a session there is the withdrawal, in which you are brought back fully to consciousness by repeating stories, pictures or sequences of numbers in reverse order.

In these cases, hypnotherapy could help you

Although hypnotherapy can be used in many areas, you should be aware that it cannot replace conventional medical treatment for serious diseases such as cancer.

Especially in the psychotherapeutic area, hypnotherapy can improve the quality of life by overcoming anxiety and attachment disorders, depression and conflicts with oneself.

Hypnosis is also suitable as pain therapy accompanying chemotherapy, after surgery and for migraines and inflammatory bowel diseases. Success can also be achieved with addiction problems.

Hypnotherapy can also be successful in people who are afraid of exams or who are about to burn out, or at least serve as relaxation therapy.

How effective is hypnotherapy?

According to the German Medical Gazette, the effectiveness has been scientifically recognized by the German Medical Association.

Withdrawal from methadone (heroin substitute, which alleviates withdrawal pain) and smoking cessation can be demonstrated by hypnotherapy.

Furthermore, the effectiveness of hypnosis in diseases such as migraines and irritable bowel is proven by the Scientific Advisory Board on Psychology.

Why do few people get involved in hypnotherapy?

Many people are very afraid of losing control in a trance-like state. However, this fear is mostly unfounded, because we do not act against our habits and morals even in the subconscious.

For successful hypnotherapy, one should also believe in the effectiveness of the alternative healing method and not avoid the incomprehensible from the outset.

The costs of treatment are usually not covered by the statutory health insurance, private patients should discuss the assumption of costs in advance. A hypnosis session costs around 80 to 120 euros for 50 minutes. Depending on the clinical picture, you should expect three to seven sessions, but treatment over several years may also be necessary.

Most psychological, mental, and physical conditions may be treated with hypnotherapy. This is used for relieving chronic pain, persistent acute pain, pain from psychosomatic disorders (e.g., headaches, migraines, fibromyalgia, cancer pain, etc.), planning for delivery, and decreasing pain relievers.

In psychotherapy, it is effective for the treatment of mood disorders (including depression) and various anxiety disorders: panic attacks, specific phobia, and social phobia, post-traumatic stress disorder (PTSD), obsessive-compulsive disorder (OCD), etc.

Moreover, hypnotherapy is particularly indicated to reduce stress and overcome addictions such as smoking and alcoholism. Children are also easy to hypnotize, and bedwetting and chronic asthma can be improved by hypnotherapy.

With most psychological and emotional issues, hypnotherapy is one of the easiest, quickest, and most successful types of care. It encourages an independence and pride mentality to deal with challenges and can also improve the healing process for many physiological problems.

Where to find psychologists trained in hypnosis

Hypnosis is also a psychotherapeutic method and should thus not be used in isolation but instead incorporated into psychotherapy. When you are interested in benefiting from this therapy, you have to be aware that not everybody who has practiced this approach is qualified to be able to cope with psychological issues.

To provide the full assurance of therapeutic hypnosis, hypnotherapists must be trained in psychological therapy, in addition to specialists in hypnosis. The El Prado Psychologists Center in Madrid, which has some of the best psychologists specializing in hypnosis, is one of the clinics that are at the forefront of this method of care.

El Prado Psychologists Center is a clinic in psychology provided by the Community in Madrid as a health center. It has a team of hypnotherapists with comprehensive clinical hypnosis training and experience who use this technique to treat different problems. The Prado Psychologists will give you ideas and help you solve the challenges you are facing, so you can recover your emotional equilibrium and live a complete and rewarding life.

Many therapeutic approaches are successful.

While we frequently equate psychological counseling with a severe problem, for the most varied reasons, many people go to the psychologist: developing social skills, getting to know each other better, optimizing personal growth or enhancing communication with their spouse. This clinic does not preclude any psychotherapeutic model, as it aims to be better able to administer individual psychological care.

The intervention approach stands out for delivering concise interventions. As a learning hub, it is at the forefront of psychology, applying the latest developments in science and integrating brain improvement methods into psychotherapy, such as brain integration techniques (ICT) or mindfulness.

CHAPTER 19

BRAINWASHING

Brainwashing, also known as reform of thought, education, or re-education, is the application of techniques often coercive to change beliefs, behavior, thinking, and behavior of an individual or society, for political purposes, religious or any other. Some common brainwashing techniques are the constant repetition of the same message along with public derision or the demonization of anyone who contradicts the message. Others include tactics aimed at nullifying critical thinking as well as preventing access to uncensored sources of information, isolation from the outside world, manipulation of language and the use of labels.

General

Throughout history, various forms of control of the thinking of individuals have been used. But it has been the totalitarian societies of the 20th century that have first applied scientific knowledge to improve brainwashing techniques. And that today is supported frequently with the use of drugs that inhibit cognitive abilities, hunger and protein deprivation, which produces confusion and credulity in the reasoning ability; and sleep deprivation, which causes stress and confusion.

George Orwell, in his 1984 novel, described various techniques used in brainwashing. The effect of these techniques on the person's image is not perceived by most people subjected to brainwashing. One's image is mainly established from two sources:

- The outside world made up of their parents, their educators, their friends, and all the people who have crossed the path of their existence.
- Their thoughts.

Brainwashing seeks to create a social framework or an environment of ideas and models to follow, to which the individual must adapt to survive, be accepted, or feel integrated into the group or society in which they live.

What Is Brainwashing?

Brainwashing is a method, more or less effective depending on the individual, whose objective is to admit any information to another person, with the technique of repetition until the objective is reached. Sometimes verbal or physical violence is used to confirm or create a defined hierarchy of superiority between the scrubber and the person being brainwashed.

There is also talk of brainwashing carried out by the media on the population, which can effectively have the effect of imposing the media's point of view on the population in the long term. The best way to avoid control of information is to use several sources within the possible informative spectrum.

Although the word "sect" is related to groups that have the same affinity, over the years, it has acquired a connotation more related to radicalized groups. Generally religious, tending to control thinking other than their own, outside and within their organization. It is present like this within some sects: brainwashing, mind control, persecution, human and sexual exploitation, slavery, and various forms of abuse. From a sociological point of view, it is a group of people with common affinities (cultural, religious, political, esoteric, etc.). Usually, it is a pejorative term, against which it has emerged, that of "new religious movements."

Brainwashing in the 21st Century

Brainwashing in the masses

The term brainwashing is sometimes applied, in some societies, when the government maintains firm social control of the mass media and the education system and uses this control to disseminate propaganda on a particularly intensive scale, with the global effect that can brainwash large sections of the population. This political interest manipulation can be seen in the case of, for example, the Soviet Union, China, or Israel, where all information is subjected to intense censorship and education.

The so-called Propaganda seeks to influence the citizen's value system and their behavior. It is articulated from a persuasive discourse that seeks public adherence to its interests. It is monological in nature and requires the resource of the advertisement. Its approach is to use massively presented and disseminated information to support a certain ideological or political opinion. Although the message contains true information, it may be incomplete, not contrasted, and partisan (disinformation), so that it does not present a balanced picture of the opinion in question, which is always viewed in an asymmetric, subjective and emotional way. Its primary use comes from the political context, generally referring to government or party sponsored efforts to convince the masses.

Thought Reform

The change of thinking or coercion, as it is often called, is an attenuated synonym for brainwashing. It is better understood as an organized method of phased coercive manipulation and regulation of behavior, intended to persuade and affect people deceptively and unexpectedly. This is usually in a scene orchestrated by the organization, for the benefit of the program's designers.

Brainwashing in youth

Brainwashing is much more effective when applied to young individuals than to those who already have a formed personality. Several programs are established in the subject during childhood, at an age when his critical sense is still very little developed, and he easily and naturally accepts all the suggestions coming from outside. These suggestions, the basis of the program, come at the beginning from the parents, later adding other adults, educators, and the individuals with whom the child is related, who may be of the same age, or even younger and of another sex.

For example, the US government uses the Holocaust Museum, built-in Washington DC with public funds, to teach hundreds of thousands of schoolchildren who visit it, at an age when the critical sense is not yet developed. Therefore, those beliefs will become deeply embedded. The German government, for its part, maintains a list of books on politics, prohibited for young people (see the case of the censorship of the writer Udo Walendy). In this way, he prevents his unscrupulous plan of political indoctrination of children and young people in classrooms on issues such as the Holocaust.

Deprogramming

Deprogramming is the process of releasing someone from the mind control to which he has been subjected. Since control is a long and complex technique, so is deprogramming; for this reason, some professionals are well versed in the field.

Circumstances

To achieve deprogramming, especially the most destructive control, the concurrence of several circumstances is necessary:

- Separation of the controlling group.
- Physical rest.
- Adequate food.
- Perseverance.

Techniques

Once the above circumstances have been met, experts in the field such as Steven Hassan follow a series of deprogramming techniques:

1. Establish relationships of mutual trust.

2. Communicate with the person to know their situation (do you want to continue? Do you feel doubts about the goodness of those who have controlled you? Are you disenchanted but fearful?).

3. Developing identity models: what the person was like before entering, how does mind control impose the personality model, and what is the personality that it adopts within the controlling structure (initiated, with some responsibility, controller...).

4. Putting people in touch with the original identity; that's why it's so difficult to deprogram children, who have no previous personality to recover.

5. Change the perspective from which the controller looks (the one imposed by the controller group).

6. Disrupt the self-deception that the controlled person has been systematically taught to do when they have doubts about what they have been taught.

7. End the phobias that have been implanted in the person so that he does not leave the group and show him the well-being that can be obtained outside the group.

8. Explain to the controlled person the characteristics of the mental control he has suffered.

CHAPTER 20

SOCIAL INFLUENCE

Social influence occurs when a person's emotions, opinions, or behaviors are affected by others. Social influence takes many forms and can be seen in compliance, socialization, peer pressure, obedience, leadership, persuasion, sales, and marketing. In 1958, Harvard psychologist Herbert Kelman identified three-wide varieties of social influence.

Social influence

In the face of a persuasive message, the recipient can:

- Process the message rationally.
- Let yourself be carried away by heuristics.

For some authors such as Allport, social influence is the central object of study in Social Psychology. Allport defines the study of social influence: I try to understand and explain how the thoughts, feelings, and behaviors of individuals are influenced by the real, imagined, or implicit presence of others. People intervene, sometimes as an influential agent, sometimes as a target that is influenced by other human beings. Influence is not always deliberate or explicit.

Intended Social Influence or Persuasion

Through the processes of influence and persuasion, our affections, beliefs, attitudes, intentions, and behaviors are configured. The intention to influence is always aimed at achieving a change in the behavior of others, individuals, or groups. Sometimes the objective is to achieve a specific behavior (that they prepare breakfast for us); other times, it is intended to influence attitudes (announcement of nature). Attempts to influence can occur: In face-to-face processes or through the media.

Typologies in The Study of Influence

DEPENDING ON THE OBJECTIVE OF THE INFLUENCING AGENT:

a) Achieve specific behavior in the receiver.

b) Get them to change their attitudes to produce, in the long run, a behavioral change.

DEPENDING ON THE SCENARIO in which it takes place:

Direct or face-to-face interpersonal communication: The interaction is bidirectional and dialectical. The influencer and his target intervene at the same time. The influence target participates by imposing his position.

Direct communication directed to an audience: One-way and little reciprocal interaction (meeting). The influence target can be expressed through reactions (applause, booing), but its influence on the agent of influence is less.

Mass communication: There is no direct contact between the communicator and the audience. The influence is unidirectional.

Social psychology analyzes the psychological processes involved in interpersonal influence and the most effective influence tactics. It helps to understand better why people behave in a certain way, to defend against manipulation, and to get experts in influencing techniques.

Influence techniques

People use tactics when we want to influence.

ROBERT CIALDINI systematized all the influencing techniques observed about a series of psychological principles. Psychological principles are understood as fundamental characteristics of the human being from which many social behaviors are derived, or that serve as a guide to act in different interaction situations. Since they are useful in interaction processes, it is easy for them to work when trying to trigger a certain response.

These tactics can be grouped, according to the underlying psychological principle, into 6 PRINCIPLES OF INFLUENCE:

Principle of reciprocity: "We have to treat others as they treat us." It is easier to convince those people who have previously been given a gift or a favor to support our purposes.

Scarcity principle: "What is most difficult to achieve is valued." Any opportunity seems more attractive to us, the less affordable it presents itself (due to its economic cost or the effort involved). Principle of social validation: Tendency to act like the people around us do. In most cases, it is usually appropriate to do what people similar to us do.

Principle of sympathy: Tendency to do what the people we like, or love want to do. The greater the attraction that a person arouses, the greater the possibility that he has to influence. The principle of authority: Obligation to obey the boss. Obedience, not only to legitimate authority but also to symbols associated with authority. Coherence principle: Importance of being consistent with previous actions and with previously acquired commitments.

Common characteristics of the previous principles:

- They are useful in most cases.
- They are rules of coexistence highly valued socially.
- They are learned from childhood.
- They serve as a heuristic or cognitive shortcut to quickly interpret and act in a social situation.
- They are usually used by conviction professionals to achieve their purposes.

The fact that they are used as heuristics means that they provoke automatic responses. This type of answer has the advantage that it saves time and mental capacity, and the disadvantage that it increases the possibility of error. Depending on the characteristics of the interaction, some principles work better than others.

The effectiveness of influence tactics depends on the influence agent using them appropriately for the situation and the people involved in the interaction. The joint use of more than one principle maximizes the possibilities of influencing.

CHAPTER 21

THE SECRETS OF SUBLIMINAL PSYCHOLOGY

The theme of subliminal messages in music began to gain importance in the early 1970s when various religious movements claimed that they were capable of unconsciously influencing people and changing their behavior. Even today, there is controversy about it.

The subject of subliminal messages in music has always been surrounded by controversy. For some, it is a simple myth, for others, a minor anecdote. Some think that it is a manipulation mechanism that is capable of changing people's behavior and influencing their values.

There is still no definitive conclusion in this regard, neither about the subliminal messages in music nor in those that have to do with the image. The available data is contradictory. Several governments have banned this type of message, but at the same time, most researchers have distorted its real effectiveness.

The subject has become fashionable at times and has caused everything from laughter to enormous concerns. At times, it has been pointed out that subliminal messages in music incite crime, practice Satanism, use drugs, etc. How true is this?

Some history

Let's say first that subliminal messages are those that are designed to be captured below the normal limits of perception. In other words, these messages cannot be consciously perceived but are received in such a way that we do not realize that we are capturing them.

Everything indicates that these messages have been spoken for thousands of years. Specifically, there are allusions by Aristotle to impulses that go unnoticed when we are awake, but then reappear strongly when we are asleep. Michell de Montaigne, O. Poetzle, and later Sigmund Freud also referred to this type of unconscious phenomenon.

However, advances in technology made these phenomena much more evident. Thus, it was in the 20th century when it became really clear that this type of communication was possible.

In 1957, a famous experiment was done with images, and almost a decade later, The Beatles got everyone to talk about subliminal messages in music or backmasking.

Subliminal messages in music

Subliminal messages in music, or backmasking, are encoded using a recording technique. It consists of recording a sound or message backward, on a track that is designed to be heard forward. This means that such a message can only be consciously picked up if the track is run backward.

There were two decisive factors in the birth of subliminal messages in music. The first was the rise of "concrete music" in France. In this genre, the sounds of electronic instruments were combined with recorded sounds from the environment or industry and combined in the recording studio.

The second incident factor was the use of recording tapes to record and preserve the musicians' original performances. This allowed fragments to be combined, cut, overlaid, and pasted to the original recording.

The Beatles and John Lennon, in particular, did several experiments around concrete music, and a new story began there.

The seventh Beatles album included, for the first time, a song that had texts recorded backward. The theme was called Rain, and it appeared in 1966. The objective of the band was to satirize, experiment, and offer new sounds. Since then, a good number of artists have resorted to the same resource, and subliminal messages in music have become frequent.

Doubts that persist

Quickly, several religious movements began to speak out against this type of appeal. Several urban legends also began to gain strength. Many people listened to the tapes backward and found hidden meanings, but most of the time, they were pure guesses, without a concrete basis.

The religious, in particular, accused various rock groups of inducing youth to worship the devil, commit crimes, or use drugs. The debate became very heated until, in 1985, the psychologists' John R. Vokey and J. Don Read experimented. They recorded a Psalm from the Bible upside down and watched the listeners' reactions.

The researchers concluded that subliminal messages in music did not cause any considerable effect on the receivers. In 1996 C. Trappery did 23 experiments and concluded the same thing. However, researchers Johan C. Karremansa, Wolfgang Stroebeb, and Jasper Claus, from the University of Utrecht, did a new experiment in 2006 and proved that these messages do change people's behavior. The debate is still open.

Subliminal Psychology in An Intimate Relationship

We know individuals appear to be drawn to, to make appointments, and to marry other people who are similar to them in terms of personality and values, in addition to their physical appearance. However, these characteristics only scratch the surface of what makes a relationship work well. The agreement in certain aspects of the style of speaking of each member of the couple is also important, according to the results of a new study in which it has been found that people who speak in a similar way regarding certain parameters are more compatible with forming a lasting couple.

The study focused on what is technically known as "function words." It is not about nouns and verbs; but the words that show how those others are related. How we use these words constitutes our style of speaking and writing, according to James Pennebaker of the University of Texas at Austin.

Function words are very social, and social skills are required to use them. For example, "the other day's" may be very clear to two people when one says it to the other, but a third person who hears them may not have the slightest idea what they mean.

Pennebaker, Molly Ireland, and colleagues examined whether the speaking and writing styles couples adopt during one member's conversations with the other predict future dating behavior and the long-term strength of their relationship. The study authors conducted two experiments in which software compared the language styles of the couples.

In the first experiment, the conversations of pairs of college students whose members had four-minute speed dating were recorded to meet and see if they liked each other. Almost all the couples talked about the same topics: What is your main subject? Where are you from? What do you think of the university? Each conversation sounded more or less the same to observers, but analysis of the spoken text revealed marked differences in the synchrony of language. Couples whose language style similarity was above average were nearly four times more likely than couples whose speech styles were out of line to expect to have further potential interactions.

A second analysis showed ten days of the same trend in online chat between couples. Nearly 80 percent of the couples whose two members' writing styles matched continued to date three months later, compared to approximately 54 percent of couples who did not match that style as much.

CHAPTER 22

HOW TO USE DARK PSYCHOLOGY IN SEDUCTION

The art of seduction is something that many long to understand and practice efficiently, and that seduction is not always for sexual gain. Unlike what many may think, it is something deeper and more complex than it seems at first glance.

A true seducer or seductress is that person capable of arousing interest in others for elements of their personality, their attractiveness, their way of expressing themselves, knowledge, etc. Many of the seducers are attractive without having a sexual interest different from the rest. However, they are capable of producing a feeling of trust in people, motivating others to do what they want, or achieving a benefit that nurtures both parties.

Seducer Features

Some studies indicate that from childhood, we acquire this capacity for seduction, but some train it better throughout their lives. We all know the typical person who, no matter where or how he is, manages to be the center of attention in a positive way without trying. These seducers produce interest or provocation in the rest in a very natural way.

The true seducer is one who seduces you without you realizing it. It can be their phrases, gestures, behaviors, education, security, etc. Each seducer has his tactics, all of them positive since they do not need to use tricks or bad arts to get what they want.

Contrary to what one might think, a seducer does not need to be particularly handsome, intelligent, funny, or overly daring. Sometimes, they don't even know what the "hook" they have with people is or why people are interested in them.

The problems seducers face

It could seem that seducers have it all in their favor and that they will run into little trouble. But the truth is otherwise. They can experience serious problems in all areas of their lives, especially in the emotional part.

When living with a seducer, problems such as jealousy, mistrust, or insecurity, among others, may arise. The couple's self-esteem will be vital to define the seriousness of these problems. A person sure of herself and the relationship will be able to bear the natural seduction of her partner and even take it with grace.

Otherwise, the seducer may face jealous scenes and unpleasant situations. The person who lives with the seducer must have high self-esteem, confidence in their partner, and the certainty that it is not the seducer who is looking for something, but other people who approach and express interest.

Enjoy the seducer

When you live with a seducer, you have to think positively because just what made you fall in love with him or her, will attract the attention of others. Learn to appreciate and be happy to be able to enjoy that person and his/her qualities.

CHAPTER 23

CONCLUSION

The dark triad is a term that emerged in the 1990s. Now, it was the studies and description of psychologists Paulhus and Williams of the University of British Columbia who coined this dimension in 2002. This should be noted as an important aspect.

When we speak of the dark triad, we are not referring to a personality disorder; they are a set of subclinical features that define a type of adverse behaviors, and that generate great discomfort in the environment.

A person who scores high in the dark triad test will generate a psychosocial impact in any scenario in which he moves. Thus, both family, emotional, and work-related relationships are affected by these antisocial tactics that these men and women make use of. Let us now analyze the signals of the dark triad.

We know that the signs of the dark triad of Psychology form a wide range. Does this mean that a person should score high in both narcissism, Machiavellianism, and psychopathy? Indeed, the score should be positive in all areas, but there are nuances. The Jonason and Webster scale is usually used to make an adequate evaluation.

In it, it can be seen that, on average, there is always one more significant area than others. An example: in a study carried out by Webster and Jonason (2013) at various universities in the United States, it was found that those with the highest scores in the narcissistic area abound.

Now, what this scale also reveals is that the most dangerous profile within the dark triad of personality is the one that shows a higher score in the area of psychopathy. In this case, it is when the most harmful and adverse behaviors appear. As we see, this is a subject as interesting as it is disturbing, especially when we consider what the psychoanalyst Michael Maccoby tells us: the dark triad of Psychology is increasingly common in the highest positions in the business field.

BODY LANGUAGE

How to Detect High-Stakes Liars Through Body Language Analysis and Everything You Need to Influence People with Emotional Intelligence, Powerful Communication and Persuasion

Blake Reyes

INTRODUCTION

A lot of research has shown that as much as 80% of our communication is through body language and facial expressions. By understanding our body language, we will understand what signals we send to the environment. Through the body, we give people what we think and feel without even being aware of it. By becoming aware of other people's body language, we can understand when someone is lying to us or giving us signals that they are attracted to us. Even with people who are in a relationship, the success of the relationship may depend on the ability to send and receive signals.

This is because it is sometimes much easier for partners to point out some problems or wishes in a non-verbal way than by speaking. When they see the person who is attracted to them, people automatically start to raise or lower their eyebrows slightly. Such a reaction takes only a fraction of a second, but if we pay attention to our own or others' behavior, we will see that it is easily noticeable and true. A raised eyebrow 100% proves that we are sexually attracted to someone.

By adjusting their clothes, men want to draw attention to themselves, while playing with buttons shows nervousness. Psychologists say it can also be a subconscious sign that a man wants to undress in front of a woman. The attitude in which a man takes off his jacket and places his hands on his hips is a clear sign that he already has concrete plans with the woman who is attracted to him. Playing with hair is a technique used by women.

By removing the hair from her face, she subconsciously lets the man know that she wants to get closer and get to know him more closely, and conveys the same message with a slight lick of her lips. In this document, you will learn a lot about body language, some tricks, and tips to get started.

CHAPTER 1

BEING A LIE DETECTOR

Tim Roth, who we know from Quentin Tarantino's 1995 movie The Four Rooms, starring in a jog, also starred in the Lie to Me series of Human Lie Detector, which encouraged me to explore human body language. So-called non-verbal communication. It has been communicated in this way since the beginning of time. It is a very important form of communication, and today many are not aware of it.

Ignorance is sometimes bliss. After acquiring this knowledge, you may be hurt when it is obvious that someone is lying to you. Various deception techniques are used by police, forensics, psychologists, security experts, and other investigators. This information is also useful for administrators, employers, as well as everyone for use in daily circumstances where separating truth from lies will prevent anyone from falling victim to fraud and other deception.

Signs of deception can be seen if one's behavior is limited and rigid, with very little movement. The liar holds his hands to his body, trying to take up as little space as possible. He avoids eye contact with the person he is lying to or stares at him without blinking. His hands touch his face, throat, and mouth. Also, he touches or rubs his nose, ear...

A contradiction in the expression of emotional gestures can be observed like a forced fake smile. The display of emotions is delayed, the reaction stays longer, then stops at once. Time is excluded between emotions and gestures, expressions, and words. For example, someone says, "I like it!" when receiving a gift, and then he smiles after that statement. Gestures or expressions do not respond to verbal statements, such as when someone says, "I love you" while frowning. Expressions are limited to mouth gestures if anyone fakes emotions (happiness, surprise, sadness, awe) instead of the whole face. Let's say when someone smiles, of course, the whole face is on—the jaw expands into a smile, the cheek is raised, the eyes and forehead are wrinkled down, etc.

Interaction and reaction - The culprit defends himself, while the innocent person responds more often with the attack. A liar is uncomfortable when confronted and often turns his head or body away from an interviewer. He unwittingly places objects (a book, a coffee cup) between himself and you, as a symbolic obstacle.

Other Signs of Lying - If you think someone is lying, then quickly change the topic of conversation, the liar will accompany you voluntarily and become more relaxed. The culprit wants the subject of the conversation to be something else, while the innocent person may be confused by the sudden change of topic and will probably want you to go back to the previous one. The use of humor or sarcasm is often used by liars to avoid talking about a particular topic.

Micro-expressions - are instant involuntary facial expressions that are drawn on people's faces when they hide emotions without even being aware of it. They are characterized by speed and tension. They occur in a split second and disappear just as quickly. They are reluctant to move facial muscles because we cannot influence them by our will.

They are usually grouped into seven universal emotions: anger, disgust, fear, sadness, happiness, surprise, and contempt.

Micro-expressions give us away when we lie. If we try to hide emotions with a fake smile, we give off hidden emotions to the involuntary movements of the facial muscles. They only show how one feels, which does not lead to the conclusion that one is a liar; they only show one's current emotional state.

(If someone saw a picture of a dog and commented that it was great and that the dog was beautiful, and the expression on the face at the time depicted disgust, it might not be a lie. Maybe that person was bitten by the dog, so the picture reminded him of that situation.)

Eyes - Eyes are a mirror of the soul, more accurately reflecting our current emotional state, the state of mind. Some scientific studies say that people unconsciously look in certain directions during the conversation and that it has to do with lying, remembering, imagining, because certain centers in the brain respond differently to certain stimuli, and this is reflected in the eye muscle. The analysis of one's diversion is not reliable to conclude as to whether one is lying or not, but it is certainly interesting. Try it.

Visually Constructed Images - If someone told you to imagine a purple boar with green tufts, as you visually construct that image, your eyes would look upwards to the right.

Visually Memorized Pictures - If someone asked you what color the house you once lived in as you try to remember, your eyes would look up to the left.

Sound Construction - When you try to imagine a sound you haven't heard before, your eyes will be pointing to the right.

Sound Recall - Remember the voice of your acquaintance, eyes will look to the left.

Feeling - Remembering the smell of a campfire will direct your gaze down to the right, as well as thinking about taste, emotion, or smell.

Inner conversation - When a person is thinking, thinking, talking to himself in his head, his eyes are directed down to the left.

Of course, when looking at the interviewee, the left is right, right is left, as in a mirror. This is true for right-handed people, and the situation is the opposite for left-handed people. If someone is staring at you in a non-moving eye, this can also be a sign of lying. All this through analysis and examples has proven more accurate than incorrect.

It is very important that body language can also be misinterpreted. Therefore, some of the ways we can apply in most cases are listed. Body language is viewed comprehensively, and we need to know one's normal behavior to notice deviations. It is not enough for someone to blink repeatedly and to think that he is impatient, insecure, or lying. Verbal speech, tone, and other things should also be included so that we can more easily assess a particular situation. Sometimes people are uncomfortable with their skin, they are unsure of themselves, some inconvenience has happened, something bothers them, and maybe they care about you, their job, etc. We cannot judge others just like that unless we know the whole story, but these gestures can also help us understand the other side.

CHAPTER 2

FOOLPROOF STEPS TO DISCOVER LIARS

Some signs can help to identify when a person is lying because when a lie is told, the body shows small signs that are difficult to avoid, even in the case of experienced liars.

So, to know if someone is lying, it is important to pay attention to various details in the eyes, face, breath, and even in the hands or arms. The following are some techniques to find out if one is telling you a lie:

1. Look closely at the face

While a smile can easily help hide a lie, there are small facial expressions that can indicate that the person is lying. For example, when the cheeks become redder during the conversation, it is a sign that the person is anxious and this can be a sign that he is telling something that is not true or that it makes him uncomfortable to talk about it. Also, other signs such as dilating your nostrils while breathing, breathing deeply, biting your lips, or blinking your eyes too quickly may indicate that your brain is working too hard to build a false story.

2. Observe all body movements

This is one of the most critical steps in figuring out whether somebody's lying and is being used by specialists in lie detection. Normally, when we're honest, the whole body works in a coordinated fashion, but when we want to trick others, it's normal not to synchronize it. The person can speak very confidently, for example, but his body is withdrawn, contradicting the feeling the voice gives. The most popular body language changes that suggest a lie is being told include being very quiet throughout the conversation, crossing your arms, and holding your hands behind your back.

3. Watch your hands

One may most likely observe the whole body to know when someone is lying, but the movement of the hands can be enough to discover a liar. This is because while trying to tell a lie, the mind is concerned with keeping the body's movement closer to the natural, but the movement of the hands is very difficult to copy.

Thus, hand movement can indicate:

Hands closed: It can be a sign of a lack of honesty or excessive stress.

Hands touching clothes: Shows that the person is uncomfortable and anxious.

Moving your hands, a lot without need: It is a movement often done by someone who is used to lying.

Put your hands on the back of your neck or neck: Shows anxiety and discomfort with what you are talking about. Also, placing objects in front of the person you are talking to can be a sign that you are lying, as it shows a desire to create distance, which usually happens when we tell something that makes us nervous and uncomfortable.

4. Listen to everything very carefully

Changes in voice can quickly identify a liar, especially when sudden changes in tone of voice occur, such as speaking in a thick voice and then starting to speak in a thinner voice. But in some situations, it may be more difficult to detect these changes, and thus it is, therefore, important to be aware of any changes in pace that occur while speaking.

5. Pay attention to your eyes

It is possible to learn a great deal about the feelings of a person only through their eyes. This is likely because the majority of people are conditioned unconsciously to look in those directions contrary to what they think or feel.

The types of looks generally related to a lie include:

Look up and left: it happens when you realize you're talking about a lie.

Look left: it's more normal when you're trying to create a lie when you're talking.

Look down and left: it indicates you're worried about something that's been accomplished. Other signals that can be transmitted by the eyes, and that can indicate a lie, include looking directly into the eyes for most of the conversation and blinking more often than normal.

That's right, whoever is telling you a lie, uses as much detail as he can, in the mistaken belief of being more credible. The liar fills his story with many (unnecessary) details. What we have to do then is to be continuous with questions that lead you to contradict yourself to lose the line of speech.

So how should you act if you have a liar in front of you? Well, that depends on the case. In fights between coworkers or in fights between couples, what you could do is perhaps ask some general questions that cannot be answered with a resounding "yes" or "no" and then ask more specific questions. But it takes a lot of work. Perhaps it is better to trust the sixth sense itself, which rarely fails, in addition to asking yourself if you would be ready for the truth and, if you would not be being deceived in the face of evident lies. Also, some believe in their lies. And what would be the truth? Follow your heart.

CHAPTER 3

SENSING LIES, AND MOST COMMON SIGNS SOMEONE IS LYING TO YOU

1. Pinocchio poses

You can be a very attentive and insightful person, but your chances of catching a liar in the act are relatively low. This has to do with the psychology of lying and body language. A layman in body language usually hits only 50% of the time when he tries to identify a liar by his posture. But not even the greatest experts are always right: your chances of success are usually around 65% or a little more. The main difficulty lies in the fact that the signs of lying are often confused with traces of shyness, anxiety, and nervousness. It is what Camargo calls "Othello's mistake," about the classic Shakespeare character. Instead of fear, the protagonist of the tragedy sees betrayal in the eyes of his wife, Desdemona, and commits a terrible injustice. In real life, miscalculations are also often frequent— especially if you are emotionally involved in the situation. The advantage of the expert who analyzes videos or interviews defendants, for example, is that he does not have a direct relationship with the liar.

In everyday work, however, the feelings and expectations you have about your interlocutor can "cloud" your judgment about his honesty—for better or worse. Still, certain classic signs often betray liars.

2. Cover your mouth

A typical gesture of someone who is not telling the truth is to touch their mouth. Stroking your chin, wiping your lips with your fingers, placing a pencil or other object in front of your mouth are very common signs. The concern with the mouth reflects the desire to prevent others from hearing the lie that will be uttered, or even the unconscious desire to suppress their own words, because they are false.

3. Avoid eye contact

Not looking directly into the other's eyes does not necessarily mean lack of sincerity: it may simply be insecurity or shyness. Still, it is common for the liar to lower his eyes to prevent the falsity of his statements from being perceived. However, this detail can be tricky. Many liars, knowing this, do exactly the opposite when they lie: they look directly into the victim's eyes in an attempt to make their statements more credible.

4. Compress the lips

A liar in action usually closes in on himself, preventing words from coming out of his mouth. A very clear sign of this resistance to communication is to fold your lips inward, squeezing them tightly. This is a common reaction to questions with the potential to expose the truth. The "disappearance" of the lips can indicate that the person was affected by the question and does not want to answer it.

5. Look up and to the right

When looking at the upper right corner, the individual usually wants to create an image. This is one of the most consistent signs of lying—the person makes a creative effort, that is, prepares something fictitious to say. Many individuals turn their heads in the same direction. In many cases, looking away also serves not to face the interlocutor directly.

6. Show micro-wrinkles on the forehead

The nervousness caused by the situation can also cause the appearance of small horizontal wrinkles on the liar's forehead. The problem is that they disappear very quickly and are not always easy to observe. But be careful: the lines on the forehead often reflect a kind of tension that has nothing to do with lies. In general, wrinkles that denote mere nervousness are well pronounced and remain on the other person's face for longer.

7. Restrict hand and arm movements

It is common for people who lack the truth to decrease their gesticulation greatly. "The hands are stuck to the legs, in the pockets, placed behind," writes an expert. "The movements are scarce and controlled." The reason for this paralysis is unconscious: without knowing it, the person believes that the more immobile he is, the more easily he will go unnoticed by the attentive gaze of his interlocutor. He also tries to reduce his body language so as not to let his gestures end up contradicting his speech.

8. Rigid and repetitive movements

242

In an attempt to close in on his own body, the insincere individual will tend to move in a hard, repetitive, and mechanical way. The more intense these gestures, the more it becomes clear that the liar is uncomfortable and wages an internal struggle to keep control of the situation.

9. Shrink your head

The liar tends to retract his own body: shrunken neck, low chin, legs together, and crossed arms indicate an unconscious attempt to control his own emotions. The behavior goes back to cave times. In the face of a predator, prehistoric man had three options: flee, fight, or be paralyzed. The third option is the one that draws the least attention. Not for nothing, the liar who wants to "survive" his interlocutor tries to shrink himself in all possible ways.

10. Often touching one's own body

Self-hugging and caressing your arms can denote insecurity, anxiety, the need for protection, and unconscious return to a childlike posture. There are several touches to the body itself that betray liars. Running your hands over your legs to get rid of imaginary dirt, for example, can denote worry and anxiety. Scratching the nose is another characteristic gesture, says an expert: During his testimony in the Monica Lewinsky case, former US President Bill Clinton touched his nose more than 25 times.

11. Shrug only one shoulder

This is one of the most classic signs of lying, according to the American psychologist Paul Ekman, considered one of the world's greatest specialists in facial and body expressions. The posture of the individual who lacks the truth is asymmetrical: one of his shoulders stands up or protrudes slightly forward. With the gesture, he tries to convey disregard and little concern for what he is saying. Often, this disguised tone of disdain also appears in the liar's voice.

12. Trying to get away from the caller

One of the techniques most used by experts to unmask a liar is to get as close as possible to him during a delicate question. This tactic can make him more anxious and prone to surrender. This is because the more removed he can be from the other, the more secure he will feel. The attempt to maintain a comfortable distance appears both physically and verbally: he will also try to stay away from the thorniest details in his story. Still, you need to be careful with that sign. Certain liars get very close to their victims.

CHAPTER 4

CLUES TO REVEAL TRUE INTENTIONS

It is not always in the process of conversation that you can learn about the true intentions of a person. What words are silent about can be told by the eyes, facial expressions, behavior, and gestures of the interlocutor.

How to know a person's intentions?

The first way: ask him about it. A person can tell the truth or can be a deceiver. So, there is no guarantee to hear the truth on the question asked.

The second way: to catch and remember the first opinion of a person when meeting. Intuition will not deceive us. If there is a negative impression wait for the trick. People at a subconscious level recognize signals using gestures, postures, facial expressions.

The third way. Observe the look of the interlocutor. Running eyes betray shame, fear, or deceit. The excessive shine of the eyes will warn about the excitement of a person; perhaps he is in a state of alcoholic or drug intoxication. Dilated pupils are a sign of pleasure or intense experience. The random movement of the pupils occurs when intoxicated. The faster they move, the stronger the interlocutor is drunk. Frequent blinking can be observed to deceive you.

The interlocutor, who prefers to look you in the eye, intends to lie or not to say anything. If he has something to hide, then he will not be completely frank with you. A

245

"drilling" gaze can give out an intention to surpass you and dominate you not only in conversation.

A direct look into the interlocutor's eyes is not always a guarantee of honest intentions. It often happens that professional cheaters spend hours honing their skills in front of a mirror. They easily control their eyes, facial expressions, and make sure that their hands do not touch their faces.

If a person is inherently shy, he will not look into the eyes when communicating. His speech may be confused, and his eyes involuntarily "run" around. The modest man has no bad intentions, and his behavior is due to a special mental organization. True, to recognize this feature, you need to be familiar with it for more than a single day.

The fourth way, the last. Closed poses (crossing arms or legs), touching during a conversation to a person, confused and incoherent speech will give the indication that he intends to lie or not to say something. Transferring from a topic you are interested in another is a signal; the interlocutor wants to escape from the discussion of an unpleasant topic for him.

Be observant with new people, but do not lose your vigilance with old friends. Perhaps you continue to communicate with them only through ignorance of their intentions. People unconsciously give signs that you can learn to "read." Having mastered this alphabet, it is much easier to see the true attitude towards yourself.

Folk rumor

Judging a person by someone else's words is an ungrateful affair; perhaps he is not at all what his neighbors, a former boss, or his wife say he is. They may have their selfish interests associated with the intentional desire to harm. But if you hear negative things about him from many people, you should be more careful. For comparison, we can give the rating of sellers on a large trading platform. If you see a particular seller having low ratings from different buyers, acquiring something from him will be very risky. Do not risk in vain.

Professional trickster

Each fraudster has his narrow specialization, and therefore they know the psychology of their victims very well. Many dodgers use the desire of women to get married as soon as possible. If you are in an active search, have a good salary, but at the same time there is little chance of a good party, you can get into the view of such a person. The first time with him will be like a fairy tale: a guy in love sings serenades to you, communication with him makes your heart tremble. But suddenly he will "happen" a great misfortune, which urgently needs money. As soon as he receives what he wants from you, he will disappear forever. Therefore, be vigilant and do not succumb to the affectionate speeches of someone who wants to use you. A man who is aimed at a serious relationship, won't ask for money from a new acquaintance, but on the contrary, will do everything to be considered self-sufficient.

Lonely women also often fall into the network of married men, spending their whole lives in the expectation that he is about to divorce. And after all, they know that their chances of moving from simple flirting to real relationships are negligible, but they still hope that in their case, there will be an exception to the rule.

"Another's soul is darkness," says folk wisdom. The way it is. Unless, of course, you have special knowledge and skills. Have you ever wondered how clairvoyants "work"? Among them are talents who have developed what nature has given them. But most of all, seers hone a couple of techniques to help them in their work. And that's all. And then a matter of practice and experience.

In this section, we begin to come close to some professional secrets of communication success. Moreover, in any place, at any time, in any state, etc. And all people know how to do it, but they do it subconsciously, i.e., without fully realizing how they succeed in communicating, acting, and opposing other people's influence so successfully. As a rule, each of us subconsciously owns a couple of three techniques at the amateur level this is a kind of our survival strategy in this world. But, since even gifted people do not train and develop their skills, they also remain amateurs, like us.

You can master dozens of effective techniques. And if you constantly pay due attention to them, then you will get everything you want in this life. This is how all famous people act. The line is yours.

Face, pose and gestures

The first indicator of a person's psyche is his face, or rather his facial expression. Indeed, a villain may be hiding behind a beautiful face, and a decent and kind person may turn out to be terrible. Therefore, everything becomes clear when a person comes to life according to his facial expressions.

Another indicator is a person's posture. If you are told about compassion, and with their whole appearance, they show indifference, then everything becomes clear to you without explanation. Gait, as a pose in motion, also very clearly characterizes the state of a person.

Most often, the process of communication is accompanied by gestures, which are also very informative. With the help of gestures, we try to convey our message more accurately and, accordingly, we perceive it more accurately.

Now, watching your interlocutor, pay attention to how his facial expressions, posture, and gestures coincide with what he tells you. How much you will discover for yourself! And this is just the beginning.

Ask questions

It is very useful to ask questions, since it is very easy for an inexperienced person to deceive himself in other people's words, not to mention other people's manipulations. This happens for several reasons, one of which is the difference in the perception of the world. Yes, we are all human, but we perceive the world differently. It turns out that we find in our interlocutor's words our meaning, which is very far from that which the interlocutor puts into his words. From here, quarrels and disagreements and similar troubles begin. It is worth noting that there are times when we understand each other perfectly.

But this is a separate conversation

If you ask questions, especially in those cases when you are not completely sure of the correct understanding of some meanings in the words of the interlocutor, then you can find a lot of interesting things about your perception, correct it and avoid unnecessary quarrels.

Do not wander in the clouds

There are no miracles in the world—in the right sense of this expression in this context. Develop sober thinking. Romance is romance, but some things and events are not even described in fairy tales. And people so willingly believe everything and anything... And why? Partly from low literacy, partly from little experience, partly from naivety, and partly from an unwillingness to sometimes think critically.

What are they telling you?

Voice is one of the individual characteristics of every living creature.

Watch what you are told. It may not be stupidity and not fairy tales, but quite real things, only little relevant. Such things are said to obscure your consciousness and further inspire you with some truths. Being not quite attentive to the words of the interlocutor, we can skip very important information, and without giving it any importance, promise something, putting ourselves in a very difficult position. And you never know...

As they say to you

In addition to what they tell you, pay attention to how you are told. The effect is the same as when watching facial expressions and gestures. Intonation must strictly correspond to the meaning. If someone tells you that he loves you, his intonation will be congruent with the words of love, and at the same time, it will have nothing to do with the intonation that accompanies the words of hatred and contempt.

Do not forget that not only you can master this skill...

CHAPTER 5

HOW TO DISCOVER DARK PEOPLE'S MASKS

Many people are successful, happy, or seem to have perfect lives. But is this the case? Not always, as many of them pretend. This is called wearing a mask.

These are depressed people who are optimistic, anxious people who seem relaxed, and people who choose to wear a mask so that others do not see what they are.

Do you want to know the different masks we wear and their reasons? We will explain everything in this chapter!

The controller

A person who controls all aspects of his life may have been betrayed before. Faced with this pain, the person develops a behavior that will allow him to ensure that others keep their promise. Thus, he will avoid being betrayed again.

The controller hides feelings of insecurity. Thus, it is essential to control everything and even sometimes in an exaggerated way.

The mask protects him from the pain of another betrayal, while he tries to do everything to prevent it from happening again.

The rigid

A rigid person has suffered great injustices before. Faced with this, he/she becomes inflexible, constantly seeking justice and the accuracy of things.

A rigid person becomes a perfectionist, to the point that it turns into an obsession. Everything must be in place!

Thus, studying everything perfectly will prevent injustice from ringing at our door. This is why the rigid act this way.

The addict

A dependent person often carries the pain of feeling abandoned. This injury generates indifference towards others, so as not to feel abandoned again. This avoids taking any relationship seriously while rejecting the idea of living with someone.

The pain of abandonment is terrible. The addicted person suffers from the depths of his or her being unable to depend on someone or failing to believe that the people who are important to them will never abandon them.

The leaker

The person fleeing rejects company. She prefers solitude and moments of calm. She rejects being the center of attention because it scares her.

A person who is fleeing behaves like this because he has been rejected and because it causes such an injury in him that he prefers to avoid it.

Leaky people cannot bear not knowing how to act in certain situations, being ashamed or feeling lost, simply because it would cause a rejection on the part of others.

In their solitude, they are neither vulnerable nor uncertain. Their mask protects them from what makes them suffer.

Would it be cowardice? No! It is simply a matter of preventing what we cannot control from hurting ourselves.

The masochist

It may be a mental or emotional masochist. This attitude is due to a feeling of humiliation and shame dating from a past situation.

This then provokes this masochistic attitude, always pushing to want to solve the problems of others by all means, regardless of whether one is humiliated or belittled.

The masochist does not act like the profiles we saw just before, and he does not try to avoid or flee his injuries.

The masochist faces what hurts him, sometimes seeking to suffer even more. He was hurt, and he had no control.

Today he is in control, and it is he who decides who will harm him or not. Deep down, it helps him to overcome the situation.

We were able to see that there are several different and varied masks, which are most often explained by a past emotional injury.

Do you recognize someone in these different profiles? It is easy to identify people who wear a mask, as they sometimes leave their true personality hidden.

It is best to overcome what causes this fear in us. Perhaps the masochist is hard on himself, but he at least faces his pain.

This can make him stronger and allow him to overcome his trauma, or, on the contrary, make himself suffer even more.

And you, what do you think of all this? What is your point of view?

CHAPTER 6

THE POKER FACE MYTHS

We have all put on a poker face sometimes even without knowing it, especially children during interrogation after some mischief. Consciously or unconsciously, we all use body expression and our gestures, voluntarily or not, to convey a message. The body speaks, and that is why in some cases, we have to make it shut up, especially if you are Patrick Antonius or if you are in a poker game where you do not want anyone to know your emotions. But this board game is not exclusive to putting a poker face, and although its use has become more popular, especially since the appearance in 2010 of the 4chan forum, putting a poker face has been used throughout history both in the gaming world as in politics, associated with well-known characters like Trump or Putin or even in anthropological studies.

An important reference is found in the British writer Henry Jones' book "Round Games at Cards," published in 1875, who describes "Poker face" as the expression we adopt when we do not want to transmit anything. What we would rather call an expressionless state.

In 1934, the novelist Graham Greene wrote a critique of Sir Arthur Conan Doyle, titled "The Poker Face," referring to his outstanding work in his novel Sherlock Homes. Here the detective and the author worked the same concept showing that who controls the true poker face, in the end, will learn how to read the opponent's face. María

256

Konnikova, a Russian-American psychologist who published an essay called "How to Think Like Sherlock Holmes," would also write about this character.

There are different types of research such as "The Poker Face of Wall Street" by Aaron Brown, where the relationship between the world of finance and the gaming system in poker is analyzed, or "Poker Faces" by David Hayano. He published his anthropological study based on the impenetrable face of poker players. Or in the artistic field like the series of photographs "Poker Face" by Ulvis Albert about the WSOP published in 1981.

Many examples of the use of the poker face as part of an emotional control strategy can also be found in sports. Grantland Rice described Helen Wills, Winner of 19 Grand Slam titles in the 1920s, including "Little Miss Poker Face."

It was precisely tennis and science that demonstrated a few years ago that our actions are evident not just on the lips, but also on our body or our movements, voluntary or not. Israeli Hillel Aviezer conducted this study as a result of a collaboration between Princeton and Jerusalem universities; it was carried out through an investigation into the expressions of Serena Williams and Rafa Nadal during moments of great tension that would be shared by photographs with 45 students. These, divided into groups, would have access either to different parts of the body, to the complete photograph, or only to the face. The result confirmed that the mind deceives us more commonly than we think and that joy and sadness are best seen in our hands, arms, legs, and even veins.

In the poker world, in addition to the necessary sunglasses, some prefer to play with a good long-necked sweater to conceal any traitorous veins that swell in us because of the stress of the table or with a cap that covers our ears. As useful information, we recommend gloves for your kit if you are one of those who sweat from the nerves or those who bite their nails.

Now you know that putting on a poker face helps but it is not everything. You must also learn to control certain unconscious movements that can give you away. Of course, do not pretend to become a mime, the strategy is important but knowing how to play is even more so.

CHAPTER 7

HOW TO UNDERSTAND AN HONEST EMOTION VS. FAKE AND MANIPULATED EMOTIONS

It seems very simple to say, and the reality is that simple: you feel good when you solve your problems easily. Without drama, you are full of energy and vitality, you feel optimistic...that is when you are using authentic emotions.

An emotion is authentic when it responds to the stimulus that mobilizes it. This demolishes the terms "positive emotion" and "negative emotion" that have become obsolete when verifying that all emotions are necessary, and that fear or anger should not always be negative.

And what stimulus mobilizes an emotion so that it is authentic?

First of all, I have to say that each emotion must come into operation with a single stimulus. In this way, we will obtain the benefits of each one, and we will be able to verify that all the emotions if used well, are fundamental for a life of well-being:

FEAR: Response to the THREAT stimulus, and its objective is to set limits to any invasion or danger to obtain SECURITY. Ana was upset that her best friend called her at any time regardless of her privacy; she began to feel angry and criticize her behind her back. Anger, in this case, would be a false emotion because the stimulus is threatening; with authentic fear, she would set limits asking for respect, and she would feel safer.

SADNESS: Response to the stimulus of LOSS, and its objective is to think to solve and thus learn and DEVELOP. José left his partner; he was afraid of being alone and not finding another love story as beautiful as the one he lived. This had him distressed. Fear was a false emotion because what he suffered was a loss, not a threat. With sadness, he would accept and look for ways to improve from experience.

ANGER: Response to the encouragement of LIE (manipulation, abuse, treason, injustice), and its objective is to take action to react and cut through deception to do JUSTICE. Eva suffered the betrayal of a colleague in her own business, and she felt sad because she did not expect such an outcome, so she felt guilty and did not raise her head. Sadness was a false emotion because we are talking about treason. With rage, she would have expressed herself and would have cut off the traitor, thus bringing justice to her life.

PRIDE: Response to the encouragement of ADMIRATION, and its objective is to dare to value greatness in others and oneself, avoiding comparisons, its purpose is RECOGNITION. Silvia was invited to participate in a Congress with a presentation, she began to feel fear, and this led her to feel inferior to the other speakers. Fear was a false emotion that weakened her. The right thing would have been to feel pride for the other speakers and also for herself, who had the opportunity to take a brave step towards her dreams.

LOVE: Response to the stimulus SAFE SPACE and its objective is the dedication to everything worthwhile to achieve BELONGING with whomever one chooses. Marta dedicated herself to "saving" all the people she saw in need and then complained bitterly that she did not receive even a small part of what she gave. Here the false emotion is love because giving someone who only wants to take advantage of it is a threat, not a safe space. The authentic emotion would be to feel afraid and to set limits when it comes to delivery.

JOY: Response to the stimulus of UNEXPECTED GIFT, and its objective is to open up opportunities and flow with life in freedom to feel FULL. Manuel was a little curmudgeon, and it bothered him that his wife went to yoga and then stayed to have a beer with her friends. He saw it as something unfair while he was bored alone at home. He felt false anger. The real thing would have been to connect with the joy of enjoyment and seek something pleasurable for him instead of angering the joy of others.

With these examples, you can see that all emotions can be very damaging when used to face the wrong stimulus. For this reason, there are no positive or negative emotions, but authentic or false, that is, adequate or inadequately used. It is just a matter of re-learning their language, being alert to the stimulus, and using the correct emotion in each case.

A false emotion is ALWAYS accompanied by discomfort, negative energy, lack of vitality and enthusiasm, problems that accumulate one after another, anxiety, and stress.

261

Also included are other somatizations that produce emotional dysfunctions caused by the use of emotions that do not respond to your stimulus.

Envy, resentment, feelings of guilt, interesting relationships, dependency, impotence, the feeling of inferiority, or superiority. All these are dysfunctions that are produced by using false emotions.

If you want your life to prosper, you have no choice but to manage your emotions. Otherwise, it will be them who will direct your life, and you will be doomed to suffer one disaster after another.

CHAPTER 8

WHEN THE LIE HITS HOME

If falsely attributing yourself to fantastic situations or characteristics turns into a compulsion, it may be a sign that there is a personality disorder that hides suffering.

The "Pinocchio syndrome," also known by the name of "pathological liar," and with the name of "mythomania," is the one suffered by those who lie consciously and compulsively to obtain a benefit.

The pathological liar lies intending to hide something that he does not accept from his story. His lies are spontaneous and unplanned, and, once embedded in this dynamic of farce and deceit, he cannot stop, which is why he maintains his deceits on many occasions for years. The pathological liar knows he is lying, but he cannot help it until he finally ends up believing his fables.

Mythomania is defined as a tendency to lie or to tell fabulous things. For the sole purpose of not engaging in naïveté, we must recognize that lying is very frequent, social, and universal behavior, both to justify behaviors and not to make others suffer. It is a common resource to hide something, so as not to hurt or harm. However, there is a type of lie that we would call "pathological" that afflicts people who invent great realities and that have nothing to do with their lives. It is the one enunciated by those who disfigure or disguise situations in their personal, economic, social, or work life. They are not people whose behavior

263

can be seen, because they do not look like unbalanced people, so it is very easy to fall into their deceptions. However, like all complexes, it has its roots in childhood, when self-esteem has had early failures. One of the possible causes is that the parents did not value their qualities or compared them with siblings or cousins; and, later, with the companions. The mythomaniac, as a compensation mechanism for his battered and devalued narcissism, invents, and fantasizes about situations to level himself out before others.

Of course, only very insecure people present this tendency and this psychic work of omitting, lying, exaggerating, and falsifying reality to try to be accepted.

Origins

This disorder can be due to different reasons, namely:

- It may be that the mythomaniac belongs to a family that lives on social simulation, on appearance, showing what they do not have and what they are not.
- It may be that his life is so intolerable concerning the ideals and fantasies that he or his family deposited in him that by not being able to satisfy them, instead of accepting the truth, he takes the path of "inventing" another reality that only exists in his head.

One of the most notable characteristics of mythomaniacs is low self-esteem, given their non-acceptance of themselves and the deep and impossible desire to be another. And the devaluation is so great that they have to appeal to anything to be admired and accepted by people.

Coexistence

In coexistence, whether family or work, with the mythomaniac, their situation becomes more difficult, since others begin to suspect and gradually discover that their word is not worth believing. The feeling it generates for who received the effects of mythomania is to feel mocked, deceived. Those who make up their environment feel that they do not know who he is or what he wants and, thus, colleagues, friends, and even family members are taking distance. Consequently, the mythomaniac is often left very alone.

Of course, it is quite complicated to live with these people. First, because they are usually very trained and used to handling. They are always pretending, cheating, omitting, inventing things from the smallest to situations that can lead to serious consequences. And because they are compelling, people tend to believe them at first.

They can even take risky attitudes, like stealing or spreading rumors in offices for the sole purpose of harming someone. Because, by not accepting any mistake they may have made, they may end up awarding it to a partner. And, since, of course, they are not willing to recognize their lies, by force of repeating them, they end up believing them. Hence it is quite difficult for them to consult their own with a mental health specialist; it is rather the family, worried, desperate, who asks for help.

265

When this happens, one of the recommendations made is to confront the compulsive liar or mythomaniac, with his long lists of deceits and omissions. In the first place, so that the compulsion to lie does not continue to grow and also because, although it is an emotional disorder in their personality, they are not crazy. And deep down they know perfectly well that they have a problem and that alone they cannot get out of it.

Compulsion

The mythomaniac cannot stop lying and, precisely for this reason, his is a true compulsion.

He does not tell a lie to cover himself or justify himself as any person can eventually do, but he does it always and does not measure the harmful consequences that it can cause.

In general terms, this condition is the expression of an alteration in the construction of the personality that leads the person to thin their ties systematically and to ensure that nobody believes anything.

Being a mythomaniac has negative consequences; the person who lies compulsively loses credibility and social prestige.

It is often said of them: "Don't believe him because he is a charlatan."

Nuances

"Whoever told the first lie founded the civil society," said Irish playwright and novelist Oscar Wilde.

266

On some occasions, the lie arises as a necessity, in the face of a possible real or fantasized threat of losing our place, our prestige, our romantic relationship. In these cases, we can think of lying as a defense mechanism against the anguish of loss, and this characteristic makes it universal, without respecting creeds, ages, and relationships.

Lying comes from the Latin word "mens" (mind). Lying well means intelligence to have full knowledge of the truth; it also means understanding what the other wants to hear or, better said, entering the mind of the person who will listen to the lie, which makes it a creative fact.

Fear is a great cause of deception, but some lies are widely accepted by society, those that are linked to the promotion of products, services, people, candidates. In this case, qualities are exaggerated, and possible failures or defects are omitted.

Socially, the lie that avoids pain or suffering is also admitted and promoted. So the nuances between the collectively accepted and rejected forms require a certain skill acquired with induction or upbringing.

In the mythomaniac, the behavior of falsifying reality, deceiving (in some cases it includes defamation or accusations against people), took root in the personality.

These people live in a state of permanent anxiety because they have reached extreme behavior, and to stop making lies is difficult, so it is a compulsion.

CHAPTER 9

THE POWER OF EMOTIONAL INTELLIGENCE

The ability to read people can also be used for the dark side of emotional intelligence.

In some jobs, the connection with emotions is essential, while in others, it is harmful. Like any skill, the ability to read people can be used for good and evil. Some of the greatest events in human history have been triggered by emotional intelligence.

When Martin Luther King, Jr. set out his dream, he chose words that would move the hearts of his audience. Instead of respecting the sacred obligation of freedom, King said, America gave blacks an uncovered check.

He believed that a country suffocated by the heat of oppression could be turned into an oasis of freedom and justice. So he predicted a future in which the sons of former slaves and sons of former slave owners could sit together for a hundred fraternities on the red hills of Georgia.

Communicating such an exciting message required emotional intelligence the ability to recognize, understand, and manage emotions. Dr. King demonstrated extraordinary ability in managing his emotions and in awakening the emotions that propelled his audience to action.

As the writer of his speeches, Clarence Jones said, King conveyed a perfectly balanced protest of reason and emotion, anger, and hope. His tone of painful indignation was completely in line with that.

What is Emotional Intelligence?

Although numerous authors have contributed to the definition of emotional intelligence, certainly, the most important is Daniel Goleman, because of which the term EI became known to the whole world. He published his first book in 1995, while his later editions were limited to establishing the existence of EI. Goleman later extended his work on EI to the field of leadership and linked EI to performance in the workplace.

Today there are several models and theories of EI. One of the definitions was given by Meyer and Saloway, who introduced the term EI into psychology:

- Emotional intelligence is the capacity to interpret emotions, analyze and produce them to help us understand emotions and emotional awareness and to control emotions to reflexively encourage emotional and mental development.
- Another definition of Mayer and Nightingale, which is also generally known, is: Emotional intelligence is a type of social intelligence that includes the ability to track the thoughts and emotions of one's own and of others, discriminate against them, and use that knowledge to understand others' opinions and behavior. Emotional Intelligence (Salovey & Mayer, 1990).

Models of emotional intelligence

269

There are three different EI models, which differ depending on the definition and operationalization of the term. Thus, there is an ability model, a mixed model, and a line model, and we will briefly look at each of them.

1) The creators of the first model, the ability model, are Saloway and Mayer, who consider EI based on four components:

- Accurate identification of emotions ("How do I feel?").
- Using emotions as an aid in thinking ("What effect do emotions have on me?").
- Understanding the effects (consequences) of emotions ("What is the cause of these emotions?").
- Managing emotions to make good choices and focus on effective action ("How do I manage these emotions?").

2) Daniel Goleman is the creator of the so-called mixed model, which includes five components:

- Self-awareness (the ability to recognize emotions when they are manifested, recognizing the impact they have on other people, is essential for psychological self-knowledge and self-understanding, the inability to recognize our emotions leads us to depend on them).
- Self-regulation (overcoming and managing emotions, adapting to new situations, people who

are better at self-regulation recover faster than life falls).

- Social skills (the ability to maintain relationships with others that largely depends on the skill of understanding other people's emotions).
- Empathy (respecting the feelings of other people, more empathetic people can better interpret existing social signals).
- Motivation (what drives us to succeed and for the sake of achievement).

Goleman adds, in addition to these five components, a set of emotional competencies that are within each of these five components. Emotional competencies are not innate, but are acquired through experience and can be developed. Furthermore, Goleman states that there is a general EI with which people are born that determines their potential to learn certain competencies.

3) The third type of model is based on the assumption that EI can be viewed as a set of personality traits, and Constantine Vasili Petrides gave the setting of the model. This model defines EI as a constellation of emotional self-perception that is located at lower levels in the personality hierarchy. Thus, EI is considered as a self-perception of emotional abilities, and another name given to this model is "emotional self-efficacy based on traits."

There are numerous findings that emotions are sometimes more important and that the rational part of the mind prevails. Various studies involving injuries to regions responsible for emotional data processing indicate that emotional intelligence is different from general intelligence.

In addition to numerous criticisms, EI has managed to find its purpose, and today it is used in many global companies to determine leadership skills, to predict violence among young people, to determine the links between emotions and prosocial behavior and the like. Although EI is challenged in terms of prediction of behavior, it justifies a significant impact when it comes to the use of psychoactive substances (which negatively correlates with EI), self-confidence (the higher the score on the EI test, the higher the level of self-confidence), business, i.e., work performance (high positive association with EI) and related areas of human behavior.

Hallmarks of the Emotional Mind

The study of emotional intelligence takes its official beginning in 1937 when approaching our topic. Hereditary psychologist, a student of his father, Robert Thorndike, published work on social intelligence of the same name. In 1940, the outstanding psychologist David Wexler (also a former student of Thorndike's father) opened the next stage with an article on intellectual and non-intellectual components. He pointed out that non-intellectual components are even more important for social adaptation than intellectual ones. It was with them that a serious study of this phenomenon began. An important milestone was also 1983 when Howard Gardner wrote about multiple intelligence and 1990 when American psychologists John Meyer and Peter Salovey introduced the term "emotional intelligence" and began a research program to measure it. We'll mention Daniel Goleman's book "Emotional Intelligence," which was published in 1995 and has become classic: even though the term itself is not his idea.

We owe Meyer and Saloway the definition of emotional intelligence. Scientists described it based on its constituent parts.

Emotional intelligence is a combination of four skills, among which:

- The accuracy of evaluating and expressing emotions is the ability to determine emotions according to their physical state and thoughts, appearance, and behavior. This also includes the ability to express your emotions and related needs to other people.
- The use of emotions in mental activity is an understanding of how you can think more effectively using emotions. Many human problems come from the fact that one does not know how to control his emotions, does not understand them, and is not able to control them. If he has such a skill, he gains an invaluable gift— the ability to stand in the other's position, look at himself from the side, and evaluate the situation from different points of view. All this is the ability to see the world from different angles. This skill is extremely productive because it allows you to

273

regulate relationships and find solutions to pressing problems.

- Understanding emotions is the ability to determine the source of emotions, classify them, and recognize the relationship between words and emotions. It is also the ability to interpret the meanings of emotions related to relationships, understand complex feelings, and be aware of transitions from one emotion to another. Researchers include here the possible further development of emotion.

- Managing emotions is the ability to use the information that they give, evoke emotions or move away from them, depending on their information content or usefulness; manage your own and others' emotions.

Emotional intelligence, fortunately, can be developed. This is not what is given to us from birth and for life. Although, for example, J. Meyer believes that it is impossible to increase the level of emotional intelligence, because, in his opinion, this is just a given. And then he admits that through training, you can increase the level of emotional competence—the ability to recognize your feelings and feelings of other people with the goals of self-motivation and control your emotions.

Among his opponents, we see a very authoritative D. Goleman, a true titan in the study of emotional intelligence. Goleman believes that emotional intelligence can be developed because the nerve pathways of the brain continue to develop until the middle of human life. The methods for developing emotional intelligence can be very different. Among them, everyone will find at least one that is most suitable: family education, relationships in society, close relationships with the opposite sex, and simply life experience itself, which, as you know, is the best teacher.

When studies of emotional intelligence became widely available, they turned out to be the missing link in a specific question: why do people with average intelligence (IQ) seventy percent of the time outperform competitors with the highest intelligence? This problem cast a dense shadow on what people have always mistaken for the only source of success: intelligence. Decades of research now point to the emotional component of intelligence as a decisive factor.

Emotional intelligence consists of four basic skills that describe personal and social competence.

Personal competence consists of our self-awareness and self-management skills, which focus more on us individually than on our interactions with other people. Personal competence is the ability of a person to be aware of his emotions and control his behavior and inclinations. Two skills belong to it:

Self-awareness - The ability to accurately feel your own emotions and track their appearance and development. We are aware of our own emotions, the way they affect our thoughts and behavior, we know our strengths and weaknesses, and maintain self-confidence.

Self-government - The ability to use an understanding of one's emotions to remain flexible and positively direct one's behavior. We can manage impulsive feelings and actions, manage our emotions (in healthy ways!), take the initiative, fulfill obligations, and adapt to changing circumstances.

Social competence consists of understanding the processes taking place in our environment and of relationship management skills. Social competence is our ability to understand the mood of other people, their behavior and motives, to improve the quality of our relationships. This also includes two skills:

Social understanding - The ability to accurately notice the emotions of other people and understand what is happening. Thanks to this skill, we can understand the emotions, needs, and problems of others, and feel comfortable in society.

Relationship management - The ability to use an understanding of one's and other's emotions to manage interactions with other people successfully. We know how to develop and maintain good relationships, how to communicate, inspire others, how to work well in a team and find a way out of conflict situations.

Emotional intelligence, IQ, and personality are two different things. Emotional intelligence is a fundamental element of human behavior that is distinct from intelligence. There is no known connection between a measure of intelligence and emotional intelligence; it is

276

completely impossible to predict the level of emotional intelligence based on how smart someone is, that is, how high his IQ is. IQ itself is misunderstood as a degree of education or as an indicator of genius. IQ in itself is your ability to learn, and at fifteen, you have the same as at fifty. Emotional intelligence is a versatile collection of skills which can be theoretically learned and developed. Although some people naturally have higher emotional intelligence than others, if you wish, you can develop emotional intelligence to a high level, even if you were not born with it.

Individuality is the last piece of the mosaic. It is a sustainable style that defines each of us. Individuality is the result of deep preferences, such as a tendency to focus on oneself or, conversely, to extrovert behavior. However, like IQ, personality cannot be used to predict the level of emotional intelligence. Like IQ, personality is stable and does not change throughout life. IQ, emotional intelligence, and individuality each of these phenomena represent a unique basis for the interaction of a person with himself and with the world around him.

Emotional intelligence affects:

Our success at work. Emotional intelligence helps to manage contacts, which is especially important if a person is working in a team or if his work is related to communication (and the vast majority of classes are suitable for these criteria). EQ helps motivate people, and if there is an element of competition in work, surpass rivals. Communicating with the heads of the personnel

277

services of large companies, you can find out that, when selecting for a job, they consider EQ the same as professional skills, and often require an EQ test before accepting a candidate.

Physical health. Modern life is stressful, and it is a fact. Of course, some people have less stress, but in general, it is not about who has more, who has less, but how much a person can manage it. If you are unable to control the level of stress, this can lead to serious health problems. No wonder they say all the diseases come from the nerves: excessive stress may raise blood pressure, weaken the immune system, raise the risk of a heart attack, lead to infertility, and accelerate the aging process. Therefore, the first step to improving emotional intelligence is to try to learn and understand how to reduce stress.

Mental Health. Uncontrolled stress can also affect a person's mental health, making them vulnerable to anxiety and depression. Unable to manage our emotions, we find ourselves subject to mood changes, and the inability to control ourselves leads to the inability to form strong relationships, which in the end can make us acutely experience loneliness.

Relationship. Understanding our emotions and knowing how to manage them, we can better express our feelings and understand what other people feel and how. This skill allows us to communicate more efficiently and create stronger relationships both at work and in personal life.

So, emotional intelligence is associated with success at work. Think about how much your emotional intelligence affects professional success. Short answer: very strongly! Because it is a powerful way to focus energy in one direction with a huge result. Social psychologists from the Aristotle University of Greece, future candidates of science, during a large-scale study, comparing emotional intelligence with thirty-three other skills important for work, found that it was emotional intelligence that is the strongest predictor of success at work. It determines fifty-eight percent of success, and in all professional areas. Fifty-eight percent—think, it's more than half! And it turns out that such important factors as IQ, profile education, previous experience, etc. account for even less than half of the merits!

Our emotional intelligence is the basis for acquiring critical skills. It affects most of what we say and do every day. Emotional intelligence is the most important criterion for success in the workplace. For those who aim at a high position, this is the most important factor in leadership and personal superiority.

Among the study participants were executives, including large international companies; it turned out that ninety percent of them have a very high level of emotional intelligence. At the same time, only twenty percent of employees holding grassroots positions have a highly developed emotional intelligence, which means that sooner or later, they will occupy a much higher position. If others develop their emotional intelligence, their capabilities will also improve markedly. You can be the main person in the company without emotional intelligence, but the chances are small.

People with a high degree of emotional intelligence obviously gain more money than people with low EQ. The relationship between emotional intelligence and income is so direct that each point in emotional intelligence adds two percent to the annual salary. Of course, two percent is not much, but this is for each point! The data obtained is stored for employees in all industries, at all levels, in every region of the world. So far, experts have not found a field of activity in which success and salary would not be closely related to emotional intelligence.

Emotional intelligence can be developed. This is certainly his most encouraging property. The actual basis of emotional intelligence is the link between our emotional and logical "brains." The pathway to emotional intelligence begins in the brain; when an event occurs with us, our primary feelings emerge here and through the limbic system breakthrough to the forefront of the brain before we can think rationally about what happened. And, before the mind can comprehend them, we have an emotional response to events. Therefore, emotional intelligence requires good communication between the brain's logical and emotional centers.

There is such a term - "plasticity." Neurologists use it to describe the brain's ability to change. The brain grows new connections while we learn new skills. Changes are gradual and occur because brain cells develop new connections to accelerate the effectiveness of newly acquired skills. Using strategies for developing emotional intelligence allows billions of microscopic neurons that pave the road between the rational and emotional centers of the brain to "pull branches" to reach other cells. One cell can grow fifteen thousand bonds with neighbors. When we train our brains constantly using new strategies of emotional intelligence, emotionally intelligent behavior becomes a habit.

Busting The Myths About Emotional Intelligence

Many people tell that they cannot develop this Emotional Intelligence "business" because they are very nervous; others say that they have tried several times and were unsuccessful. Some say that they have tried to like everyone around them and have not succeeded.

The three great myths about emotional intelligence:

1 - You won't be nervous anymore, or you won't be angry anymore: Lie!

Emotional Intelligence does not lie in failing to feel what is natural for us human beings to feel in different situations in our lives, such as anger, hurt, sadness, disappointment. What changes with Emotional Intelligence is that you will start to notice that you feel a certain way and will start to measure your words and attitudes. For example, instead of yelling at that annoying coworker who keeps disturbing your performance, you may even feel irritated in the same way, but you will be able to consider the best attitude to solve the problem. Not just to vent the irritation that caused you.

It is important to know that having Emotional Intelligence does not mean becoming a cold person. Without feelings, quite the contrary, you will be even more connected with your emotions. However, aware of what you are feeling and how each emotion influences your attitudes, you will refine your reactions, stop acting on the emotional impulse, and act in an increasingly balanced and effective way.

2 - Understanding what Emotional Intelligence means will make you balanced: Lie!

It is not enough to read all the literature that exists about EI and think that this will be enough to become an emotionally balanced person. Your emotions cannot be mapped, understood, and managed overnight, and this is a job for every day of your life. You will always be learning new things about yourself, even because we are beings of constant change. What makes you feel good today, may be what hurts you tomorrow and vice-versa. If you wait for a magic book, a magical consultation with a renowned psychologist, or even with a miraculous guru to achieve emotional balance overnight, I'm sorry, but I need to ask you to "take the horse out of the rain."

Dedicate yourself to self-knowledge and never give up on being a better person, be patient with yourself, and seek learning in each of your mistakes. Think of it as a journey of a thousand steps where each small step brings you closer to a lighter and more successful life.

3 - You will like everyone around you: Not even close!

When talking about balanced people who get along with everyone, there is a great tendency to interpret that these people like everyone and that everyone likes them. That does not exist! There will always be that person that your "saint" just doesn't hit or even that person who doesn't like you no matter how well you treat them. EI only contributes so that you can get along with all these people and get along well!

Imagine that coworker who keeps talking bad about you to the whole office and the worst, in front of you still pretends to be your friend. It's bad to have to look at him every day, isn't it? A lot of people just can't even look, talk then becomes impossible. However, EI allows you to separate the chaff from the wheat and still create an environment of light coexistence with everyone, opening the door to good communication and, in the vast majority of cases converting boring colleagues into great work partners.

Just respect that no one is obliged to like you and vice versa, but in 99% of the cases, it is possible to maintain coexistence on a light and productive level. But if you want that, you will have to start from yourself, whoever waits for others is always living according to what they have to offer when you could offer something much better to yourself and the world.

Many demand that the world is a better place, but few are those who exchange posters for attitudes!

283

CHAPTER 10

SCHOOLING THE EMOTIONS

Educate emotions for what? Development of emotional intelligence, emotional competence, awareness of our emotions, quality of life.

Many people still don't understand the importance of developing emotional intelligence. A survey shows that in the last 30 years of the last century in the USA, 87% of people who lost their jobs lost them due to difficulties related to the lack of good use of emotional intelligence. The consequences of the lack of emotional education, just citing the data collected in developed countries, according to Claude Steiner, include delinquency, increased abuse of licit and illicit drugs, traffic accidents and conflicts. Also included are violence at all levels and social sectors, homicides and suicides, physical and sexual abuse of women and children, abandoned children, and unemployment at all levels. Further, conduct problems and dropping out of childhood and adolescence in all social classes, marital problems, separations, conflicts between parents and children, depression and psychosomatic illnesses were noted. It is easy to see that these situations happen precisely because of the lack of emotional intelligence development.

Emotional competence is an essential component of personal power. By making our relationships stimulating and mutually rewarding, we feel encouraged, optimistic, and powerful. It enables any dialogue, human contact, or

284

association to provide greater rewards to all involved. Good communication makes it possible to confirm perceptions, give and receive feedback effectively, and honesty of feelings are essential elements for a person to live in balance.

Emotional competence is made up of the ability to get to know each other, understand emotions and feelings, and expressing them productively. It also involves having self-control and empathy with other people, and thus understanding what they feel and interacting with them. Being emotionally competent is being able to deal with emotions in order to develop your personal power and the quality of life that surrounds you.

When we educate our emotions, our relationships expand. We create the possibility of affection between people, cooperative work becomes more viable, and the sense of community is facilitated. Many people, especially men, imagine that emotional education will result in a loss of power in their personal and professional lives. But the truth is that we all have something to learn from our emotions.

As we learn to read and write, we can develop the ability to deal with our emotions and feelings, and for this, there are a series of simple methodologies and techniques that allow this development at any age. The development of emotions begins with the awareness of our emotions and feelings, a differentiation between them, and learning to name each of them. It also involves understanding where they come from and how they work, learning to talk about what we feel, overcoming fear and inhibitions, and directing them positively. As we do this, natural empathy and intelligent interaction with other people develop, and we develop relationship skills. Naturally, the levels of stress and anxiety go down, and we can live with more joy, health, and quality.

What Is Emotion?

Emotion is a response from our body to an external stimulus. The relationships with others or the events that surround us cause an impact, which is translated into some kind of emotion.

The emotion we feel, for example, the sadness after receiving bad news, has physiological consequences such as a shaky voice, the pallor on the face, or the change in gestures. On the other hand, there are psychological consequences, that is, the feelings that remain as a result of some emotion.

Why Do We Need Emotions?

The human being is the most evolved being by nature. This being has a body that comprises exclusively animal parts and exclusively human parts. Almost every organ in the human body is anatomically analogous to that of other animals in its class. Although some animals have some organs with greater capacities than humans, they have a developed anatomical set that surpasses all the capabilities of all others.

Result of thousands and thousands of years of natural evolution, the human vocal apparatus that produces dozens of phonemes and its brain that memorizes them, formed the ideal duo for the creation of rationality. Speak and think, and memorize what you think and say, only man can do it.

Human rationalization has created new values, new ideas, and new realities. And these new realities have reinforced the growth of others. The language has forced the development of the brain and vice versa, and both forced to the development of the entire human body. The human senses have become the most developed - the refining of taste, smell, hearing, and especially touch, is very developed in man, as well as vision, namely in their sensitivity to colors.

All of these aspects create new needs for human beings, including ways of expressing themselves, not only what they felt for their animal nature, but also for what they felt for their capacity for mental creation. For this reason, nature has endowed human beings with unique characteristics, such as the ability to blush because they lie, cry because they are sad or laugh because they are happy.

Any emotional feeling is an accumulation of tension that comes from everything around us, or from ourselves, and goes against our ability to react or to understand immediately. Emotions are the way to defuse that tension.

Animals have no understanding, so they have no feelings, so they do not accumulate emotional or nervous tension, and therefore they do not laugh or cry.

If a person wants to do something but does not do it because conscience society, culture, religion, the law and everything that is of human origin do not allow it, then a certain emotional tension will be created that it can be expressed in the most varied ways: with depression, violence, apathy, and usually accompanied with sadness because it is a negative tension. In the same way, if a person is calmed by something he did not expect, or feels a satisfaction greater than imagined, he is also unable to understand and react. It also builds up tension that needs to be emptied equally by emotions now with joy. It is the body's return to a healthy balance.

We have feelings and emotions because we understand some things, but we don't understand others. If we understood everything, we would also have no emotions. Emotions are closely linked to the unknown, the doubtful, the ambiguous, and the uncertain. There are no emotions regarding what we know or are totally unaware of. What is fully conscious or unconscious does not move.

Emotions can be pleasant or unpleasant, but they are all adaptive; that is, they guide us towards our survival. Emotions are like a complex communication system, which regulates how we interact with the environment.

The basic emotions are Joy, Love, Surprise, Wrath, Sadness, and Fear. Each of these emotions has a function. They are like "software" that serves not only to communicate, but to propel the action, and fast.

In most everyday situations, these behaviors are extremely useful to us. For example, if we see a snake, fear (it has the function of protection and survival) will tell us to flee; if we lose a loved one, sadness (it has the function of personal reintegration, "motivates us to") guides us to leave work and stay at home to seek "support"; when we are happy we are more willing to explore and try new situations, it is easier to plan and make decisions faster, etc.

But sometimes, our emotions get deregulated in patterns that don't help us. For example, fear pushes us to run away from everything, the sadness of withdrawing from activities that help us to feel better, and shame (feeling secondary to sadness) to hide from everything, so that we never have any chance of getting away from it.

The impulses to avoid emotional discomfort at all costs can make our lives difficult: when we avoid undesirable emotions, we end up losing all the dimensions that animate them too. This is when we need to activate our brain's highest level, the prefrontal cortex, to reflect: Do these emotions push us in a useful direction? Are they allowing us to live the full life that we want to live?

If the answer is no, our prefrontal cortex, the anatomical structure of the brain most recently developed in the evolutionary process, where functions such as complex thoughts, behavior planning, personality expression, decision making or modulation of social behavior reside, overlap up to our limbic system ("emotions," the amygdala, the "emotional heart" responsible for

289

emotional processing, or the acquisition of fear responses, playing a central role in the body's alarm and reaction responses to certain stimuli). This pushes us to act in the opposite direction of how we feel, even if we are really uncomfortable at the moment.

Why Are Some People More Emotional Than Others?

People are unique and different from each other, there is no doubt, but some are much more intense and, when something negative happens, they despair, cry, suffer. When something good takes over, they skip around the world. On the other hand, there are those who react more sparingly. I wonder why?

A new study suggests that this difference in the emotional reaction may have to do with genetic issues. For this, tests were carried out to assess the processing of emotions within the brain, which may explain why some people are more susceptible to post-traumatic stress, for example.

People really see the world differently. For those who have this genetic variation, the emotionally relevant things in the world stand out much more.

Hereditary

The studied gene is ADRA2b, responsible for the regulation of the neurotransmitter norepinephrine. According to another research leader, Professor Adam Anderson, emotions are not processed purely in the way they happen but are also influenced by the way the brain perceives them.

Anderson explains that it shows us that our genes really interfere with how we view the positive and negative aspects of life and that some people tend to see bad experiences as major threats.

Todd explains that although it seems bad to have more intense responses to emotions, the truth is that this can have its positive side too, as this genetic variation helps people who react with more emotion to realize what is, in fact, relevant in the world. She cites Marcel Proust as an example of a highly sensitive person who transformed what he felt into creativity and literary production of excellent quality. Now tell us: what type of person do you fit in with?

Useful Tips

When building relationships with others, you should pay particular attention to what type of people they are. What for? It's simple: to interact with emotional people, you need one approach, and with logical people another.

For example, a logical person in decision-making is more guided by facts, figures, depth of evidence, and other reasonable parameters that lead him to the goal. And an emotional person, on the contrary, pays more attention to the states that he lives in the moment and which, having reached the goal, he will experience. A large amount of data and numbers can confuse or alienate.

Objectively, it is important to understand that both logical and emotional people experience emotions. Believe me; piss off, piss yourself off, touch, inspire, make laugh and

291

various other feelings can be evoked with anyone. It's just that logical people have lesser feelings and emotions and pushing them to the impulses of the soul will be noticeably more difficult than those who, from birth, are more likely to reveal their inner world to others.

And one more important point. Emotional people, in contrast to logical ones, make most decisions at the level of emotions. They are more susceptible to psychological effects. This is a payment for their creativity and profundity of life perception, because they see the world from a different angle, not like logical people.

The Roots of Empathy

Empathy is built on self-awareness. The more we open ourselves to our own thoughts, the more capable we will be of reading other people's feelings.

The alexithymic, who do not know their feelings, feel lost when it comes to knowing what someone who is with them feels.

They are emotionally deaf. The notes and chords of emotion, which slip into people's words and actions, the revealing tone of voice or change of posture, the eloquent silence or a revealing tremor, go unnoticed.

Confused about their feelings, alexithymic are equally bewildered when other people express theirs to them.

This inability to register the feelings of another is a significant deficit of emotional intelligence and a tragic failure in what it means to be human. Because all rapport, the root of interest in someone arises from emotional attunement, from the capacity for empathy.

That ability, the ability to know what someone else is feeling, comes into play in a wide range of life situations. From sales and administration to idyll and parenthood, through compassion and political activity.

The absence of empathy is also revealing; it exists in psychopaths, criminals, abductors, and child molesters.

People's emotions are seldom expressed in words; much more often, they are manifested through other signals. The key to intuiting another's feelings is in the ability to interpret non-verbal channels: tone of voice, gestures, facial expression, and the like.

Just as the rational mind expresses itself through words, the expression of emotions is nonverbal. When a person's words conflict with what is manifested through tone of voice, gestures, or other non-verbal channels, emotional truth lies in the way the person communicates something, rather than what they say.

A rule of thumb used in communications research holds that 90 percent or more of an emotional message is nonverbal.

Those messages, the anxiety in the tone of voice, the irritation in the abruptness of a gesture, are almost always perceived unconsciously, without paying specific attention to the nature of the message, but receiving and responding tacitly.

The skills that allow us to do this right or wrong are also, for the most part, tacitly learned.

In general, women are better than men for this kind of empathy (Daniel Goleman).

Managing with Heart

We are talking about those who are cold, have very little compassion, and may even appear indolent. These are people who have a heart so hard that few emotions seem to be able to cross their borders and cross the layer of consciousness. We are, of course, referring to ice hearts.

Eyes that won't cry, lips that don't usually smile, hands that don't touch. To those who never give up their role as spectators, who give the impression that nothing that happens to them is important to them. However, these people are fragile while they do everything to appear strong.

We sometimes hide behind a shell, thinking that we will no longer feel the pain, but we do not see that by isolating ourselves, we are already hurting ourselves.

How are ice hearts?

When we talk about "ice hearts," we are looking at those who find it difficult to express how they feel. Here are some of their features:

- **Assumption.** These people may think that others already know how they are feeling. Therefore, they stop showing it.

- **Perfectionists.** They find it difficult to admit that they make mistakes. Besides, being weak is one of them.
- **Low self-esteem.** This prevents them from showing their feelings; they think that they have little or no value and therefore believe that it is useless to express themselves.
- **Fear.** They can be people who are afraid of facing conflicts and showing their emotions.
- **Catastrophic thinking.** They may also end up believing that everything is lost in advance. So what is the point of fighting?
- **Ignoring.** These people may not know how to communicate properly.
- **Timidity.** People with a heart of ice can hide how they feel to protect themselves. They use it as a defense mechanism against the possibility of being vulnerable.
- **Difficulty feeling.** They find it difficult to listen to themselves and, therefore, to determine what they feel.

Ice hearts have many feelings

Each person is a world. Those with ice hearts can display either of these characteristics. However, the common denominator of all these points is that they are unable to open a space for their emotions.

However, the fact that they do not express them does not mean that they do not feel them. People with a heart of ice have feelings, but the problem is that they don't know

295

or don't want to communicate them. The mechanisms that drive them to do so may be conscious or unconscious.

But how do ice hearts work? These people can be strong or distant. They, therefore, give the impression of being insensitive.

There can indeed be people as cold as ice cubes, so much so that they do not feel the slightest compassion or empathy for others. These people suffer from psychopathy. However, not all ice hearts are like this. As we have already explained, some are so out of timidity, fear, perfection, etc.

How to manage your emotions?

It is important to learn to manage your emotions. Why? Because we then become more assertive in our relationships, with ourselves and with others. Let's see how to get there:

Accept our feelings. Recognizing and accepting our emotions will help us grow and get to know each other better.

We focus on self-esteem. When we recognize our worth, we realize our importance. This will help us to know that our emotions are just as important. We can, therefore, focus on them when necessary, to grow as people, and improve our relationships.

Release. Sometimes when shyness rules us, we lock ourselves in prison and throw the key out because of this anxiety, which arises from the meeting with the other.

Face our fears. We may be afraid; however, in addition to recognizing this fear, we need to understand why it arises and why we let it out. By doing this, it will be easier for us to express what we feel. On the other hand, if we leave opinions aside and stop assuming that others will react in this or that way, we will more easily experience authentic moments and will be able to express ourselves without pressure.

Try to express our emotions. When we have spent a good part of our lives, not showing what we are feeling, starting to express our emotions can seem extremely difficult. So, to make this task a little easier, we can start by doing it with understanding people who are close to us.

Self-awareness. By getting to know each other, we will be able to identify our emotions and express them assertively more easily.

Emotions form a real universe. Managing them is not an easy task, but neither is it an impossible challenge. The main thing is to recognize them, to live them, to know how to express them, and when.

We are not all the same. Everyone expresses their emotions in a particular way. However, there is one thing to watch out for: this accumulation of feelings can end up suffocating us.

Putting ice hearts aside: the benefits

When we talk about "putting ice hearts aside," we are not

talking about people but the stiff, cold hearts that we sometimes have. This will bring us great benefits. Here are a few:

- Reduced anxiety.
- Increased empathy.
- Reduced stress.
- Better self-awareness.
- Strengthening relationships with others and with ourselves.
- Improved self-esteem.
- Better assertive communication.

To be able to know these benefits, it is good to follow or to have followed certain educational practices from an early age. These help us to become more aware of our emotions. This is what Arís Redo suggests in his article for the journal Vivat Academia, in which he explains the importance of emotional education for teachers and students.

If it is true that there are people with hearts of ice, that does not mean that it is impossible to soften them. Through emotional management, they will become more assertive when expressing their emotions, and, little by little, they will remove this heavy armor that makes them seem insensitive.

How to Get the Best out of People

Surely at some point in your life, you have been frustrated because you saw how someone with great human potential was not giving you his best. Even some disappointment may have led you to wonder if it is enough to put the best in one to be able to bring out the best in the other.

The truth is that when we talk about interpersonal relationships, although we cannot always put a label on that relationship, everything positive adds up. In some cases, perhaps we will not be able to promote the relationship so that it is as good as we would like since the last word is from the other, but we will get closer.

Remember that the important thing is that the other treats us to the best of his ability, although sometimes he is not able to contribute as much as we would like. Patience, in this case, can be an ally, let's remember that relationships also need to develop and grow to shine.

You deserve as much as the others

In our relations with others, it is convenient not to demand the exact fulfillment of our wishes, since this demand may have the opposite effect. Think that a healthy relationship is one in which both parties feel completely conditioned and even lacking in freedom. Instead, putting your best foot forward with flexibility and patience may be the best invitation for others to do the same for you.

And isn't it true that, whether in a friendship, in a loving relationship, or even a family one, we feel loved when we both strive? Taking this reciprocity into account is also beneficial to us: just as you put your best foot forward, you are also able to see equitable behavior in the other.

The balance of the asymmetrical relationship will help us to develop the best version of ourselves in it, even unconsciously. This will mean that we perceive that the other person is worthwhile and that we form a good team.

Putting the best of yourself is a sign of trust

Stephen Covey said that "if you want to awaken trust, you must be trustworthy," and indeed, for others to open up, we may have to be the first to embrace one-way. Do not be afraid to do it, since knowing your fears and your virtues will make others place their trust in you to reveal theirs, and it is very gratifying that someone considers us worthy of it.

Being able to do your best means being confident enough to know that those inner fears, shortcomings, or darkness are not big enough to overshadow all the good we can offer. So do not fear, since knowing and valuing yourself will allow those around you to see every one of your virtues.

"Trust is a two-way road," he said harshly.

"What are you suggesting?"

"That trust cannot be demanded when it is not granted."

-Dolores Redondo, from Legacy in the Bones-

Everyone will appreciate your trust in you, and therefore they will feel safe in your company: in the ties we have, a kind of closed circle is created in which several people move in unison and the edges soften.

Offer without interest, receive with gratitude

We all know the saying, "each one collects what he sows." Have you ever felt that way? We may not see results in the short term in putting the best of ourselves, but in the long run, it will be another reason for happiness.

First, how good it feels to give; secondly, because our relationships will be stronger; thirdly, because others will give themselves to us honestly and without asking.

Probably, once we have experienced this feeling with the rest and they have also done it with us: if we continually demand and do not recognize what they do to make us feel better, they will end up having a hard time giving us everything they could. However, usually, others do their best when they see that we do it too.

Discovering what is inside those we love is as nice as realizing what is in ours. Reciprocity is the key between two people who strive to maintain strong and healthy ties: it ends up becoming what saves us as Neruda would say from life, love.

CHAPTER 11

THE ART OF PERSUASION

Persuasion is not just about discovering a person's emotional profile. You have to look for unsatisfied emotions and give them a way out. Listen to what they are concerned about and come up with solutions. Persuasion, in a sense, is also a task that involves creating a desire in others.

Whether it is about closing a deal, asking for a fee increase, motivating a sales team of 5,000 people, negotiating on an individual basis, acquiring a new company, or scrapping an outdated one, situations, contingencies or conjunctures almost always come down to relationship problems and personal treatment.

These unavoidable problems of relationship and personal treatment require persuasive action for their correct resolution since the other paths involve the curtailment of the freedom of others, such as threats, coercion, the use of force, etc.

Persuasion is necessary because individuals, communities, nations, often have different interests, customs, points of view, etc. When the achievement of one person's goals is blocked by the behavior of another in pursuit of their goal, persuasion is used to convince the offender to redefine his goal or modify the means to achieve it.

Persuasion is necessary because there is resistance. To resist is to oppose a force or a body to the action or violence of another force or another body. Many physical phenomena are based on resistance, and thanks to them, we can live. Why do you resist? On the mental plane, resistance is also an inevitable phenomenon: through resistance, we create lasting impressions, impact, persuade, convince, and negotiate.

Resistance, on the psychological plane, is illustrated by the principle of "cognitive dissonance." Psychologists call "cognitive dissonance" the phenomenon by which our minds instinctively reject the possibility of containing two opposing thoughts or beliefs.

Therefore, in our human relationships, we exchange dissimilar thoughts, feelings, and beliefs that resist each other. That is why all human beings exercise resistance. And when you study why you resist yourself, you understand why others resist.

And that understanding is very important because it doesn't seem very skillful to resist resistance. As the repetition of the words themselves seems to graph it, it is like "condemning a sentence," or "shouting saying that one should not shout." Resistance must be allowed to flow, that is, it must be allowed its full expression, even allowing it to reach its limit.

The resistance is moderated with "lubricants," with "shock absorbers," listening and giving space to the other. Resistance is a thought, almost always accompanied by a feeling. By subtly changing that thought, resistance can disappear.

The First Element of Persuasion is nothing but influence. And the influence begins with what matters to your potential ally. Professor Harry Overstreet, in his illustrative book Influencing Human Behavior, says: "Action stems from what we fundamentally want (...) and the best advice that can be given to those who seek to be persuasive, whether in business, at home, at school or in politics, it is this: first, to awaken in the neighbor a frank desire. Whoever can do this has the whole world with him those who cannot walk alone along the way. Therefore, the strength of mutual exchange consists in obtaining what one wants and giving others what they need."

Persuasion is a mere intellectual exercise: How to persuade is to make the feelings and ideas that we would like them to have appeared in the spirit of another or other people. And we must always keep in mind that our actions do not come only from abstract reasons, cultural patterns, etc. They mainly come from our desires, interests, and emotions.

If I could describe in one sentence the art of persuasion, that phrase would be the following: persuasion is to convert people, not in our way of thinking, but in our way of feeling and believing.

People do things for emotional reasons. Therefore, persuading is also influencing the emotional attitudes of others.

Persuasion is not just about discovering a person's emotional profile. You have to look for unsatisfied

304

emotions and give them a way out. Listen to what they are concerned about and come up with solutions. Persuasion, in a sense, is also a task that involves creating a desire in others.

The History of Persuasion

Do you know what a speech by Barack Obama, an announcement by Chanel, a gamification campaign for the VW Polo, and a press release by Repsol have in common? The answer is found in work written over 2,300 years ago! Its title is The Rhetoric and the author, Aristotle. This treaty establishes the foundations of corporate advertising, political, institutional, emotional, and journalistic communication.

Through this Section, we will try to discover how the theoretical precepts and the methodology exposed in The Rhetoric are applied daily and in a multidisciplinary way in the areas of professional communication. The conceptual basis of the work revolves around the command of the word and discourse—discursiveness—as instruments to exercise persuasive communication. Along with these elements are the arguments or reasoning that will be presented to the public to convince them by appealing to their feelings and emotions. Likewise, Aristotle determines and analyzes the protagonists of this process: sender, receiver, message, and channel or medium.

The issue is you must project an image of credibility, authority, and moderation that facilitates the acceptance of your messages by the interlocutor. As for the recipient, it will be essential to know their approximate age and social status. In this way, the contents will be adapted to the particularities of the audience. El message is characterized by a simple style but elaborate. However not conveying the feeling of artificiality. The vocabulary will be clear and intelligible for all audiences.

And the use of 'linguistic' resources that attract the attention of the interlocutor will be pertinent. Aristotle defines the structure of the messages in preamble, proposition, and epilogue. The preamble will capture the attention of the public to present the topic that will be addressed later. In the proposition, all the argumentative and narrative force of the exhibition will be overturned. The epilogue will contain a synopsis to summarize and consolidate the transmitted message. The message will appeal to the rational and emotional component that predisposes the interlocutor in a sense desired by the sender. Finally, it specifies that the message and its structures will always be adapted to the channel or medium through which it is transmitted.

As a result, this section constitutes a look at the past that takes us back to the original concepts of persuasion. This appeal is relevant in the prevailing digital environment in which we are located. In fact, at present, we use the infinity of supports and technological channels that are within our reach. Thus, we are present in traditional social networks (Facebook, Twitter, Instagram, Pinterest, YouTube, etc.) and other emerging ones (Periscope, Meerkat). And we are up to date with private messaging systems like Telegram and innovative applications like Snapchat. Of course, we know the trends in the creation of branded content (storytelling, scroll telling, etc.)

And we try to approach the public through personalized, gamified, and quality themes, thus developing the cross-cutting nature of the information. But, simultaneously, we must not forget that the means—technological support— is not the end, but must be a tool in the exercise of our profession. And we must remember that assertion of the classical thinkers: 'the oldest is the most modern.' Past and present shake hands, since the final objective—to guide, influence the interlocutor's will using persuasive stimuli and appealing to his emotions—continues to be the same twenty-three centuries later.

Psychological Trick to Get People to Say Yes

Each of us, at least once in our life, thought about what would happen if we could become the ruler of the whole world. Often we want our opinion for other people to be perceived as the only correct one. We want people close to us always to be able to help in any situation. To realize all this, we all ask the same question - How to make a person say "yes" to us? In this chapter, you will see a couple of tricks, thanks to which people will not be able to pass by you and your requests.

Here we go!

"The one for whom you have done good is ready to answer you with even greater good," said the famous American politician Benjamin Franklin. A series of different experiments show that if we render a service to a person, he can almost immediately tell us "yes" to our request, or he can take the initiative in his own hands and offer to do something for you. This is because the person for whom we rendered the service does not want to remain "in debt," even if we deliberately warned him that we did not need anything. It will be much easier for him to agree to your request, no matter how financially or psychologically expensive it is.

When you are talking with someone and want to receive a positive response to your request, mention the name of that person as often as possible. There is no greater delight for a person's ears than repeating his name in a conversation. In this way a person understands how important he can be for you and how much the fulfillment of your request depends on his answer.

Always overstate your requirements and requests. Yes, it is very likely that if I now ask my friend for 10 thousand as a loan, she will refuse me. But after a while, the friend's guilt will take up, because she will begin to realize that I needed the money for definitely urgent purposes, and with a 95% probability she will lend me a smaller amount, but it will turn out to be the same right amount. Overestimating our requests, we receive an immediate refusal, but then the person who refuses us offers us another condition, which is most optimal for use in the current situation.

It's much easier for us to say "yes" to someone we have sympathy for. Almost everyone is familiar with this trick, and just the same people use it most often. The phrases "You are my friend" or "We are friends with you, right?" increase the chance to get a positive answer at times because we appeal to the most expensive features that a person has—his conscience and relationships with others.

One of the features of a person is to relate well to those who are somehow similar to him. If we know the manner of communication and the character traits of our interlocutor, then we can begin to carefully "copy" them, but so that it doesn't catch the eye. Our interlocutor will begin to notice that you are similar in some ways, and with a further request, he will be happy to help.

Positively use gestures, i.e., constantly try to show how interesting the conversation is to you: nod, show something with gestures. A person will begin to notice that you are interested in a conversation that you are listening to him, which means that he will listen to your request.

Listening is one of the most important persuasion techniques. If a person only pretends that he is interested in conversation and only occasionally gives "signs of life," then this can be noticed right away, and you can't count on a positive answer.

Listen to what your interlocutor is talking about, and you are more likely to get a solid "yes" to your request.

How to build lasting Relationships

The quality of any relationship is hard to predict: often completely impossible relationships last for years, while others that seem to have all the advantages collapse.

309

Nevertheless, the practice of marriage counseling and the analysis of the causes for marriage breakdown suggest that some factors predispose either to improve or break up relationships. If you are interested in your own chances of forming a successful partnership, consider some of the main factors below.

Do not bind yourself when you are too young. Early marriages are at greatest risk. Each serious study of marriage issues shows that marriages concluded before the age of 19 are least preserved (especially if the marriage is completed because the woman is already pregnant). As you reach maturity, you change, different needs and interests develop, diverging from partners. Two people can develop more or less in one direction, continuing to coordinate changing needs with each other, but much more often, they grow apart.

Do not commit too quickly. You should not decide to create long-term relationships until you know each other for at least nine months. It is this period that allows most people to find out each other's best aspects and shortcomings and, living together, in practice to find out whether the partnership will stand the test of time.

Violent involvement in sexual union is a sign of danger. If you often quarrel and especially if one of you repeatedly breaks your connection, this is a bad harbinger for the future, since such a behavior pattern tends to take root. Putting off formalizing relationships can also be worrying. If you agreed on a joint life, but postponed the design of permanent relations for a couple of years or more, carefully consider your motives. This may mean that you are not yet ready to give up your independence.

Look for similarities. Surveys show that there is a tendency to marry your own kind. Although some marriages of dissimilar people turn out to be successful, life together, not accompanied by friction, is easier for a couple who have common interests and views, who want to get the same thing from life. It is useful to have at least one or two "cross-cutting" interests, as well as match each other in age. If the difference between you is more than ten years, it is likely that such differences of opinion will be inevitable that will create excessive difficulties for the normal development of relations.

Look for harmony between the sexes. Gender does not display its intrinsic binding power if your opinions on it are somewhat different or if in your life it plays a far greater (or much smaller) role than in your partner's life. Sexual compatibility is not a technological problem, because in the course of mutual adaptation the "mechanics" of love can be discovered. It is much more important that there is a real attraction to each other and a mutually stimulating effect, only on this basis can each of you fully satisfy the sexual needs of the other. On the basis of mutual attraction and love, almost all sexual problems are solvable, and without it, they are likely to be insurmountable.

Searches for emotional maturity. Some personality traits are extremely harmful to long-term relationships in the future. Anger is probably the most potentially destructive force for a lasting relationship in the future. Perhaps a violent clash with a partner who is trying to dominate is an aggressive and malicious tendency. If you can still hope that the relationship will remain with one psychologically immature partner, then with two, they are irrevocably doomed to failure. Low self-esteem also does not bode well, as it creates insecurity and jealousy, making it difficult to create relationships based on love and trust.

A mature and long-term relationship may not be possible if you are overly addicted. A partner who remains highly dependent on parents may require more support from you than you are willing or able to provide. In certain circumstances, when you need assistance, even temporary, he may not be able to take the burden of responsibility on his shoulders as a mature person.

Make sure your partner can provide you with physical intimacy and emotional support. A person who is emotionally isolated and who is difficult to show feelings or accept them physically has few prospects for maintaining a full relationship.

The search for flexibility. The ability to adapt to change is one of the most important features that must be considered when choosing a partner. Neither individuals nor couples remain unchanged, and an uncompromising person may have difficulty meeting with changing needs and circumstances of a long-term relationship. It's good if your current or potential partner agrees to think over new ideas or try new forms of activity.

If you have serious doubts about this relationship, do not have the hope that your partner will change. Hoping that under your influence, he will become less gloomy or extravagant, less angry, and not so prone to jealousy, you doom yourself to a significant risk. Some people have great potential for change, others the other way around. Thus, if the ability to change is essential for you, and you look for your partner's signs and do it before, rather than after, you have seriously linked yourself to a close relationship.

It is your own confidence in the existing relationship and the resulting determination to translate your intentions into reality. If you have doubts, they will intensify, preventing you from completely surrendering to creating relationships that could help overcome all problems and survive.

CHAPTER 12

SOCIAL INFLUENCE

Social influence occurs when a person has emotions, opinions, or behaviors that affect others intentionally or unintentionally. There are multiple types of social influence and can be considered as consistent, socialization, peer pressure, obedience, leadership, persuasion, sales, and marketing. In 1958, Harvard psychologist Herbert Kelman identified three-wide varieties of social influence.

- Conformity, when it comes to people, agree with another matter itself to keep their particular opinions private.
- Identification is when people are influenced by someone who is loved and respected, such as a celebrity.
- Internationalization is when people accept faith or behavior and agree as publicly as privately.

Morton Deutsch and Harold Gerard have identified two psychological needs that lead people to live up to others' expectations. They include our need to be right (informational social influence) and our need to be loved (normative social influence). Information Impact (or Social Evidence) is the influence of accepting information from another as evidence of reality. Informational impact comes into play when people are not sure, either because the incentives are internally ambiguous or because there are social differences. Regulatory impact: so that they meet the positive expectations of others. From Kelman's typology, regulatory influence leads to public compliance, while information impact leads to private acceptance.

Types

Social influence is a broad term that refers to many different phenomena. Listed below are some of the main types of social influence that are currently being researched in the field of social psychology.

Kelman varieties

There are three processes of attitudinal change, as defined by Harvard psychologist Herbert Kelman in a 1958 article published in the journal Conflict Resolution. The purpose of defining these processes is to help determine the influence of social influence: for example, to separate social correspondence (behavior) from private reception (personal faith).

Compliance

Compliance is the act of satisfying an explicit or implicit request proposed by others. From a technical point of view, compliance is a change in behavior, but not necessarily in relation; it can be performed because of simple obedience or otherwise prefers to retain personal thoughts due to social pressure. According to article 1958 of Kelman, the satisfaction received from compliance is determined by the social effect of the host influence (i.e., people are responsible for the expected reward or punishment, disgust).

Identification

Identification is a change in attitude or behavior due to the influence of someone who is admired. Ads that rely on celebrity endorsements to market their products take advantage of this phenomenon. According to Kelman, the required relationship is that the identifier refers to a behavior or attitude change.

Internationalization

Internationalization is the process of adopting many norms established by people or groups that affect the individual. A person accepts influence because the content of the influence accepted is internally useful. This is comparable to an individual's value system, and according to Kelman, the "reward" of internalization is the "content of new behavior."

Conformity

Conformity is a type of social influence associated with changing behavior, beliefs, or thinking to align with other states or with regulatory standards. This is the most common form of social influence. Social psychology research in accordance, as a rule, distinguish between two varieties: information correspondence (also called social evidence, or "internalization" in Kelman terms), and normative correspondence ("correspondence" from Kelman's point of view).

In the case of peer pressure, the person is convinced to do what they may not want to do (for example, take drugs), but which they perceive as "necessary" to maintain a positive attitude with other people (for example, their friends). Correspondence from peer pressure is usually the result of identification with group members or with the observance of some members to reassure others.

Compliance may be in appearance or may be more complete, influencing an individual both publicly and privately.

Correspondence (also referred to as mute) demonstrates the public conformity of the group to the majority or norms. At the same time, the individual continues to disagree privately or dissent, holding on to his initial beliefs or an alternative set of beliefs that are different from the majority. Correspondence appears as conformity, but there is a separation between the public and private self.

The conversion involves the private recognition of what is missing in compliance. Coordinating the original behavior, belief, or change in the thinking of the individual with that of others (influencing), both publicly and privately. A person has adopted behavior, beliefs, or thinking, and assimilates it by doing it on his own. The transformation may also apply to individual group members, changing from their initial (and diverse) opinions to accepting the opinions of others, which may differ from their original opinions. As a consequence, the group's stance can be a combination of various aspects of initial individual views, or it can be an alternative based on the initial positions reached by consensus.

What seems to match in reality may be coherence. Coherence occurs when an individual's behavior, faith, or thought is already aligned with the activities of others, and no changes occur.

In situations where there is no conformity (including conformity, transformation, and comparison), there are non-conformity processes, such as independence and anti-conformity. Independence, also referred to as dissent, includes an individual (either through his actions or inaction, or through a public expression of his beliefs or thinking) aligned with their standards, but incompatible with other members of the group (or all groups or the majority). Anti-conformity, also referred to as the counter-argument of conformity, may appear as independence, but it lacks consistency with personal standards and to challenge the group. Actions, as well as reported views and beliefs, are often contradictory to group norm or majority norm.

Minority influence

The influence of a minority occurs when the majority is influenced by the belief or behavior of the minority. The influence of a minority may depend on the size of the majority and minority, the level of coherence of the minority group, and situational factors (such as the affluence or social significance of the minority). The influence of a minority most often acts through informational social influence (as opposed to normative social influence), since the majority can be indifferent to the soul of the minority.

Prophecy itself

Prophecy is a prediction that directly or indirectly calls itself to become true because of the positive feedback between faith and behavior. The prophecy is proclaimed as truth (when it is a lie), may influence a person enough, either by fear or logical misunderstanding, so that their reaction eventually fulfills a false prophecy once. This term is attributed to the sociologist Robert C. Merton from an article he published in 1948.

Reactance

Reactive is the acceptance of a vision contrary to the belief that a person is under pressure to accept, perhaps because of an alleged threat to behavioral freedom. This phenomenon is also called anticonformity. Although the results are the opposite of what the Influencer intends, reactive behavior is the result of social pressure. It should be noted that anticonformity does not necessarily mean independence. In many studies, reactance manifests itself in the deliberate rejection of influence, even if the influence is correct.

Humility

Obedience is a form of social influence, derived from an authoritative figure. The Milgram experiment, the Zimbardo Stanford prison experiment, and the Höfling hospital experiment are three particularly well-known obedience experiments. And they all conclude that people are surprisingly obedient in the presence of perceived figures of legitimate authorities.

319

Persuasiveness

Persuasion is the process of directing oneself or others towards accepting relationships by rational or symbolic means. Cialdini identified six "weapons of influence": reciprocity, commitment, social proof, authority, taste, and rarity. This is a "weapon of influence" of an attempt to achieve correspondence of directed means. Persuasion can occur through calls for rationality or calls for emotion.

Psychological manipulation

Psychological manipulation is a form of social control that attempts to alter other people's behavior or attitude through strategies that are offensive, deceptive, or behind-the-scenes. These strategies may be called exploitative, coercive, manipulative, and misleading by promoting the manipulator's interests, often at the detriment of another.

Social influence does not inherently have a negative effect. For example, doctors may try to convince patients to change bad habits. Social influence is generally perceived as harmless when it respects the right to accept or reject it adversely and is not too coercive. Depending on the context and motivation, social influence may constitute backroom manipulations.

Offensive Nutrition and Management

Controlling rapists use tactics to exercise power and control over their victims. The abuser aims to manipulate and threaten the victim, or to force them to believe they have no fair voice in the relationship.

Propaganda

Advocacy is information that is not objective and is primarily used to influence the audience and further the list, often presenting facts selectively encouraging a particular synthesis or perception. Or use a loaded language to produce an emotional response to the information presented, rather than a rational one.

Hard power

Strong power is the use of military and economical means to control certain political bodies' actions or desires. This form of political power is always violent (coercion), and is most successful when it is enforced on another lesser military and economic force by one political entity. Hard power is in contrast to a soft power derived from politics, culture, and tradition.

Emotions

Emotions and disposition can affect an individual's likelihood of matching or anticonformity. In 2009, a study found that fear increases the likelihood of agreement with the group, while romance or lust increases the chances of going against the group.

Social networks

A social network is a social system composed of nodes (representing individuals or organizations) linked (through ties, also called edges, ties, or links) by one or more forms of interdependencies (e.g., friendship, shared interests, or values, sexual relationships, or kinship). The study of the social network uses the network theory lens to research social relations. An analysis of social networks as a field has become more visible since the mid-20th century in determining the channels and consequences of social influence. For example, Christakis and Fowler found that social networks convey status and behavior, such as obesity, smoking, drinking, and happiness.

Determining the degree of social influence, based on large-scale observational data from a latent social network structure, is related to various collective social phenomena, including crimes, civil unrest, and voter behavior in elections. For example, methodologies for unraveling the social influence of peers from external influences—with a latent social network structure and large-scale—were data applied by US observant presidential elections, stock markets, and civil unrest.

CHAPTER 13

THE ART OF BODY LANGUAGE

Body language is a non-verbal communication channel that allows you to see what the other person is thinking about. A lot of manuals have been written on body language because this topic is quite extensive and fascinating; Those who wish can study them on their own. In this chapter, the applied use of body language is considered only in one area of interest to us.

A person in defense often stands in a closed position, with a cross of arms, and even legs.

Deviation of the body back and a large distance in communication more often indicates that the person does not trust you, does not consider you completely his own.

Touching a person's nose often indicates that a person doubts something, and a woman's correction of her curls in front of a man usually indicates that she rather likes the man.

Why learn body language?

People who set the task with the help of sign language to calculate those who will deceive and manipulate them do not protect themselves with this knowledge. The programs that teach "to recognize fraudsters and manipulators" lead to the exact opposite result: the number of people deceived as a result of these programs is only growing. Nevertheless, to understand sign language (more broadly—body language) is necessary; this is a natural moment of the general psychological culture. Knowledge of gestures is not a block or a master key, but a bridge to people and proximity.

Body language and the relationship between soul and body

Body language is not interested in body features that speak about the individual characteristics of a person, about his potential, about the possibilities of his growth and development. Body language does not always indicate what is happening in the soul, and often it's just a cultural or social convention. The science of body language is the science of non-verbal communication. About how, observing a person's body and gestures, to unravel what a person is hiding from us. Or how to use a body, without actually speaking, using the capabilities of gestures, facial expressions, and intonations, to convey to him some message from us.

Interpretation of gestures and gait

Human gestures are very diverse. To learn how to interpret them, it is necessary to understand for what purposes this or that movement serves. Gestures in the process of communication perform four main functions. First, they replace words with signs. You will probably understand the person you are talking to if he wants to say "OK" without words, showing you the thumb and forefinger connected. Secondly, they control the attention of the interlocutor and clarify what was said. If you need to show where the store that a passerby asks you about is, instead of long explanations, you will show with your hand the direction where he needs to go. Thirdly, they illustrate and reinforce what has been said. When the fisherman shows what kind of fish he caught, he will show it to you with his hands, and whether you believe the scope of his hands is up to you. Well, and fourthly, gestures adapt a person's body to the process of communication or express a person's state. Crossed arms create a state of security for a person, and lowered shoulders indicate that a person is tired or has lost faith in himself... It is these gestures that are most interesting for interpretation, and it is most difficult to interpret them since many of them are individual and often unrecognized. Nevertheless, it is quite possible to give some clues.

Interpretation of facial expressions

Simple emotions, expressive movements (joy, surprise, resentment) are easily understood, but in other cases, interpreting and decoding facial expressions can be a daunting task requiring attention, knowledge, and professionalism. When interpreting facial movements, it is important to adhere to the following rules:

1) Observe facial expressions in dynamics. "Video is always more informative than the photo."

2) For interpretation, it is necessary to track at least three parameters of facial expressions.

3) A statement about the emotions experienced by a person should be formulated in a hypothetical form. For example, "Based on the observed mimic movements (the

325

eyes are wide, the muscles of the forehead are stretched in an upward movement, the lips are half-open, the corners of the lips are raised), we observe the face of a person who is more enthusiastic than calm."

Sleep and body language

The falling asleep and sleeping person chooses this or that position of a body depending on the personal features and a state at the given moment.

The Five C's of Body Language

Body language Communication strategies are essential for companies to obtain good results. It is necessary to know the client and that the client knows the company and its products, and it is the responsibility of the company to know how to communicate it well. Several points can help with this task. They are known as the 5 C's of effective Body language communication.

- **Control:** There needs to be self-control in the communicator, both in body language and in verbal language.
- **Conversation:** More than a speech, the listener must have the feeling that he is having a conversation that is bringing him new and interesting knowledge. Otherwise, you can get bored and not get the message across.
- **Confidence:** It is an important C in many situations, but when it comes to communicating a message, it is even more so. If you want the

speaker to believe what you are saying, you must also believe it yourself.

- **Competence:** You have to show a professional attitude that conveys that you have full knowledge of the topic or product you are talking about. To transmit a message effectively, there has to be a product behind it.
- **Calm:** Anyone who speaks calmly tends to transmit that same calm to the rest and therefore creates an environment of greater receptivity to what is being said.

Extra

Clarity: Being clear is essential. The more an argument is bundled, the worse the message will get to the interlocutors. It is best not to overdo the subject and go directly to the fundamental idea.

The interlocutor will appreciate having time to discuss or ask questions on the subject, for that you have to express the message concisely and leave time for the rest.

Mastering the Secrets of Non-Verbal Communication

If you want more performance in your presentations, relying on non-verbal communication will increase your chances of success. Check out the secrets to being successful with this technique.

Communicating clearly and effectively is essential during presentations, either to your classmates or to a team of executives at work. However, relying only on words is not the most recommended method of seeking success in your way of communicating. You've got to rely on another tool to be successful: non-verbal communication. Although it is despised by many, non-verbal communication techniques can contribute greatly to the efficiency of presentation.

Eye Contact

To ensure efficient non-verbal communication, you must make eye contact. If you are in a presentation, you can use much more than words to express the importance of what you are saying. Try to make eye contact with as many presents as possible in your presentation, and this will make them take what you are saying seriously.

Voice fluctuation

Another way to emphasize what you are saying is to use your voice as a resource. A monotonous and constant tone will make people distracted, regardless of the content of your presentation. If you know the right time to increase or decrease your tone of voice, emphasize one word or another and even pause, your viewer's attention will be completely focused on you.

Positioning

Like the monotonous tone of voice, standing next to your presentation will make it boring. If you want to make your viewers interested in what you have to say, be dynamic. Walk around and in front of the room, point out examples. And never, under any circumstances, make your presentation sitting behind the computer. This is a bad practice.

Facial Expressions

For your audience to be enthusiastic about what you do, it is essential that you get excited about presenting it. If you stay with the famous "wake man" for as long as you are in front of them, there is no reason for them to feel the least bit interested in the subject. If you show how exciting the topic can be, more and more people will pay attention to the topic discussed. So, smile at the right moments, show animation, and even features of annoyance if that is the case.

Gestures

It is useless to walk around the room while presenting if your hands are kept in your pockets, crossed, or stuck to your sides. This shows discomfort. It makes people feel insecure about you. Try to count on the help of gestures; remember that your hands are not still during normal conversation. Just be careful not to overuse the feature and become a reason for jokes.

How to Interpret Verbal Communication

If we are more aware of this communication and understand what it means, we can better understand the people with whom we interact. This fact allows us to communicate more efficiently, and we can improve our communication with others and be more aware of what they are transmitting to us.

Sometimes we send out contradictory messages: we say one thing, but our body reveals a different message. This

329

non-verbal language can affect how we act and how others react to us.

Situations where signs and signals will allow us to communicate more effectively:

First impression: trust

Remember, for example, the day you met a new coworker. What was your first impression? Did it give you confidence? Would you associate with him/her? Did he convince you? Did he walk steadily into the office, keep his gaze on you, shake your hand firmly, or did he come in with hardly a sound, look away, and extend a weak hand? While you were talking, was he keeping your gaze, or was he looking away? Did his face look relaxed or tense? What were the movements of his arms, broad gestures, or rather close to the body?

When you look at other people, it is easy to identify cues that show how that person is feeling at the moment, either through posture or tone of voice. If you are about to enter a situation where you do not feel as safe as you would like, for example, to give a conference or attend an important meeting, try to adopt these signs and signals that project confidence:

- Posture - forehead high, shoulders back.
- Eye contact - solid with a "smiling" face.
- Hand and arm gestures - determined.
- Speech - slow and clear.
- The tone of voice - moderate to low.

A difficult meeting: tension

Think of a time when you've been in a tough meeting—perhaps an evaluation, a negotiation of deadlines, responsibilities, or a contract.

In an ideal world, both you and the other person should be open and receptive to listening to what the other has to say to end the meeting successfully. However, the other person may be on the defensive and is not listening.

For this reason, it is important to identify if your interlocutor is receptive to what you are saying. How do you know if your message is falling on "deaf ears"? Some of the signs that identify the person they are talking to are on the defensive include:

- The gestures of the hand and arm are small and are kept close to the body.
- The facial expressions are minimal.
- The person is physically away from you.
- Crossed arms in front of their body.
- Their eyes maintain little contact or avoid your gaze.

In interpreting these signals, it is wise to change what is being said and how it is being said to help the other person feel more comfortable and more receptive to what they are hearing. Likewise, if you feel that you are somewhat defensive when facing a negotiation situation, you can monitor your body language to make sure that the messages you are transmitting are the ones that you expose in words and that you are open and receptive to what is discussed.

Working with groups: disconnection

Have you ever found yourself presenting a project and had the feeling that your audience was not interested in what you were saying? Have you ever found yourself having to lead a team to reach a consensus on responsibilities and deadlines? Was everyone lined up to come up with a solution, or was there some disconnect between team members?

Ideally, when you have to make a presentation or work with a group, you want 100% participation by everyone. This does not always happen, and sometimes it is necessary to involve the audience, for this act, you must identify the signs of their "disconnection":

- Low heads.
- Staring or distracting with other things.
- Hands playing with clothes or pencils.
- People may be writing or scribbling.
- They may be sitting sunk in their chairs.

When you identify that someone doesn't seem to be involved in what's going on, you can do something to get him or her back on track and focus on the topic of the meeting again, for example, by asking them a direct question.

And while all this is happening, don't forget that your own body must also show the confidence and security you want it to express.

Detect the lie

Of all the non-verbal body language that we can observe, being able to perceive whether a person is lying or not, puts us in a very good position. Some of the signs that indicate when someone is lying are:

- The eyes maintain little or no contact, there are usually rapid movements of the eyes, and the pupils are constricted.
- The hands or fingers are in front of the mouth when speaking.
- The body turns physically away from you, or there are unusual/unnatural body gestures.
- Increase in breathing rate.
- Changes in skin tone, turning red on the face or neck.
- Increase in perspiration.
- Changes in voice, such as a change in tone, stuttering, or clearing their throat.

It is important to remember that each person's body language is slightly different. If you do not find any of these signs, you must not tiptoe what your interlocutor is saying, nor the contrary. Even if you identify some of them, it does not always mean that they are lying, they can be a reflection of other symptoms, such as nervousness.

What you can do is use these signs as a claim, to go deeper into the subject and thus get out of doubt. Asking for more

333

details on some issues is always helpful to contrast the information with the person's body language, especially in job interviews and in negotiation situations.

Interpretation of body language: do not fall into generalizations

We have already mentioned that each person is unique and that their signs and signals could have a different underlying cause than we suspect. This is usually the case when people have different past experiences, and especially when the cultural differences are great. For this reason, it is important to check that our interpretation of body language is correct.

You can do this by asking new questions, but it will be important for your body language to help the other person open up. To develop and put into practice body language interpretation skills, it is important to observe people: on the bus or television (removing the sound), trying to find out what they are saying, or what relationship there is between them.

Although you may never know if your assumptions are true, this exercise will help you pick up signals when you are interacting with other people.

And remember, if you need to convey confidence: eye contact, open posture, and smile. It never fails!

CHAPTER 14

THE SUBCONSCIOUS MIND AND THE LIMBIC BRAIN SYSTEM

Accumulated fears, beliefs, and previous experience largely determine our future, and that is why we need to work with our subconscious. Together with a specialist, Maria Samarina, we try to understand the issue.

Our brain is stunning—its capabilities have not been explored to the tenth. But what we already know about it allows us to manage our own life, to create it of our own free will. We can change our reality by influencing the subconscious, and this is not fiction at all.

Where do consciousness and subconsciousness live?

For our mind—logic, knowledge, and thought process— our consciousness is responsible. It is concentrated in the neocortex, the largest part of the brain. The same one, with convolutions. It is with the help of the neocortex that we read, write, solve logical problems, set goals, and think through strategies. While we are awake, the consciousness is with us, and in a dream it also rests.

The subconscious mind hides deeper—in the reptilian mind and limbic system. These parts of the brain are billions of years older than the neocortex. Therefore, the subconscious mind does not understand human speech. It only responds to images, emotions, and bodily sensations.

Initially, the task of the subconscious mind was to ensure survival; therefore, it stores all the information that a

335

person receives throughout life, without sorting it at all—what if it comes in handy and helps the owner? The subconscious does not need rest; it always works.

When compared to a computer, consciousness is RAM, and the subconscious is a hard drive of infinite volume. All information that falls into the subconscious is processed by it and stored later in the form of programs—ready-made options for a person's reaction. Remember that it seeks to make our lives easier? In the future, we act according to the schemes.

You once burned your hand grabbing a hot pot—now you come to all pots with a towel. A boy you liked laughed at you when you first went skating—and now you don't like the rink, even if you learned to ride.

96% of what we call our personality, all our habits, fears, addictions, spontaneous reactions, are determined by the subconscious mind—that part of the brain that we do not control.

How programs are formed

How is the formation of programs (or attitudes) of the subconscious? Information in the form of a nerve impulse is transmitted to the brain through chains of neural connections. They are created and destroyed constantly. The more often the same information arrives, the stronger these chains become. There is a "beaten path"—a steady program of the subconscious. That is why repetition becomes the easiest way to get hold of the installation.

Most often, they turn out to be strangers, especially if

acquired in childhood. It is at this age that we are most susceptible to the opinions of other people. What parents, relatives, or teachers inspire in us for many years defines our life. Well, if a child was told that he is capable, that he is loved and appreciated, then he is more likely to grow a confident person and not be afraid to do something new.

But phrases like "you are not given," "you are so stupid," or "you can't do anything" can easily give rise to future failure and fears just because the subconscious will be programmed like that.

We perfectly take root settings with the help of emotions. Children's fears can interfere with the rest of their lives for many years. Even if an adult knows that this is nonsense, he still tries to walk, for example, without stepping on cracks in the asphalt. Or does not like to fall asleep in the dark. Everyone knows that there is no real danger here, but anxiety remains.

How to deal with harmful programs?

Changing the settings of the subconscious, we reprogram the brain. Since the information will be processed using a different algorithm, we will get a different result. It turns out, changing our beliefs, and changing our whole life.

First, identify the settings that bother you the most. It's not hard. Almost all have a lot of restrictive programs. For instance:

- To Earn A Lot, You Need to Work Hard
- Big Money Can Only Be Stolen
- There Is Always Little Money

- Talent Is A Rarity, And Without It, Success Is Impossible
- In Our City (Village) There Is No Good Work
- A Woman Should... (And A Million Options, What Exactly)
- A Man Should... (Similar)
- There Are No Good Men/Women
- Luck Is Not For Me
- No One Can Be Trusted
- I'm Not Good Enough To...
- Ashamed to Have / not have something

You can write a list of several hundred installations! Think about which ones of yours—these or others? What do you want to replace them with? Try on a new program—do you feel warm from it? Listen to the sensations, and you should be comfortable.

If you want to replace programs, you need to be prepared for the resistance of your brain. This is not an easy job. The subconscious mind seeks to preserve everything that has been accumulated, so just a strong-willed effort here is not effective—you have to fight with yourself. Affirmations, if you simply pronounce or read them without using special techniques, will not help either—the subconscious of words does not understand, remember?

How to Speed-Read People

Sooner or later, everyone comes to the idea that it would be good to know how to speed read a person. Because it allows you to be, if not one step ahead, then at least not one step behind. If someone is trying to deceive, and you know how to recognize a lie, then you can protect yourself from the sad consequences of deception.

Example No. 1. A person asks to borrow money and promises to return it, but if you notice the gestures of lies and understand for yourself that a person is lying, then you can refuse a loan without remorse. This is not even saving, but the safety of one's money, which is usually obtained with difficulty.

Example No. 2. The head suggests heading the department on unfavorable conditions and voices that there are no alternatives. But if you can read a person like a book, and notice that the leader is nervous, you can assume that there are alternatives and begin to agree on the best conditions for themselves.

Reading a person like a book is not so much a dream in modern society as a necessity for those who communicate with people! And it doesn't matter where you communicate: at home, on a date, at work or somewhere else. During communication, people have gestures and facial expressions that say a lot.

Some believe that there are gestures of lies—gestures that indicate a person's lies and, having seen these gestures, you can find out when a person is lying, and when he is telling the truth.

Others believe that there are facial expressions of lies— facial expressions and micro expressions that help to recognize a lie.

Gestures of lies

Alan Pease and several other authors wrote about poses and gestures. They wrote a lot about lies in particular. However, they were mistaken in many ways. They could not give much that was known for a long time in neuro-linguistic programming.

For example, Pisa has a collection of so-called "closed poses," which supposedly indicate that a person is closed to communication or critical. The simplest and most obvious thing that comes to mind is to use the knowledge of people reading Pisa against themselves: close the position—the person changes communication, thinking that you are critical.

Some people think that touching your nose, eyes, or ears during an explanation always means it is a lie. This is nonsense!

Touching any part of the body is not always a sign of lies. This can be a symptom of a disease (scabies, acute respiratory infections, mental illness). It can be a manipulative gesture or simply an unconscious movement that is not related to the topic of the conversation. There are many options. It's funny when people read a small book and believe that they know everything about a lie, and everyone knows about a person's gestures, including lies. Not just funny - funny!

It's even funnier when such people participate in talk shows on TV channels.

Facial expressions of lies

Paul Ekman became famous for studying facial expressions. It was his life that formed the basis of the plot of The Theory of Lies (rumored). It would seem that here it is - the whole person's face is accessible, and the question of how to read a person will no longer be. But the first 5 minutes of talking with people show that in people, during communication, the face moves as smartly as the leaves of trees in the wind, and this is very confusing.

It seems that many micro expressions are visible and macro expressions too. But there are so many of them that there is often the disappointment that what is described in books is not at all like the reality. By the way, most books do not describe very, very much.

For example, when a person lies because he believes in lies, or because now the mood is lying in jest, or because of resentment, or something else, is it considered a lie, and how can it be noticed at all?

And how do you recognize a lie by voice, if you get acquainted with pointers (markers) of lies in books? No way. This can only be heard live. When a person lies, his voice changes, his voice can flinch, stammer, and in other ways give lies. It is useful to know what to notice, and even more important to be able to notice it, especially for cases of communication by phone or Skype (vibera and so on), when you only hear a person. It's like reading people's minds, only you are not reading their minds at all, but rather the ideas that are hidden behind the phrases voiced. Moreover, it is important to be able, not to know!

Books provide knowledge, and skills give training under the supervision of a professional.

How to find out if a person is lying if the person is not visible and not heard? It can actually be done. There is a technology that allows you to find a lie in the content of words. It is useful to be able to identify a lie in the content of words or the text if you conclude contracts, for example. Not to mention the analysis of the words of politicians, sellers, and many others.

By the way, in very rare cases, lies can be defined outside the meaning of words, without sounds, without seeing a person.

If you remember that people do not always lie, then how do you read people's thoughts and feelings? People have thoughts and emotions, and they may want to hide them, rather than deceive others about how they feel and think. This is not a lie!

Example No. 1. The girl was offended by her boyfriend because he forgot that they had been dating for six months. She may not tell him anything, but her resentment can be noticed. If the guy notices on time, then he can talk and apologize or otherwise correct the annoying misunderstanding. And if he doesn't notice, the scandal smells like bonfires.

Example No. 2. The guy is not ready to actively get closer to the girl and does not want to get together with her. But she talks nonstop about plans for living together, describing where the furniture will be, where the children will be, and so on. Perhaps in time, he would have agreed, but not now. In such a situation, her dreamy songs about the future will repel the guy, the tension in the beginning of the relationship will increase, and the negative will firmly bond with the girl.

Example No. 3. It is necessary to agree with the person that he should do some work (issue the necessary document, or sign it, and so on). When there are several such people, a choice arises – whom to approach? People who know how to read a person's train of thoughts and emotions often choose those people who are more likely to perform the actions they need. From the outside, it looks like a "good choice," but the matter is only in the technological determination of the right person.

So, how to speed read a person?

You need to be able to notice what is happening with emotions, mood, and everything else! To know that this is possible, to know what some kind of lips, some kind of forehead, or some pose will say about mood and emotions! Namely, to be able to read a person!

Literally, "I notice that something is not right," even with the slightest muscle movement on the face, subtle at first glance (and at the second too). The ability to recognize a lie and read a person like a book is easy to develop in a couple of days of training.

Is it possible to read a person like a book in ordinary, everyday situations? Not just possible, but necessary!

Situation 1. You come with a company of 5 people to a cafe to order food, and you have little time (an hour). The waiter offers you dishes, mentioning the cooking speed of 20 minutes. It seems that he didn't lie—a fresh dish in their establishment can certainly be ready in 20 minutes, but only one of those ordered! The rest of the people in your friendly company will be forced to wait. As a result, someone will already finish eating, and someone will just start, and someone will generally swallow saliva, and remain hungry.

Situation 2. You are on a date, and the person with whom you spend time is trying in every way to please you. Or just portray sympathy? As long as you do not know how to determine this, you are blind! You rely on your feelings (including intuition), and feelings can fail. Skills are more reliable, but only when they are good. Without them, dates are held in the "it seems like it" mode, but for many, they end unsuccessfully. It's a shame to spend time and money on a person to whom you are indifferent, right? How to understand what you like? To be able to read a person like a book, you must pay attention to his mood, emotions, condition, and train of thought. Without skills, there is only the impression of clarity—the illusion of understanding the situation.

Situation 3. Your child screams and cries in every possible way. Is the parent worried because the child is in trouble, or is it a blatant hysteria for the sake of getting candy, toys, cartoons, and everything else? A parent who does not know how to determine emotions, in almost all cases accurately, goes towards the child, becoming an obedient ward of a small trainer. Further, the child is called "howls of rope" from the parent and "sits on the neck." Most often, such a child's tantrum ends up with problems for the parent and the child.

The most powerful techniques you can use to fake your body language and manipulate Anyone's

The most typical question is, "Is it possible to fake one's body language?" The usual answer to this question is negative because you will give out contradictions between gestures. For example, open palms are associated with honesty, but when a deceiver opens his arms to you and smiles at you, at the same time telling a lie, the micro signals of his body will give out his secret thoughts, such as narrowed pupils, raised eyebrow or curvature of the corner of his mouth. And all these signals will contradict open arms and a wide smile. A person is inclined not to believe what he hears.

There are cases when body language is specially trained to achieve a favorable impression. Consider, for example, Miss America or Miss Universe beauty contests, in which each contestant is trained in such body movements, which radiate warmth and sincerity. The more skillfully a contestant can transmit these signals, the more points she will receive from the judges. But even experienced specialists can imitate the necessary movements only for a short period because soon the body will involuntarily transmit signals that contradict its conscious actions.

Many politicians are experienced specialists in the field of copying body language and use this to get the favor of their voters and make them believe their speeches. They do it successfully, and they say that they have a "divine gift." The face is more often than any other part of the human body used to hide false statements. We smile, nod and wink in an attempt to hide the lie, but, unfortunately for us, our body speaks the truth with its signs, and there is a mismatch between the signals read from the face and body, and words.

Studying facial expressions is an art in itself. It is difficult to imitate and fake body language for a long period, but it is useful to learn how to use positive, open gestures for successful communication with other people and to get rid of gestures that have a negative connotation.

This will make you feel more comfortable in the company of people and will make you more attractive to them.

The problem with the lie is that the subconscious mind works automatically and independently of the person; therefore, body language gives people away. That is why it is immediately noticeable when people who rarely tell a lie, try to lie, no matter how convincingly they present it. At the very moment when he begins to lie, the body begins to give opposite signals, which gives a sense of the speaker's lies. Some people's professions are directly related to deception in various forms, such as politicians. Lawyers, actors, and television commentators have trained their movements to such an extent that it is difficult for people to notice that they are telling a lie and people fall for their bait, and trust them.

They train their gestures in two ways. First, they work out the gestures that give credibility to what was said. But this is only possible if one practices lying for a long period. Secondly, they almost eliminate gestures so that neither positive nor negative gestures are present at the moment they lie. But to do this is very, very difficult.

You can experiment—deliberately tell a lie to your friend and make a deliberate attempt to suppress all kinds of body movements. You are in a full review of your interlocutor. Even if a liar deliberately restrains bright, catchy gestures, the body will somehow transmit a lot of tiny micro signals.

This can be either a curvature of the facial muscles, an expansion or narrowing of the pupils, perspiration on the forehead, a blush on the cheeks, rapid blinking, and many other small gestures that signal fraud. Only people, such as professional interviewers during a conversation, experienced business people during negotiations, and those people who, as we say, have developed intuition, can notice them. The best interviewers and salespeople are such people.

How to Influence and Subdue the Mind

Before you begin, it is important to note that none of these methods are intended to influence other people with obscure intent. Anything that could be harmful to someone in any way, especially their self-esteem, is not included here. These are ways of making friends and influencing people who use psychology positively and without making someone feel bad.

1. Benjamin Franklin effect

We can get someone to do us a favor using a trick, and this is also known as the Benjamin Franklin effect. Legend has it that when Franklin was in the Pennsylvania Legislative Assembly, there was an opponent who had once spoken against him (Franklin does not say his name), someone very influential. Franklin was very uneasy about this opposition and hatred and decided to win over this gentleman. What occurred to him is very curious and intelligent. Instead of doing this gentleman a favor or service, he induced the opponent to do him a favor by borrowing a rare book from his library. The gentleman in question immediately lent it to him, and Franklin returned it one-week-old with a note in which he greatly appreciated the favor. When they met again in parliament, the gentleman spoke to him (which he had never done before) and, above all, with a great education. From then on, this gentleman was always ready to help Franklin, and they became great friends, a friendship that continued until his death. This fact demonstrates the truth of a maxim that Franklin had learned as a child that says: "It is more likely that someone who has already done a previous one will do you another favor than not one who owes it to you."

There is another very illustrative example of this phenomenon in The Karamazov brothers of Dostoyevsky.

Fyodor Pavlovitch recalls how, once in the past, he was asked why he had hated a person so much. And he replied: "I will tell you. He has done me no harm. I was very dirty with him once and have hated him ever since." Just as in these examples, we get a vicious circle, the Benjamin Franklin effect shows that it is also possible to generate virtuous circles.

The scientists decided to test this theory and found that those who were asked by the researcher for a personal favor, made much more favorable assessments of him than the other groups. It may seem contradictory since common sense tells us that we do favors for people we like, and we annoy those we don't like. But the reality seems to be that we tend to like people with whom we are kind and to dislike people with whom we are rude or misbehave ourselves.

2. Too much

The trick is to ask at first for much more than we want or need to lower our request later. You start by throwing an exaggerated request at someone, and the request will most likely be rejected. He then turns back soon after and wonders about something much less extravagant, which is actually what we wanted in the first place. This trick may also sound counter-intuitive, but the idea behind it is that the person feels bad about denying our first request, even though it was not reasonable. So when they ask for something reasonable, they will feel more compelled to help this time.

3. The proper name

Using a person's name or title, depending on the situation is another tool to gain trust. Dale Carnegie, the author of "How to Win Friends and Influence People" emphasizes this. Listening to us validates our existence and leads us to have more positive feelings about the person who validates us. The use of a title or a nickname can also have very strong effects. This can be as easy as calling an acquaintance and calling him "mate" or "partner" whenever we see him, or referring to a person we want to work with or continue to work with as a "boss." While this might sound quite corny, it works in practice. "How to Win Friends and Influence People" demonstrates why it is incredibly necessary and successful to make friends use someone's name. A person's name is said to be the sweetest sound in any language for that person. The name is the fundamental part of our identity.

4. Flattery

Flattery opens many doors. This may seem obvious at first, but there are some important caveats to be aware of. For starters, it is important to know that if flattery is not seen as sincere, it will do more harm than good. Researchers have studied the motivations and reactions behind flattery and have found some very important things. People tend to seek cognitive balance, always trying to keep their thoughts and feelings organized similarly. So if we flatter someone who has high self-esteem and finds it sincere, they are going to like it very much, as we are validating their feelings. However, if we flatter someone who has low self-esteem, there is a chance that it could backfire, because it interferes with how it is perceived. That, of course, does not mean that we should degrade a person of low self-esteem.

5. Mirroring or the mirror technique

Mirroring, also known as mimicry or mirror technique, is something that some people do naturally. People with this ability are considered "chameleons"; they try to fit in with their surroundings by copying the attitudes, movements, and even speech patterns of other people. This ability, however, can also be used intentionally and is a perfect strategy for becoming more friendly. Researchers studied mimicry and found that those who had been imitated were much more likely to act favorably towards the person who had copied them. Even more interesting was their second finding, that those with someone who mimicked their behavior seemed more interesting and more personable in front of others. Probably the reason this is so is that the reflection of someone's behavior makes them feel validated. This validation is positively associated with feeling greater self-esteem and greater security, more happiness, and feeling a better disposition towards others.

6. The use of fatigue

People are more sensitive to something that anyone can say when they are tired, whether it's a comment or a question. The explanation for this is that mental energy levels drop significantly when people are tired. When we request from someone who is tired, they will probably not have a definitive answer, and we will probably get an "I will do it tomorrow" answer because they do not want to face the decisions at that moment. The next day, they are more likely to be inclined to help us, as people tend to keep their word; it is psychologically natural to want to go ahead with something you said would be done.

7. Offers that cannot be rejected

It consists of starting with a request that they cannot reject. This is a reverse "aim high" technique. Instead of starting with a large order, you start with something very small. Once someone has agreed to help us or agrees with us, they will be more likely to be more receptive to fulfilling a larger request. Scientists tested this phenomenon in advertising. They started by getting people to express their support for the environment and rain forests, which is a fairly simple request. Next, they found that once someone had come to express their agreement to support the environment, it was much easier to convince them to buy products that supported rainforests and whatnot.

8. Know how to correct

Correcting people when they are wrong isn't a smart idea. In his popular novel, Carnegie also pointed out that telling others they're wrong is usually pointless and makes people stay away from us. There is a better way to show disagreement and turn it into a polite conversation without saying they are wrong, as it affects the essence of their ego. The idea behind this is quite simple: instead of arguing, listen to what they have to say, and then try to understand how they feel and why. Then discover the common ground that you share with him and use it as a starting point to explain your position. This makes the other person much more likely to listen to what you have to say and allow you to correct him without losing your position.

9. Repeat things

Repeating something that our interlocutor has just said is one of the most positive ways to influence others, since we show that we understand what they are saying to us and how they feel, thus manifesting our empathy. One of the most effective ways to do this is to paraphrase what they say and repeat it, also known as reflective listening. Studies have shown that when therapists use reflective listening, people tend to reveal their emotions more and have a better therapeutic relationship. This can be transferred by talking to our friends. If we listen to what they tell us and rephrase it as a question to confirm that we understand it, they will feel more comfortable talking to us. They will also show more friendship and will be more likely to listen to what we have to say, as it showed that we care about them.

10. To agree

This involves nodding as we talk, particularly when we want to ask for a favor. Scientists have found that people are more likely to agree with the other person when they nod while listening to something. They have also seen that when someone nods a lot in front of us, we end up doing the same. This is understandable because human beings are well known for imitating behaviors, especially those that we consider having a positive connotation. So if you want to be very convincing, nod regularly throughout the conversation. The person who is speaking will find it difficult not to agree, and they will begin to feel good vibrations towards what is being said, without even knowing it.

CHAPTER 15

HOW TO USE SUBLIMINAL MESSAGES AND HOW TO USE THEM TO MANIPULATE PEOPLE

Do you want your life to embrace new possibilities? Want to widen the horizons and crack the walls around you?

The power of subliminal messages is still to be discovered.

The Subliminal Messages Force-What Is It?

Subliminal signals act like magic wands. Wield them, and things are going to go your way unexpectedly, miraculously, and you don't even have to expend too much effort to control things. And that works on all facets of your life, including your job, financial status, personal and professional aspirations, dating, social life, etc. Your life is plentiful, and full, and you don't need to break your back to make that difference.

Subliminal messages in videos make all of that possible with one strong weapon: your subconscious.

Sounds almost surreal? Well, numerous experiments and trials have proved and tested the phenomenon. If you need to be convinced, here's a short response to the question, "How do subliminal messages work?"

How Do Subliminal Messages Work?

Subliminal signals are brief or secret orders in music, videos, and other artistic mediums. Their primary aim is to influence a person from within or the subconscious outwardly. Instead of actively forcing you to change your

355

mind, the messages cultivate, strengthen, or improve subconscious-level thoughts to facilitate the change from deep within your mind. This is more powerful as it can change habits and control thoughts and emotions that we don't have full control over sometimes.

You do not hear or see any subliminal video messages while listening to subliminal music or viewing subliminal videos; these function very stealthily, in secret, and can be understood only by the subconscious mind.

And the best thing about them is that they function even without your understanding, so you won't be able to combat the messages' impact with harmful habits of thinking that we can't keep out of our minds at times.

Subliminal video messages, when used correctly, hold power over everything you have ever wanted to achieve in life. And even if they don't make all that you want to materialize, the messages can create such a perfect and content state of mind in you so that you can see things positively and powerfully.

Is there anything you'd like to achieve? Make sure that you have a chance for subliminal video messages.

Do subliminal messages work fast?

Now, the next question is, "Do subliminal messages work fast?" What if your next day's coming up with an exam or a big job interview? What if you give a really important client a presentation? What if you're about to sign a big deal? What if you're sick of life, and want more? How long do you have to wait until you can experience the beautiful impact of subliminal video messages?

Subliminal messages are often used, mentally or otherwise, as remedies or therapies for different problems. They can help with weight loss, sleep disorder recovery, depression, anxiety, phobia, trauma, stress, and so on, for example. And they are highly successful and helpful because in only a few days they are not only healthy and normal but also known to start having positive effects.

Listening to subliminal music or watching videos will make you experience the impact right afterward. But if you want the optimistic state of mind to be a constant in your life, cultivating the habit of the subliminal message will cause changes in your life in no time!

How to Decode Micro Expressions

Under the influence of feelings experienced by a person, coordinated contractions and relaxation of various facial structures are born. They define a facial expression that perfectly reflects the emotions experienced. Since it is not difficult to learn how to control the condition of the facial muscles, the display of emotions on the face is often tried to mask, or even imitate. Knowing facial expressions with different emotions is useful not only to understand others but also for the most thorough working out of your working imitations.

The sincerity of human emotions is usually indicated by symmetry in displaying feelings on the face. The stronger the falsity, the more different are the facial expressions of its right and left halves.

Even easily recognizable facial expressions are sometimes very short-lived (fractions of a second) and often go unnoticed; to be able to intercept it, you need practice or special training. At the same time, positive emotions (joy, pleasure) are recognized more easily than negative ones (sadness, shame, disgust).

The lips of a person are distinguished by special emotional expressiveness, which is not difficult to read. For example, enhanced facial expressions or biting the lips, for example, indicate anxiety, and a mouth twisted to one side indicates skepticism or ridicule.

A smile on the face usually shows friendliness or a need for approval. A smile for a man is a good opportunity to show that he owns himself in any situation. A woman's smile is much more truthful and more often corresponds to her actual mood. Since smiles very often reflect different motives, it is advisable not to rely too much on their standard interpretation:

- Excessive smile - a need for approval.
- Crooked smile - a sign of controlled nervousness.
- A smile with raised eyebrows - a willingness to obey.
- A smile with lowered eyebrows - showing superiority.
- A smile without lifting the lower eyelids – insincerity.

- A smile with a constant expansion of the eyes without closing them is a threat.

Typical facial expressions that report experiencing emotions are:

Joy: Lips are curved, and their corners are pulled back, small wrinkles have formed around the eyes.

Interest: Eyebrows are slightly raised or lowered, while the eyelids are slightly widened or narrowed.

Happiness: The outer corners of the lips are raised and usually laid back; eyes are calm.

Surprise: Raised eyebrows form wrinkles on the forehead, the eyes are widened, and the parted mouth has a rounded shape.

Disgust: Eyebrows are lowered, the nose is wrinkled, the lower lip is protruded or raised and closed with upper lip, eyes are as if mowed; the person as if choked or spits.

Contempt: The eyebrow is raised, the face is extended, the head is raised as if a person is looking down at someone; he is as if removed from the interlocutor.

Fear: Eyebrows are slightly raised but have a straight shape, their inner angles are shifted, and horizontal wrinkles pass through the forehead, the eyes are widened, the lower eyelid is tense, and the upper one is slightly raised. The mouth can be opened, and its corners are pulled back, stretching and straightening lips over the teeth (the latter is just talking about the intensity of emotion...); when only the mentioned position of the eyebrows is available, then this is a controlled fear.

Anger: The forehead muscles are shifted inward and downward, organizing a threatening or frowning expression of the eyes, the nostrils are widened, and the wings of the nose are raised. The lips are either tightly compressed or pulled back, taking a rectangular shape and exposing gritted teeth, the face often turns red.

Shame: The head is lowered, the face is turned away, the eyes are averted, the eyes are turned downward or "run" from side to side, the eyelids are covered and sometimes closed; the face is quite reddened, the pulse is rapid, breathing is intermittent.

Grief: The eyebrows are lowered, the eyes are dull, and the outer corners of the lips are sometimes slightly lowered.

Knowing facial expressions with different emotions is useful not only to understand others but also for the most thorough working out (usually in front of a mirror) of your working imitations.

1. Sight and eyes

This openly shows the inner experiences of a person—not without reason experienced "players" try to hide their expression behind the lens of dark glasses.

People are usually given out:

- Any changes in the usual expression of the eyes - the emergence of a certain emotion, a response signal to the stimulus.

- Involuntary eye movements, noticeably "rolling eyes" - anxiety, shame, deceit, fear, neurasthenia.
- Brilliant look - fever, excitement.
- A glazed look - extreme weakness.
- Pupil enlargement - a sense of interest and pleasure from information, communication, photography, partner, food, music, and other external factors, the adoption of something, but also severe suffering.
- Narrowing of the pupils - rolling irritation, anger, hatred, initial negative emotions, rejection of something.
- Chaotic movements of the pupils - a sign of intoxication (the more such movements, the more drunk a person).
- Increased blinking - agitation, deception.

People always prefer to look at those they admire or at those with whom they have a close relationship, from close range, while women show greater visual interest than men.

In the course of communication, they often look at the partner in the eye when they are listening, and not when they are talking. However, when carrying out the suggestion, sometimes they use a direct look in the eye during dialogue.

A person who looks into your eyes noticeably less than one-third of the entire period of communication is either dishonest or trying to hide something; the one who stubbornly stares into the eyes has increased interest in you (the pupils are dilated), shows outright hostility (the pupils are narrowed) or seeks to dominate.

Modifications of eye contacts have the following decoding:

- Absent gaze - focused thinking.
- Looking at the surrounding objects and the ceiling - a drop in interest in the conversation, an unnecessarily long monologue of the partner.
- Persistent gaze in the eyes (pupils narrowed) - a sign of hostility and a clear desire to dominate.
- Persistent gaze in the eyes (pupils dilated) - a sign of sexual interest.
- Looking away and lowering one's eyes - shame, deceit.
- Side view – distrust.
- The gaze is either diverted or now returned - lack of agreement, distrust.

2. Pose and its details

Significant information about the inner mood of a person gives a static position of his body. At the same time, the often-repeated pose informs about the stable personality traits.

Since people usually have better control over their face than the body in the extremes of feelings, it's often not a facial expression at all, but a pose that can tell about the individual's true experiences.

Possible bindings of body positions to the mental state of a person are as follows:

- Hands clasped behind the back, head high, chin up - a feeling of self-confidence and superiority over others.
- The body is forward, hands (akimbo) on the hips self-confidence and willingness to take action, aggressiveness, over-agitation during a conversation, the desire to defend one's position to the end.
- Standing with your hands on a table or chair - a feeling of the incompleteness of contact with a partner.
- Hands with apart elbows wound behind the head - awareness of superiority over others.
- Putting your thumbs in your belt or the slit in your pockets is a sign of aggressiveness and demonstrated self-confidence.
- Protruding thumbs from pockets - a sign of superiority.
- Crossed limbs - skeptical protective installation.
- Non-crossed limbs and an unbuttoned jacket - the establishment of trust.
- Tilting the head to the side - an awakening of interest.
- Head tilt down - negative attitude.
- The slight deviation of the head back is a sign of aggressiveness.

- Sitting on the edge of the chair - the willingness to jump up at any moment to either leave, or act in the current situation, or to calm down the accumulated excitement, or to attract attention and connect to the conversation.
- Throwing one leg on the other with arms crossed on the chest - a sign of "disconnection" from the conversation.
- Throwing a foot on the arm of a chair (sitting on it) - neglect of others, loss of interest in the conversation.
- Crossed ankles of a seated person - restraint of disapproving attitude, fear or agitation, the attempt of self-control, negative protective state.
- Position (sitting or standing) with legs oriented toward the exit - a clear desire to end the conversation and leave.
- Frequent change of poses, fidgeting in a chair, fussiness - inner anxiety, tension.
- Getting up is a signal that a decision has been made, the conversation is tiring, something surprised or shocked.
- Finger grip - frustration and the desire to hide a negative attitude (the higher the hands are located at the same time, the stronger the negative).
- The tips of the fingers connect the hands, but the palms are not in contact - a sign of superiority and confidence in oneself and one's words.

- Hands rest with elbows on the table, and their hands are located in front of the mouth - hiding their true intentions, playing with a partner in cat and mouse.
- Supporting the head with a palm – boredom.
- Fingers clenched in a fist are located under the cheek, but do not serve to support the head - a sign of interest.
- Propping up the chin with the thumb is a sign of some critical assessment.
- Clasping his glass with two hands - masked nervousness.
- Smoke upward from a cigarette - a positive attitude, self-confidence.
- Blowing smoke from a cigarette down is a negative mood, with hidden or suspicious thoughts.

3. Gestures and body movements

"A gesture is not a movement of the body, but a movement of the soul." It reports on the desire of the person and what he is experiencing at a particular moment, and the gesture familiar to someone indicates the trait of his character. Externally, the same gestures of different people can mean completely different things, but there are identical moments:

- Active gesturing is a frequent component of positive emotions, understood by others as showing friendliness and interest.

- Excessive gesticulation is a sign of anxiety or insecurity.
- When determining the thoughts and emotions of an individual, only involuntary gestures should be noted:
- Open hands demonstration - an indicator of frankness.
- Clenching of fists - internal arousal, aggressiveness (the stronger the fingers clench, the stronger the emotion itself).
- Covering your mouth with your hand (or glass in your hand) at the time of speech - surprise, uncertainty in the spoken, lies, confidential message, professional safety net from reading lips.
- Touching the nose or lightly scratching it - insecurity in the message (both by yourself and the partner), a lie, a search for a new counterargument during the discussion.
- Rubbing the eyelid with a finger indicates a lie, but sometimes - a feeling of suspicion and lies on the part of the partner.
- Rubbing and scratching various fragments of the head (forehead, cheeks, nape, ear) - concern, embarrassment, uncertainty.
- Stroking the chin - the moment of decision making.
- The fussiness of the hands (pulling something, twisting and untwisting a fountain pen, touching parts of clothing) - alertness, nervousness, embarrassment.

366

- Pinching the palm - readiness for aggression.
- Biting nails - internal anxiety.
- All kinds of movements of the arm across the body (adjust the watch, touch the cufflink, play with the button on the cuff) - masked nervousness.
- Picking up villi from clothes is a gesture of disapproval.
- Pulling from the neck a disturbing collar - a person suspects that others have recognized his deception, lack of air with anger.
- Rubbing the glasses or placing the temples of their frames in their mouths - a pause for reflection, please wait.
- Removing points and throwing them on the table is an overly sharp conversation, a difficult and unpleasant topic.
- Quenching or snoozing - the period of maximum stress.
- Knocking down ashes from a cigarette too often - a painful internal state, nervousness.
- Tilting the head to one side - awakening interest.
- A quick tilt or turn of the head to the side - the desire to speak out.
- The constant casting of supposedly "interfering" hair from the forehead is a concern.
- A clear desire to lean on something or lean against something - a sense of complexity and unpleasantness of the moment, a lack of

understanding of how to get out of the situation (any support increases self-confidence).

Body Language Mistakes to Avoid

Body language plays an important role in the communication process. Our postures and movements while communicating with other people, can both improve one's opinion about us and worsen it.

It is logical that, in this case, you need to work on yourself and concentrate around controlling your gestures. But there is one caveat: as a rule, habits associated with the "wrong" body language are very difficult to eradicate. We don't even notice how often we look away, cross our arms, or stoop for no reason.

Let us now pay attention at least to the main mistakes in facial expressions and gestures, because of which everyone has problems. If you can get rid of them, then this will make your communication much more productive.

1. Fussiness

If nervous fussiness has become a habit, then it will be hard for you to abandon it.

When you fuss, you show nervousness and weakness.

It would help if you learned to control this bad habit.

2. Game with hair

You do not know where to put your hands and constantly reach for your head to wind a lock of hair on your finger?

368

From the outside, it looks very incomprehensible. Also, because of this, you cannot focus on the conversation. In the end, you not only spoil your hair but run the risk of harming your hair. Therefore, it is better not to touch them at all.

3. Closed poses

If you cross your arms over your chest, this is interpreted as an attempt to distance yourself from reality and protect yourself. But many people perceive this as a comfortable pose, which is easiest to take if you don't know where to put your hands.

Nevertheless, all protective postures have negative consequences. Crossed arms and tightness make us unconvincing and cause suspicion of the interlocutor.

Body Language Specialist Patti Wood says: "You need to keep your hands in sight during the conversation. When the interlocutor does not see your hands, he thinks that you are trying to conceal something."

4. Gestures too active

People have different attitudes to the use of gestures. Someone may not gesture at all during a conversation, but someone else may spin in different directions and constantly wave his arms.

In this case, the main role is played by a person's temperament. But at the same time, experts say that gesturing is the most effective way to draw public attention to your words. But here it is very important to avoid gestures that discredit you.

You can't poke your finger, imagine yourself in the role of a conductor, and use dance moves.

5. Uncertain gait

People are prone to pickiness and strict criticism. We are confident that we can learn everything about the interlocutor, making conclusions only based on his manner of walking.

According to statistics, our walk even affects the risk of being robbed on the street. Therefore, it is important to make your walking style more refined and coordinated. This is not an easy task, but you can't walk shuffling all the time.

6. Lack of a smile

We often underestimate the importance of a smile and even consider that a smile for no reason is a sign of cunning and hypocrisy. Sometimes we are proud that in dealing with people, we constantly use the so-called "poker face."

We use the phrase "on-duty smile," by which we mean something insincere and false. So far, there is no need to talk about social politeness at all. But in many other countries, a smile is appreciated very highly. So a sincere smile can be of great benefit to you.

A laid-back smile is a sign not only of friendliness but also of confidence, honesty, warmth, and affection for a person. Do not forget that a smile has a mirror effect and makes the interlocutor smile back. If you do not smile, then you look detached and gloomy.

7. Distraction for extraneous things

Most of all, people are annoyed when the interlocutor does not pay due attention to them during a conversation. Sometimes people get distracted for a good reason. Sometimes they have important things that they cannot postpone for later.

Nevertheless, in most cases, they check the mail, unsubscribe to friends in instant messengers or leaf through the feed-in social networks. If you are in company, it is better to learn to restrain yourself from these impulses. Otherwise, they will begin to consider you impolite and disinterested in them.

8. Stoop

Straighten your back! Bad posture can occur out of the blue, especially when you spend most of the day in the office at your desk.

Stooping not only makes us look insecure but also harms our backs. After abandoning it, you will benefit in two ways: take care of your health and improve your reputation in the eyes of others.

9. Averted eyes or aggressive gaze

This is one of the most common mistakes, moderation, and meaningfulness of actions that will help get rid of it. The author of the book, "What your body says," Sharon Sailer believes that the perfect eye contact of the

371

interlocutors implies a series of long glances and not a game of peepers.

If you look into the interlocutor's eyes for too long without looking away, you make him feel awkward. At the same time, the desire to avoid eye contact indicates insecurity and even contempt.

10. Excessive calm

This is still better than an emotional explosion, violent gestures, or energetic movements in the process of business negotiations. But you still don't need to become like a statue, because otherwise, the interlocutor will think that you are not interested in the conversation.

It's worth using mirror tactics. No, you do not need to completely copy the gestures and facial expressions of another person, as he may be offended by this. Carefully repeat the main gestures, maintaining the proper level of expression. Proper mirroring will make you seem positive and confident.

Refusing stone expression and making your facial expressions natural is a difficult task, especially for those who, by nature, are not emotional and open people. But efforts will bring good results.

CONCLUSION

Our nonverbal or body language is one of the most powerful forms of communication that we use in our day-to-day experiences. It is the contact mode that ignites our emotions and responses at the "healthy level." Research has shown that having an understanding of body language improves one's potential to be effective in getting out of any given situation whatever one wants.

Have you ever seen a couple sitting together and had a sense of just how good or bad their relationship was in minutes? Have you ever wondered how you could arrive so easily at this conclusion without any direct interaction? If you are aware of it or not, we spend our days listening to non-verbal signs of people interpreted by their body language and drawing conclusions from our assumptions about them.

Our body language shows the reality that we conceal from the world with our expressions, including our feelings towards ourselves, our relationships, and our circumstances. The people we associate with will evaluate our motives, the strength of our relationships, how masterful we are in any given circumstance, our level of trust, and what our true motivations and desires are through our eye contact, movements, body posture, and facial expressions.

The strength of body language is contained in the resulting emotional reaction. In nearly every situation, emotions influence decisions and reactions. Non-verbal signals trigger emotions that define an individual's core assets, such as truthfulness, trustworthiness, honesty, skill level, and capacity to lead. The perception of these signals will decide who we are going to meet, the work we are being hired for, what degree of success we are having, and even who will be elected to powerful political positions.

Why don't we spend years studying and improving successful body language abilities with such an essential skill? The truth is that most people underestimate the importance of body language before they try a deeper understanding of human actions in a personal relationship, or gain an edge in a competitive business setting.

Mastery in body language provides the keys for people to perceive the context behind particular movements and body movement, as well as to provide an understanding of how to project and convey messages while communicating with others effectively. The cumulative success of interpersonal partnerships is, therefore, significantly improved. The best way to start this learning process is to learn the basic understanding of the two styles of core body language-open presence and closed presence.

The closed body language form of presence is found in individuals who fold their bodies around the centerline of the body, which runs straight down the middle of the body from the top of the head to the feet. The physical features that produce this form of appearance are feet positioned next to each other, arms held close to the chest, hands crossed on the chest or held together in front of the body, slight hand movements kept close to the body, shoulders rolled forward and eyes fixed below eye level.

The signals sent to the world by the body language form of closed presence are a lack of confidence, low self-esteem, powerlessness, and lack of experience. In extreme cases, the message of wanting to be invisible may even be produced. The consequences of this kind of body language on the person projecting can range from simply not having the best possible opportunities to a worst-case scenario of harboring a self-fulfilling image of victimization.

The open presence, by comparison, is featured in individuals who build a sense of authority, control, and leadership by projecting mastery of confidence, achievement, energy, and ability. The physical features are feet held hip apart, open hand movements used in speech away from the body's centerline, elbows held away from the chest, shoulders pulled back, upright postures and eyes fixed on their listeners' eye level. These individuals are viewed as desirable, competent, intelligent, and are easily seen as having success. We see this form of body language as the 'leaders' body language.'

The secret is eye contact to develop body language and to start projecting an open presence. Eye contact is one of the social devices that we own most. Someone can alter the way others see them by using direct eye contact while communicating with others. When people start looking directly into the eyes of an individual, they are seen as confident, trustworthy, and professional.

Hand movements and facial expressions are the second forms of transition that one can render with accessible presence to be seen. Both modes of communication improve the ability to efficiently convey messages.

Through skillfully using open hand gestures away from the body and expressive facial expression, the greater impact is produced while speaking making the audience more visually relaxed and increasing the amount of information presented during the conversation.

As kids, we are told from an early age that healthy boys and girls sit together correctly with legs and hands crossed in front of them. The desire to restrict physical space as children will establish some of the characteristics of the closed presence at adulthood found in body language. To combat this effect, one can start adopting the characteristics of body language of the open presence and integrating these manners into one's natural state of being. After this behavioral shift has been achieved, it should have the same non-verbal experiences and signals as its counterpart's inaccessible contact.

Body language mastery is essential to creating the most powerful presence in all interpersonal interactions. Individuals lacking this knowledge are vulnerable to confusion and find their attempts inadequate in expressing their ideas. With the ability to distinguish between the various body language styles, everybody can achieve the mastery required to succeed in whatever endeavor they want.

EMOTIONAL MANIPULATION

All You Need to Know for Mastering Weapons of Influence and the Art of Mind Control Using Dark NLP, Brainwashing, Hypnosis, and Persuasion Techniques

Blake Reyes

INTRODUCTION

As human beings, we respect one another. There are certain rules of life in society, rules of collaboration (you have to help each other to reach an objective), reciprocity (you have to know how to give as much as to receive), empathy (I put myself in the place of the other), trust and many others, which we apply daily.

You could say that the manipulator rather than respecting the collaboration rule, will try to get the other to do things for them. Rather than respecting the rules of reciprocity, they try to get the other to give to them, without giving in return. Rather than being attentive to what the other feels (empathy), they try to play the rule of empathy in one direction (if you do not give me what I want, you will make me suffer).

After all, the manipulator, and to put it a bit differently, does not consider the other as an end in itself, but considers them a means to gain personal benefit. They make a compliment, not just for the pleasure of the other, but because they hope to get something as well.

In extreme cases, for example, we find crooks or psychopaths (who sometimes are one), who play with intelligence on these social standards of reciprocity, trust, and collaboration.

We all manipulate others. But while respecting certain limits. It is a 'normal' aspect of human relationships. We will speak of a manipulator when the personality of an individual is globally organized around such social relationships. It is the constant character that makes the manipulator. Not the manipulation itself.

Some people, by their function, are likely to manipulate others. The word manipulation does not have the same meaning here! This is the case, for example, a manager leading a team and wishing to do it pleasantly and gently rather than by giving direct orders. Not always the healthiest mode of management, which seeks to conceal the relationship of authority, and which can be compared to an iron fist in a velvet glove. There are manipulative bosses, but because a boss asks you to do something without reciprocity, he does not manipulate you. Everything is, therefore, a matter of context. We will discuss all this in this eBook.

CHAPTER 1

WEAPONS OF INFLUENCE

Would you like to know how to influence other people? Who doesn't, right? Having the power to direct others' actions is something that many of us would like on some level. Knowing how to do it would be like a superpower, perhaps stronger than that of Superman. Just imagine being able to make your wife or husband do what you want. WOW.

Influence is probably one of the most frequently cited books in marketing for its accuracy in exploring the hidden forces behind the decisions we make.

Before exploring these weapons, we must take into account that the fundamental principle of this chapter is that, although many believe that we act rationally, this is far from the truth. Our decisions are mostly emotional. We are pre-programmed to act in certain ways, according to certain external stimuli.

Premise of Influence

By studying people with brain damage to their emotions, the famous neuroscientist Antonio Damasio showed that these people were practically normal, except that they couldn't make any decision. Despite being able to solve problems logically, when choosing, people are deprived of their emotions. These discoveries have caused a revolution in human behavior because they have allowed us to understand better how humans act. Under this premise, the first weapon of influence is reciprocity.

Reciprocity

An American scientist did the following experiment:

He sends Christmas cards by mail to strangers. To his surprise, most of the people he sends these cards to send him a card too. Why? We are pre-programmed to be reciprocal. If someone gives you a gift, you feel a sense of indebtedness and want to give something back. This is why we tend to reject gifts from companies that we know want to sell us something we don't want (maybe you rejected an air purifier from Rainbow vacuums?).

The force of reciprocity in action is very powerful, and it works, not only when we receive gifts, but when we feel some kind of indebtedness. For example, if I ask you to buy me tickets for a charity raffle for $ 5 and you tell me that you do not have $ 5 at that time. I could then ask you to buy me something of lesser value. How about a $ 1 bar of chocolate? The fact that you said "no" to me the first time can make you feel indebted and increase the probability that you will follow me if the second order is less.

Try it with your partner. Think of something you want and:

- Give him a gift
- Request something that you know he will say no to
- Wait a moment and ask for what you wanted

- The sense of reciprocity for the gift and the saying no will be so great that you have a good chance of receiving a yes.

Against this background, consider how you could use the weapon of reciprocity in your marketing and sales activities. For example, today, it is very common for companies to give free advice, an eBook, or downloadable help material, to start building a relationship in which the prospective client feels some kind of psychological indebtedness or a need to be reciprocal by buying something.

Commitment and Consistency

A Canadian study showed that immediately after gambling, people are more confident that they can win their bet than before. This seems simplistic, but it has profound implications. Humans have an almost obsessive instinct to be (or appear to be) consistent in our words and actions and maintain our status.

For example, once we state that we believe in a political idea publicly, it is extremely difficult for anyone to convince us to explore alternatives. On the contrary, in the face of any opposition, we will look for reasons to justify our belief. In the same way, when we identify with some group or ideology (people like us do things like these), we can become illogical in our decisions with the desire to be consistent and do things like we think our group does.

Do the following experiment. Ask your friends how many are considered collaborators. After their response (almost always yes), ask them to collaborate on something small. Sure, your friends will be more likely to help after your question versus if you hadn't asked them anything previously. This is because consistency goes hand in hand with commitment.

When we take small steps (commitments) towards something, we gradually develop beliefs consistent with the steps we have taken. For example:

Q: Do you think drinking water is good for your health?

A: Yes.

Q: Do you think you are drinking enough water in a day?

A: No.

Q: Would you like to find ways to drink more water during the day?

A: Yes.

After only two questions (commitments), suddenly, the person being questioned wants to find ways to drink more water during the day. What would have happened if we asked the last question directly? The results would be mixed. The same is true for testimonials. Customers who give positive testimonials generally become fans of the products or services they testify about. After publicly saying something good about a product or company, they will defend their belief.

You should be careful in using this technique, as it is the tritest in the sales arsenal. It has been used a lot unethically by direct selling companies, and we are on the defensive when it comes to answering questions that lead us to commitments that we do not want to make. Anyway, used ethically and looking for the benefit of the consumer, this weapon of influence is super powerful.

Ask yourself, how can you make your prospective clients take small steps (actions or commitments) and gradual steps towards the purchase? What is the purchase journey that leads a prospective customer to become a customer? Also, consider what behaviors are most consistent with the personality or status of people like the clients you seek? For example, if your client is looking for luxury and your proposal is not consistent with luxury, no matter what kind of questions you ask, you will not be able to convince him/her.

Social Forces

You see someone laugh, and it makes you laugh. You see someone yawn and you yawn. In a stadium, everyone stops to make a wave, and you also stop. They are not just reflex effects. This is also a social influence.

When we feel uncertain about how to act, it is easiest to do it in a similar way to what other people do. This is why we buy items marked as "best-sellers," or we let ourselves be carried away by what the most popular figures say or do.

Nike Sponsorships offers are a great example. Nike has created a whole brand ideology behind the celebrity endorsement of each sport. Why are Jordan shoes so successful? Although we know, on a conscious level of Jordan shoes, they WILL NOT make us play like Michael, that MJ wears them is reason enough for us to want to buy them. True? It doesn't matter if other basketball shoes are identical at a fraction of the cost (a better logical decision).

To use social forces in your company, you can show your portfolio of satisfied customers, put certifications you have obtained and awards you have earned on your website, or even invite an influencer to use your products or services. The more you assure your prospective clients that other people in similar situations benefit from your offer, the more you can use this weapon of influence to your advantage.

Like or please

It is no surprise that we want to do business with people we like. It is also no surprise that we like things that we feel familiar with. What may be surprising is that "pleasing" or "being familiar" can be derived from repetition. For example, the more we listen to a new song, the more we like it. And once we like it, we buy it, we recommend it, and we even identify with its letter.

Why? Because it is a survival mechanism. Approaching the safe and familiar, as well as exploring the new and unknown, are part of us. Whenever something is unfamiliar, we have to experience it (see it, feel it, or hear it) several times to feel safe and to feel familiar.

Why do you say "YES" to someone who seems attractive to you? We tend to say yes to people we like physically more than people we don't like, because, generally, we like people who assimilate to a familiar face more than we consider beauty. We have a hidden need to want to please the people we like.

In this same sense, we tend to relate better with people with whom we share interests, antecedents, or points in common: SIMILARITIES. For example, we relate better to people who went to our same school even though they have not been our friends before, who like our same soccer team, or even who use the same brand of cell phone, simply because these similarities make us feel that we have things in common.

Here is the key to pleasing, what if you do not know what things you have in common with a prospective client? Simply frequenting places (where they can see your face several times), having continuous communication (such as emails where they see your name), and adopting mirror behaviors (reflecting movements and postures when meeting) are all "repetitions" that will make you more familiar to the moment to influence. Ask yourself: How can your company have more contact with the people or companies that you would like to reach?

Authority

Perhaps one of the easiest weapons of influence to understand is that of authority. In one experiment, social researchers asked an actor to make requests, similar to those made by a police officer, to passers-by on the street, requests such as picking up litter from the ground or not walking through certain sectors. The actor first made these requests dressed as normal and then dressed as a guard. The results?

When the actor was dressed as a guard, people obeyed his requests. But, when he was dressed normally, people saw no reason to fulfil his requests. This happens at all levels. For example, we trust the doctor's authority to the point that a white coat is sufficient for us to take medicines, of which we do not know their side effects.

We trust that a person dressed as a mechanic knows more about cars than we do, or that a person with a helmet and jeans on a construction site knows more about engineering than the average person. In a sense, we are programmed to trust authority.

But authority goes beyond what is apparent. For example, a study done in the San Francisco Bay found that car drivers whistle less for luxury cars when the light turns green than for cheap cars. Titles, clothing, vehicles, followers, are all signs of some kind of authority.

This is a topic of utmost importance for companies. If you are looking to grow your company, sell more with fewer objections, you must be an expert in your field. Ask yourself: how can you show authority?

Shortage

Last places. Only five items in stock. We have limited edition products. Make your pre-order today. These are all ways to demonstrate scarcity. The idea of a potential loss plays a fundamental role in our decisions, much greater than the idea of winning something.

Would you rather get a $5 discount or avoid being charged an extra $5 for a fine? In most cases, even though the result is the same, people would rather avoid losing than have a chance of winning. This is known as "loss aversion."

In an experiment by Stephen Worchel, volunteers were asked to give their opinion on a chocolate-chip cookie. The volunteers in one group were given one cookie, and they could see that there were ten more sample cookies. The other group was also given one cookie, but they saw that there were only two more sample cookies. The results? The group that saw fewer sample cookies rated the cookie better than the group that saw more sample cookies.

If your prospective client feels like they are going to lose something if they don't work with you, they will be much more likely not to let you go. Ask yourself how you can include scarcity elements in your offers. Prices or premium content, limited editions, exclusive programs, limited time offers, among others, are all actions that you can include in your commercial proposals.

When we make decisions, it is difficult to evaluate all our options logically. Generally, we use pieces of information that we consider relevant and make highly emotional calculations. Although each of the weapons of influence studied is valid, they usually do not happen in isolation. On the contrary, many elements are playing an important role simultaneously.

In this sense, to apply these concepts in business, we must visualize a global environment, taking into consideration the mission and vision of the company, and why a client would buy from our company and not from another. Once we have a clear picture of this, the application of weapons of influence can be ethically adapted within a process that helps generate a win-win situation.

The most Powerful Mind-Power Tool

You have the most effective resource for your journey to an enhanced life. Your mind is the tool.

Mindpower techniques can and will enrich your life.

Are you one of the many millions of people who are not satisfied with their lives?

Then there is hope.

Mind energy techniques are scientifically proven to improve the unconscious mind.

How can you be part of the most enriching phase of your life?

It is easy! Read on and see how you can increase the power of your subconscious mind.

Mental Power Techniques- Panorama

Just look around you at the wonders of modern society, technology, and development.

All those miracles are the creations of the human biological mind's most powerful tool.

You can imagine that the human mind has essentially no limits as to what it can achieve.

Supersonic airplanes, super aircraft carrier cargo ships, and automatic vehicle transmission engines all are the penultimate results of the power of thought and imagination.

A truly wonderful tool of the human mind has no limits to the progress and development it can generate.

A profoundly unfortunate fact is that the vast majority of individuals do not exploit the human mind's incredible capacity.

People of all ages and from all walks of life do not use the full potential of the mind, and there is a good chance that you are one of them.

How can you harness the full power of your mind?

Are there any power techniques that can be used?

Mental Power Techniques- Science And Medical Bases

The brain is a bioelectric machine. The impulses that are generated are the products of conscious and unconscious thought.

Your healthy and functioning mind generates electrical impulses, the healthiest thoughts in mind.

On the opposite side of the spectrum, those individuals who do not use or do not challenge their minds have a strong tendency to lose the benefits of it.

It would help if you exercised your mind to get the most out of the benefits it could give you.

Exercising- psychologically, which is the key to a healthy mind.

However, it is very sad that most of the jobs and professions out there are just not conducive to exercising mind power.

Let's look at this example; the comparison of a gardener and an accountant.

The gardener uses less of his mental faculties in his line of work while the accountant solves countless complex math problems in daily work.

It's recommended that the gardener perform some recreational IQ or brainpower exercises to enhance brainpower.

His brain is enclosed in an imaginable hard protective skull layer.

The human skull can withstand a great deal of mechanical damage, but the brain cells it encapsulates can destroy a demanding and unhealthy lifestyle.

Life itself and the stress it generates creates detrimental factors for our brain capacity.

You may have previously experienced mental blockages, or you couldn't remember certain information when you needed it most.

Scientific studies have indicated that much of this is psychosomatic — it is caused by mental factors that are of your own free will and within your control.

This lower mental functioning is caused by low self-esteem and a negative global outlook on life.

So how can this be avoided?

Through exercise, and training through mental energy techniques, you preserve and improve your mental health.

Just as you exercise your body, so you must do mind training exercises to increase your conscious and subconscious mind.

Mind Energy Techniques To Promote A Better Life

Happiness and well-being are bi-products of the mind.

Your happiness and well-being are focused on your state of mental health.

A healthy mind is bodily sound — this is the wisdom of the ancient Greeks — which is still definitely true today.

There are proven methodologies today that have been shown to design or redesign your mental process.

Doing meditations and optimistic everyday affirmations are very powerful methods of mind energy to activate the subconscious' reprogramming cycle.

Meditation helps to calm down the brain activity of the conscious mind, which in turn opens the door to easily influence and impress more desirable thoughts in your subconscious mind.

393

Meditation also enables you to focus on a relaxed mind-state. A relaxed mood will give you the ability to stay focused, driven, and on track.

Furthermore, meditation is also highly recommended by the medical profession as a means of relieving tension and stress.

Strengthen the meditation process with daily positive and constructive affirmations that will give you a positive overview of yourself, your life, and your ability to achieve your goals.

Continuous repetition of affirmations to yourself during meditation will help you communicate to the power of your subconscious mind the positive thoughts and images of you living that life that you desire.

Audio technologies such as binaural beats have been seen emerging to change a person's mood.

They affect our brain waves directly through tones of different frequencies to aid our brain by improving brain function, motivation, memory, and more.

There are other techniques that you can use to harness the incredible powers of your mind, but just to get started, these are some simple but effective mind power techniques that can be used to propel your life to levels of unlimited success, happiness, and prosperity.

How To Increase Your Social Influence?

Social influence is the ability to awaken other people's behaviours, actions, and consumer desires. This social factor is the basis of Marketing strategies that use influential people to represent brands, helping these companies to gain engagement and generate more sales.

With the advancement of social networks as Marketing and business platforms, the importance of social influence has become increasingly clear to companies in their quest to understand and impact consumer behavior.

As long as brands know how to use this factor, it is possible to reach specific audiences and, above all, create genuine connections with their audience.

To influence others in favour of a business, it is necessary, first, to know well who you want to conquer, retain, or what the company's objective is.

From this, the strategy develops when there is a centralizing figure, someone capable of exercising this social influence on the public that your brand wants to impact.

Social influence has always played an important role in society and consumer relations, whether in simple opinion analysis or the chain reaction. Therefore, this section will cover the subject in detail and discuss the strategy and how it should be executed.

What is social influence?

Social influence is the ability to generate decisions and actions based on other people's behaviors, indications, habits, and customs.

Influencers, people who manage to rise to these

movements, have a high power to generate repetition of their actions or to simply direct people to actions within a certain social niche.

This is a very common construction in society, and it has always been happening, no matter how few times it has been debated, until the emergence of digital influencers.

Each social niche has its influencer; that is why the ideas of influence are so broad and fit in so many scenarios.

Social influence as a strategy

A good example is the action of major suppliers in the sports sector, which sponsor not only football clubs, but also athletes.

Over the years, players have constantly appeared on the pitch with different cleats, always with different colours, shapes, and designs.

From a strategic point of view, brands have used this feature for years because they know the power of social influence that these athletes have, especially over fans of the team in which they play.

This rotation of boots is a way of associating a product with an influential figure, generating the desire to buy in people who are adept at the social niche in question.

The strategy is repeated in droves, in all possible markets and with actions from the simplest, as the example mentioned, to the most complex — more and more present in the digital age.

Without a doubt, it is the time for "digital influencers".

The rise of Influence Marketing thanks to digital

Marketing Influence is a strategy that has already been implemented for a few years now, the first place among the favourites of companies thanks to its effectiveness. The formula is simple: it is possible, with investment within the budget, to have an advantageous return, reaching the right audience.

There is simply no company that is unable to influence action, even though its audience is very small.

The micro-influencers are a category of people who can have a high level of social influence, even within a small niche. For many companies, this is enough to bring great results.

The high adherence to the strategy can be better understood in numbers. We separate some:

- In the USA, the ROI of campaigns with influencers is 6.5 (Tomoson);
- 49% of Americans claim to be influenced by a purchase (Influencer Orchestration Network);
- 8, out of 10 influencers, are micro-influencers; that is, they have 15 to 100 thousand followers.

How can social influence benefit companies?

Social influence, as the basis of Marketing strategies, can bring direct and essential benefits to companies that want to strengthen their brands and generate more sales.

More than gaining visibility, it is necessary to remain relevant in the market and count on the public's loyalty.

Understand how this strategy helps you achieve all these

goals!

Accurate targeting

Social influence is the basis for strategies that put people as the "face" of their brands to generate the public's desire for consumption or, simply, sympathy.

The most important thing is not this power to influence, but who this influencer can reach.

The choice of this representative must be made in line with the target audience. It doesn't matter the size of the audience: the influencer has a great capacity to talk to whomever you want.

That is, an effective strategy provides highly accurate targeting. This ensures that the investment in the shares has an optimized ROI: the campaign will be able to generate more engagement and conversions, regardless of which ones.

Greater engagement

Followers are not always a faithful translation of your brand's growth. Often considered vanity metrics, these numbers do not necessarily represent what matters most: engagement.

This means that people are open to hearing about your brand, learning about new products, following everything that is launched, and consuming.

When social influence is high, the chances are high that this chosen figure will be able to transmit the message of your brand and, above all, generate a desire for consumption and replication of their attitudes.

While these people can be true curators within their segments, they can also be brand ambassadors.

More sales

Sales are the most important and desired consequences. Although they are not the only ones since it is also important to ensure that the target audience is engaged and ready for more than an isolated purchase, companies depend on good sales.

The best way to generate your audience's desire for consumption is to use the capacity of social influence that someone has.

Whether using influencers or running campaigns in specific locations, especially those where your audience is and values, the chances of increasing sales increase.

Imagine that a certain brand has as its target audience the so-called geeks and decide to exhibit a new product in a Comic-Con Experience (CCXP).

The place, of course, is frequented by people from this niche and, being a specialized festival, creates a perfect environment for consumption. Through this strategy, the chances of generating social influence increase considerably.

What are the main ways to apply social influence in the Marketing strategy?

Social influence can be applied in Marketing strategies to generate results and make it possible to achieve the advantages that we have already discussed in this chapter. However, for this to be possible, it is essential to structure a plan and then start the work.

Next, through 4 tips, learn how to apply social influence in Marketing strategies using a complete and effective process!

1. Know your audience

Knowing the audience you want to influence is a priority requirement. This should be the starting point, and to further facilitate the understanding of who the brand's average consumer is, a persona well-defined is of great importance.

Only then is it possible to understand which traits of this audience can be exploited as triggers for consumption. Surveys are a great way to better understand the aspirations, preferences, expectations, requirements, and details of the average consumer.

A persona is built by analyzing a good volume of data in a relevant sample before the public. From this, it becomes easier to define a strategy to generate social influence.

2. Set goals

Companies have different objectives when implementing Marketing strategies.

Each brand can be at a different stage in the market, and that is precisely what will guide your intentions through campaigns and actions.

Thus, to decide how to exercise this social influence, it is first important to decide the objectives, the main ones being:

- increase brand engagement;
- increase e-commerce traffic;
- gain more followers on social networks;
- generate more sales;
- launch a new product.

3. Make the right choice of influencer

One of the most important parts of the strategy, the choice of the influencer needs to be someone who considers the factors that we have already covered throughout this chapter.

The impact of this person needs to be relevant within the niche, with adequate communication and the real ability to not only introduce brands or products but also to generate influence for consumption, concretely.

In this choice, it is also necessary to assess your audience's size, not just who these people are. The choice between large or micro-influencers is crucial since this segmentation is not always large and requires so much investment.

Remember: the chosen influencer must already have a previous relationship with the target audience, exercising the role of social influence.

4. Plan your actions

Once it has been decided who will be this brand ambassador, it is time to think about actions that promote the brand and its products.

Undoubtedly, posts on social networks such as Twitter, Instagram, YouTube, and Facebook are the ones that give the most results today.

Different formats can perform well for each of them either in specific actions or in continuous campaigns, which have several presentations of brands and products.

Social influence is one of the great tools of persuasion that brands have to generate the desired impact on their target audience.

With the help of influencers, it is increasingly possible to create a legion of supporters of the brand and, of course, consumers.

CHAPTER 2

HOW TO INCREASE YOUR POWER WITH
PSYCHOLOGICAL TRICKS

Some thoughts heal and others harm. The power of your mind can protect you like a fortress, and its absence, on the contrary, will make you fragile.

In addition to artificial intelligence, our natural intelligence can reach new heights. We are the first generation to benefit from the accelerations of time, space, and knowledge. We can move faster and faster and get all the information we want with one click. This speed leads to flexibility. The faster we evolve, the more we manage to carry out several operations simultaneously. But we must constantly adapt to stay in the race. You also need to know how to get out of your comfort zone. Education should give the child the desire to discover and venture into unknown territories. Sometimes, you have to embark on paths that seem closed and dangerous, but which can lead to other universes. These experiences will make you stronger, and you will, therefore, have an iron mind. You are the source of your invincible energy armor.

Your mom was blowing on your little sores to make them disappear, and it worked: you were no longer in pain. If you suffer from small daily ills today, do not rush to the drugs. You risk addiction, not to mention harmful side effects. Instead, learn to mentally "breathe" into these momentary pains. If you divert attention from what is hurting you, you will feel less harm. By focusing on one

403

activity, you will forget the pain. For example, if you burned yourself lightly while cooking, try a new recipe that is a little difficult. After five minutes, you will no longer think about what should make you suffer.

It's proven, the body secretes its remedies to relieve itself. This is the case with endorphins, which are equivalents of morphine. Experiments have also shown that subjects relieved by a placebo (a fake medicine) have an increased level of endorphins, which makes it possible to erase the pain. Moreover, when developing a new drug, we know that just with the placebo effect, it will have at least 30% success.

Forgetting can make you smarter

Red squirrels have a habit of carefully hiding their supplies at the onset of winter, and then forgetting about them. Above all, do not panic if facts, names, places escape you. We immediately think of threatening specters like Alzheimer's disease or degenerative pathologies when this is often not the case. On the contrary, these oversights prove to be excellent for your brain. They allow memory to be erased to erase the least important details and focus on those that allow effective decision making. Forgetting is the tool for good memory storage, like computer hard disks, which have to eliminate data to store new ones.

Let's take an example: your doctor changes address. There is, therefore, no point in reminding you of the contact details of his former office. In other circumstances, you will erase memories of painful moments, which does a lot of good. When you happen to forget the name of a person, a film, a singer, ask yourself once found why you had temporarily erased it. Sometimes it's your subconscious that manifests itself to mean something to you. In his work, Psychopathology of Daily Life, which includes a chapter called "The forgetting of proper names," the famous Doctor Freud evokes his tendency to forget names or appointments. He interprets it as the unconscious expression of a repressed desire.

We get faster when the light is intense

Light can make us smarter, acting directly on our brains. We become faster when it is strong. American scientists have shown that under too weak lights, certain functions of our brain decrease in capacity. They discovered that staying in poorly lit rooms decreases our ability to learn and memorize. Thus, the researchers demonstrated that in a muskrat subjected to weak lightings, the hippocampus' capacity decreases by 30%. Located in the brain, the hippocampus plays a key role in memorization. The good news is that this impact is reversible. If rats having lived in the dark are exposed to powerful lighting, they recover their intellectual alertness after a certain time.

In children, scientists again noted that school performance was better in very well-lit classes. This is cured by exposing oneself to special lamps easily found in the market or by walking as much as possible outside as soon as the sun points at the tip of one's nose. Instead of looking for existential reasons when your morale is low, treat yourself with a light cure. A final example: after spending two hours in the darkroom of a cinema, some people find it difficult to remember where they parked their car. The memory is disturbed. We feel "funny" at the exit. According to the researchers, the lack of light slows down the production of orxin, the hormone that acts on the proper functioning of memory and learning. The impact of light on morale is well known. From November to March, some suffer from seasonal depressions due to lack of sun. This syndrome is called SAD. If you want to be successful and happy, put yourself in the light. You will shine intellectually and morally.

Learn to get stronger effortlessly

Is it possible to get stronger without exercise, simply by the power of the mind? Developing muscle mass without doing anything, sitting on your sofa watching television, looks like a science fiction dream. British scientists wanted to find out. They selected volunteers who did no more than two hours of exercise per week. They took measurements of the perimeter of the calves and their functionality, evaluated by electromyogram. The researchers then asked the participants to imagine that they contracted the calf muscles for fifteen minutes, 50 times in succession, after having indicated the force of contraction desired by small electric shocks. The volunteers had to repeat the exercise five times a week for a month. The results showed an 8% increase in muscle strength. This preliminary result opens up several areas for reflection. Imagining your muscles developing would unconsciously encourage you to mobilize them better later, for walking for example. Mentally anticipating what we are going to do improves the quality of the forces involved. Try to imagine yourself swimming: when you are at the pool or sea, you will evolve more efficiently. By adopting this method, you will become like these Olympic athletes mentally focused on the performance to be achieved, and then give the best of themselves.

Go in search of your dark side

There is something evil in you. Dare to recognize your dark side. You are sometimes selfish, manipulative, and mean. You are insensitive to the despair of others when they suffer or experience, on the contrary, a certain enjoyment in the face of the misfortune of others. You enjoy watching "disaster" news or movies in which poor victims are terrorized. You can even find a good side to bad boys. You laugh when someone stumbles and falls, not to mention questionable jokes, like reversing salt and pepper by watching the trapped one's disgust. You are, however, neither a psychopath nor a serial killer!

If you hide these trends in yourself, you might as well recognize them and not repress them. What we refuse to highlight always ends up being expressed: reactions of aggression and anger, flushes of anxiety which translate into self-destructive attitudes like obesity, tobacco or excess alcohol, missed acts... Instead of suffering, become an actor in your life by agreeing to explore these forbidden territories. It is not possible to help others by remaining comfortably on your couch, inactive. Devilish impulses can become a motor if one becomes aware of them. It is not a question of choosing a profession where you can abuse the limits of your power by making others suffer but from another dimension. Instead of looking at the victims as a happy spectator, recognize at this precise moment that your dark side is expressing itself. Then go beyond this reflex by thinking about the help you can bring. Your bad inclinations will serve as a spring to give birth to the best of yourself.

Your diabolical side is, in short, a potential of energy that only asks for a release to give meaning to your life and act on the world.

Alluring scams

It has become a global epidemic. The 2 billion smartphone users use a formidable function: image filters to erase imperfections and look more beautiful. Formerly reserved for professionals to correct the faults of stars, they are now in the public domain. What may seem like an innocent game is not. Boston scientists have discovered that these practices cause significant damage to the personality of users, affecting the overall image of their bodies.

These retouched photos, widely disseminated on social networks like Instagram, convey a false self-image. The more perfect they are, the more they move away from reality. This shift ends up creating dysmorphophobia, a syndrome consisting of being obsessed with imaginary faults and focusing only on one's small imperfections, magnifying them with a mental magnifying glass. This results in permanent stress and a decline in self-confidence, with the risk of social withdrawal. This phenomenon is particularly dangerous in adolescents, who are vulnerable and fragile in terms of the appearance they wish to give themselves. I advise not to pull the trigger of these fault correctors. Otherwise, when you meet people in "real life" after sending them these images, they will be disappointed. You will lose more confidence.

Instead, do the opposite. Find what you don't like in yourself, and make it a force to distinguish yourself. Think of Serge Gainsbourg's nose: if he had corrected it, he would have lost his exceptional personality. Value what you think are your faults, and you can climb mountains rather than hiding underground. If you love yourself as you are, others will love you too. You will live in reality, real feelings that bring joy and happiness. You will also sweep the artificial side that the company is trying to sell you. By removing the gap between what you appear and what you are, you will be doing yourself a favor.

CHAPTER 3

WHAT IS EMOTIONAL MANIPULATION?

For starters, there are many reasons why people feel the need to control people, places, and things, as well as to manipulate others to meet their personal needs, wants, and wishes. We must put to the surface the most common issues on the grounds of a battered ego with no self-esteem and, therefore, little autonomy. The people in control will always use manipulation tactics. It can be subtle techniques or master manipulators like many narcissistic personalities. Manipulation refers to the idea of trying to influence or control someone else's behavior or actions indirectly. As human beings, our pessimistic feelings sometimes affect our discernment so that it becomes impossible to see the truth behind hidden motives or intentions in different types of action. The controlling aspects of the complexity of perpetuating deception are linked to emotional manipulation, to lying techniques, and are sometimes very subtle and can easily be overlooked. Often, bad habits have been taken up through a negative ego that we have not worked on, whose control behaviors are driven away by feelings of guilt, low self-esteem, fears, and unethical behavior.

As the chaos generated by planetary ascent accelerates, many people are influenced by negative forces which they do not understand. Some of these negative forces come from their Unconscious and their Negative Ego, which have strengthened a life made up of negative habits and behaviors. When people feel insecure inside themselves, they will easily resort to controlling and manipulation behaviors. It is useful to educate yourself about this behavior to protect yourself and create the necessary healthy limits.

People who are in control will always assume that their needs, wants, and goals are more important than yours. No matter what you can do or your responsibilities, they claim that you need to focus on them and their problems, no matter what the cost may be.

Even if the cleverest of them aren't going to say it directly, the use of emotional manipulation will show you exactly what they're trying to accomplish. Through emotional manipulation, a person in control will use the empathy and compassion of others. He's a type of emotional vampire. Control behaviors are found in injured personalities of people who have low self-esteem, thoughts of fear. When these fears are not addressed and resolved, this need to control others can evolve into narcissistic behaviors and psychopaths.

The need to exercise control over others leads to the perpetuation of forms of manipulation. Manipulation of others leads to different degrees of deception and lying.

Motivation of Manipulators

What are the possible motivations of a manipulator?

- The need to put forward their own goals and personal gain no matter what it costs others.
- A strong need to reach feelings of acceptance,

411

power, and superiority about others.

- A desire and need to feel in control of people and the environment.
- A desire to gain a sense of power over others to increase their perception of self-esteem and worth in the world they create.
- A childish need to get what they want, coming from a high idea of themselves and no control over their impulses.
- The need to free themselves from inner anxiety and fear by projecting obligations on others to complete personal needs.
- The boredom of their environment, the desire to be entertained, or preoccupied with dramas.

Causes of manipulation

Why do some people so easily resort to emotional manipulation?

When a human being was never able to develop, from childhood to adulthood, with loving parents who support self-esteem and know how to set healthy boundaries, he will be easily manipulated. When someone is easily manipulated by their unhealed pain, violence, disability, and lack of self-love, he or she will become a cynical person with a damaged and fragile mental (suffering) body. Some individuals claim to be teenagers, but they are severely mentally damaged and go back to young, childish emotional states. Severe emotional wounds create a disconnection between the feelings of the soul and the spirit. Generally, the age at which the most unhealed

412

trauma occurs in childhood is the age at which the adult returns when the injury is triggered in his adult life. When this accident is caused, most of the time, instead of taking responsibility for this suffering, the person assumes the need to exploit others because of their pain to get what they want. Then we can see a person acting like a little child having a crisis to get what they want. Both parents know what it's like to have a two-year-old kid who calls out, "To me! Give it to me!"

Most healthy people understand that pretending to act to feel a certain way, or to play with someone else's emotions, is not morally ethical. But some people are so preoccupied with what they want and have such a high idea of their importance that they are not aware of manipulating or deceiving others. Worse, some people have severe psychological schisms that create personality disorders that make them manipulate for fun. When dealing with narcissistic people and psychopaths, it is important to remember that they are masters in manipulation techniques and protect themselves against their antics. Set healthy boundaries and do not accept the emotional manipulations and dramas of other people, and make this a priority of your life, or they're going to assert what they're doing. It is important to be a loving and caring human being, but not a rug that is mistreated by psychic vampirism, which is the direct result of emotional and psychological manipulation. Many manipulation techniques are very intelligent, and we can be stunned by the layers of complex deception techniques. However, the more educated we are about this, the easier it is to be aware of this behavior in others and to get rid of it yourself. When we embark on the Krystic path, we must consciously stop using manipulation techniques and control behaviors over others. This will minimize the chance of using emotional manipulation repeatedly to vampirize the energies or control one's feelings of empathy for others. We also have the right to protect the room that belongs to us and to have the capacity to live without being used as a shield to exploit others. The obscure controllers are not in agreement with this freedom and are the promoters of this manipulation technique.

Common Handling Techniques

What are the most common manipulation techniques?

GUILT: Most of us know what it's like to be guilty of someone else; often, we learn this behavior from a family member early on. But many manipulators are gifted and cleverly making a person feel guilty when they are open at heart and compassionate. In general, this is like making you feel bad or sorry for something you have not done or for which you are not responsible. In the heart, in care, and giving to others, they must remember that their feelings and energies are also important. Often what you can give is not enough, so the manipulator will make you feel guilty to show you how bad you are because you didn't give him what he wanted, whenever he wanted. I have often noticed that when I do not jump when someone tells me to jump, he will use guilt with manipulation. It often happens in spiritual communities.

CLAIM TO WANT TO HELP: It is a big problem in all groups, communities, or organizations. It is undoubtedly a painful problem that we have faced in our community. Manipulators and bullies like to pretend to be useful even when it is not their real motivation. What they want is a feeling of control over something or having access to someone. There may be a desire for power, status, or personal goal that the person thinks they can achieve by claiming to be useful to someone else. Often these people create a lot of destruction and extra work on the pretext of being "useful." Then when the person/ organization who is supposed to be receiving the help is left with additional problems, the person uses guilt to say how unappreciated and underestimated he is. Open communication and the assessment of qualifications and emotional maturity are a necessity in any organization that concerns a group.

NO RESPONSIBILITY: When we understand how manipulation works, we want to discern responsibility for the situation or the person. Manipulators will always blame others for their wrongdoing, bad behavior, or unhappiness. If they fall into narcissism, they may think they are perfect and beyond reproach. Putting an end to the manipulative blame game is the key to preventing this kind of deception from taking hold. If someone starts to blame you when they don't, don't be afraid of telling the truth.

DOUBLE SPEECH: Manipulators like to take anything that has been said and turn it around, or twist its meaning to use it against you. Often with manipulators who are good at the double talk, the conversation will be mixed with confused and ambiguous language that does not make sense. It is often a lot of words, without meaning or substance. Sometimes a part may make sense, but the rest of the conversation has no connection to what was said. Double talk is a lack of consistency; the person may appear intelligent by using certain words, but they are often either confused or trying to confuse others to prevent them from seeing the truth. You may have listened to this person to speak for an hour and have no idea what it is they're saying. It can also happen a lot in relationships with strong emotional ties, and it will destroy trust and intimacy between people.

PSYCHIC VAMPIRE: A psychic vampire is a person who drains the energies of others and can intentionally drain positive energy and happiness in the other. In the manipulation tactics used to make a generally happy person feel bad or take their energy, the vampire will use condescending and demeaning behaviors. They can use bullying and harassment to make the other person feel insecure or completely dependent on them. Generally, with these people, we feel that we have to take tweezers not to irritate this person, or to awaken their rage. You don't know what can trigger them at any moment. If you notice that energy is drained when a person enters the room, you should protect yourself and amplify your shield.

Setting healthy boundaries and being able to exist in the space where we can breathe, relax, and be comfortable

416

with ourselves is the right we all have. Often as loving beings, we forget to take care of ourselves in the face of manipulative and controlling people. It is an important time to take care of yourself and to note that this phenomenon of control and manipulation will intensify in the environment due to fear, insecurity, and confusion among the masses. Many people have traumas and emotional crises and return to childish behaviors. Dark forces take advantage of this vulnerability in people who have not made an effort to understand and cleanse their negative ego. By becoming aware of how emotional manipulation works, make sure to end all of the manipulation behaviors within yourself. It's critical right now.

Types of Emotional Manipulation

We all want our needs to be met. However, manipulators use methods to fulfill their desires, and involuntarily, all the people around them, including those closest to them, become the means at their disposal to reach these desires. Often, this influence goes through a friendly tone. That's why it is worth learning to identify the main signs of manipulation so that you don't act as someone's puppet.

According to Jacques Regard, there are three types of manipulation distinguished by the specific and particular intention of the manipulator:

- Positive manipulation (known as "type I"), where the manipulator's intention is always good, useful, or pleasant for the person who is the subject of it.

- Egocentric manipulation (known as "type II"), where the manipulator turns the world around his interests, without worrying about the consequences for his victims.
- Malicious manipulation (known as "type III") where the intention of the manipulator, of a paranoid, conscious and voluntary nature, is malice, the destruction of others.

Positive manipulation

This manipulation is not always perceived as a manipulation since its intention always appears good or pleasant. This is the case of a surprise made for a friend or a gift given to a child. This is also the case when a nurse says that everything will be fine before injection, that a mother uses gentle persuasion to encourage her son to do homework: "If you finish your homework this morning, you will have the whole afternoon to do whatever you want. Otherwise, you will have to spend the day there without being able to please yourself." Finally, this is also the case of an individual who seeks to show the positive aspects of something a priori unpleasant: "I'm going to have to come home late tonight, I have to stay at the office... It's annoying, but it will allow me to be on leave tomorrow noon, that way we can leave for the weekend earlier!" The manipulation is undeniable, but the intention always starts from the heart, it is not to be condemned, but it may be useful to recognize it.

Egocentric manipulation

In this type of manipulation, the manipulator is an individual who thinks only of his interests without caring either for others or for the discomfort that his conduct can generate. It is this manipulator who will do everything to sell encyclopedias to the elderly, without worrying about the interest of these, it is this manipulator who puts a stick in the wheels of his colleagues to make himself "seen well" to management or to get a promotion from them. It is this manipulator who makes promises with flying colors to be elected or this teacher, who terrifies his class to establish his authority. The type II manipulator does not act out of wickedness; he does not seek to harm anyone: but by thinking only of his interests, he inevitably harms others.

Marketing has become an expert in this type of manipulation for the customer to buy products.

When they were offered a sample of pizza at the entrance to their supermarket, one in two agreed to try it. But if the demonstrator touched their arm when making their tasting proposal, two out of three accepted their offer and especially twice as many then put the same brand of pizza in their shopping cart.

Malicious manipulation

This last type of manipulation is marked by the conscious and voluntary attempt by the manipulator to destroy others. Its purpose is to ruin the actions of an individual, to destroy an aspect of his personality, to harm his interests. It is a malicious and concealed intention.

Recognize a manipulator

419

Even if the manipulator can hide under very diverse and even familiar features, the author Jacques Regard has identified a certain number of characteristics and character traits that the manipulators can share.

- The manipulator is often imbued with excessive pride: he tends to belittle others.
- He regularly uses misinformation, lying, or slander.
- He insidiously harasses by never intervening directly, preferring to push others to act for him.
- He always pretends to act for a good cause and rarely recognizes his wrongs.
- He often speaks in a roundabout way, never asserting anything categorically but sowing doubt in others' minds.
- He spreads the rumors and conveys the worst slanders without ever giving the impression of doing so. He sometimes sends messages under the guise of frankness or clumsiness. He says nothing, repeats what he heard or what public rumor says.
- He is instantly angry when we try to unmask him. He does not assume his words or his deeds and turns everything to his advantage.
- He does not know how to listen to others' problems, except when it allows him to achieve one of his goals.
- He devalues a lot, often belittles with incredible balance, can contradict himself, or disavow what he just said a few minutes earlier.

- He likes to surround himself with incompetent people at work: "by rewarding those who work poorly, he ensures allies who are very devoted to him because, without him, they would be nothing."
- He depletes the energy of those who are in contact with him.

Manipulated?

Take this example:

For this year's Christmas, you have no intention of spending it with the family. Instead of your sister-in-law's devious reflections and your father's existential monologues, you prefer a romantic week in Marrakech. Personal desire versus family duty... Which of the two will prevail?

Julie, your best friend, asks you to lend her your car. Since you are going on vacation the day after tomorrow, you don't want to take any chances. You refuse. "Too bad," replies Julie. "I will not be able to go to this very important meeting for my job..." Worse still: "When you need help, I am always there." Immediately, you start to feel guilty ...

Attention, you are being manipulated! Besides, we all are. Just as we manipulate others in our turn, without necessarily being aware of it. Why? Quite simply to get the other to satisfy our desires. For this, guilt — or how to make the other responsible for our discomfort — is ideal.

Spot the blackmailers

The eternal victim

Let's take the family Christmas example again. Desiring to gather all her family on this occasion, the mother will sow doubt in her rebellious daughter: "You know, my darling, the family is sacred. We are getting old... Christmas together, there may not be many left... Your brother, he comes back from London, especially..." A classic case of emotional blackmail, with an implicit threat: "If you don't come, we will be very unhappy." The mother adopts the typical behavior of the "victim" to obtain the desired behavior from the other.

Susan Forward distinguishes four types of "blackmailers":

The executioner, who threatens to punish you ("If you leave me, you will no longer see the children").

The flagellant, who turns the threat against himself ("If you leave me, I commit suicide").

The martyr or the eternal victim, who brandishes his suffering ("How can you do this to your poor mother?").

The merchant of false hopes, who makes you dangle a promising future if you answer his request ("If you agree to set up this business with me, you will earn a lot of money").

The trapped gift

Another common process: the false gift. "By an abusive use of the principle of reciprocity — which is also essential for good social cohesion — the "donor" keeps the "recipient" in a debtor position. The implicit market is as follows: Since I gave you this, I have the right to demand that in return. The problem is that the donor chooses when and how the recipient must give him the change for his coin.

Example: a grandmother who, because she regularly takes care of her grandchildren, allows herself to land at her son's house unexpectedly as if she were at home. "How can I say no, she's so sweet!"

False Beliefs

Why is it so difficult for the person who is manipulated to react healthily? "Because the manipulator uses family and social beliefs to induce a heavy feeling of moral fault in his victim," says Isabelle Nazare-Aga.

Examples of typical beliefs: children are debtors of their parents (because the latter gave them life because they sacrificed themselves for them, etc.); it is in misfortune that one recognizes one's true friends...

"The guilt that the blackmailer instills in the minds of his victims undermines the positive image of themselves that they seek to build," explains Susan Forward. Abandonment, selfishness, injustice, betrayal are the sensitive points on which the manipulator presses to hurt. He often proceeds by innuendo. He never expresses a clear request and reduces you to impotence. Example: a sick mother, coughing very loudly on the phone, manages to slip in a sad tone to her daughter, that she has not eaten for three days because she does not dare to do her shopping. But, above all, she doesn't ask for anything...

Outsmart the traps

Get clear with yourself

Do a self-examination. Find the beliefs about yourself that spontaneously come to mind: I am selfish, ungrateful, I never measure up, I am worth nothing ...

Then stop focusing on the situation and try to change your perspective to make an objective statement about yourself: "Is it true that I am selfish?" "That's all I have done for her for three years... "; "Is it true that I am not up to the task?" "These are the elements that I can put to my credit..." Because the manipulator uses a single act of the person to judge him as a whole.

Then sort out what is and is not your responsibility: "Does his problem exist independently of me or am I really at its origin?" Indeed, the characteristic of the manipulator is to blur the boundaries by putting his needs before yours. "How far can I respond to his request while respecting myself?" Once you have assessed your limits, you will be able to make a clear decision. Two strategies are then available to you: counter-manipulation or confrontation.

Learn to counter manipulate

In order not to give a grip to the manipulator, do not justify yourself, because this would only weaken you even more. On the contrary, suggests Isabelle Nazare-Aga, simulate indifference — even if you are torn inside! — and refer him to his own beliefs with the help of a few calmly stated standard sentences:

"I have a clear conscience."

"Everyone does not think like you."

"That's your opinion."

"I do not think so."

"To each his own."

"Yes, I don't do anything like everyone else!"

The goal: protect yourself by not reacting to the provocations of your interlocutor.

Example: your friend Marianne, alone and depressed, accuses you of not having invited her during your last dinner.

"When you were bad, I introduced you to my friends; you let me down."

- It is not because I did not invite you to dinner that I let you down. When you need to talk to me on the phone or come to the house, I'm there.

- Yes, but that's the minimum a friend can do.

- If you don't value what I bring to you, it's a shame. I feel like you are demanding a refund from me for what you did for me.

- No, but, for you, it was not much to add cover. For me, it meant a lot.

- You count on your criteria what others must do for you. I'm sorry for you.

Dare to confront

This is the second possible strategy. Here, it is a question of referring the other to his need, therefore, to his responsibility. More implicating, the confrontation risks bringing you to position yourself on the nature of the link that you wish to maintain with the person who manipulates you.

Example: you are married, father of two young children and passionate about soccer, horse riding or tennis. Unfortunately, every time you plan to indulge your passion, your wife bullies you: "You leave me in the lurch with the children!" "Can you imagine if I did like you? ... "

"Any reproach expresses an indirect request," notes Jacques Salomé, author of To No Longer Live on The Planet Taire (Albin Michel, 1997). We must, therefore, try to get the other to formulate his need. "When you have fun without me, I feel abandoned, unloved." You can start a substantive discussion on the nature of your relationship: "Do I have to give up my passion to prove my love to you?"

"Doesn't the development of our relationship go through the well-being of each one?" This could also lead to negotiation on time spent together and separately, sharing of tasks, etc.

Refusing manipulation is accepting to pass for a "bad girl," a "selfish husband," a "difficult colleague." So give up an ideal self-image. You will do this by realizing your value. And it works. You may become less "lovable" in the manipulator's eyes, but by freeing yourself from this external gaze, you will gain a precious asset: your freedom.

Facing a tyrannical boss

Colleagues, little chefs, bosses... Everyone at the office manipulates everyone. Some calmly resist ("Sorry, but this week, I don't have time to deal with this additional file"), while others give in without saying a word for fear of being dismissed. How to achieve a modus vivendi with a boss who keeps imposing additional workloads on you? "Go for the temporary accommodation strategy," advises Susan Forward.

Here are the basic rules:

Do not tolerate anything that could harm your health — no question of accepting requests that would jeopardize your physical or mental balance.

Stay confident. Do a self-examination and see if you can improve the way you work or not to meet the new demand. The important thing is not to let negative beliefs undermine your views about yourself ("I'm too slow, I'm not up to par," etc.).

Consider modest actions that could improve the situation. Instead of rushing the confrontation with your boss, test the ground to clarify your position. For example, ask him to explain to you concretely what he would do to "get better organized" ... Or turn away from your usual behavior of submission by announcing to him that because of important projects planned for a long time, you will not be available when he needs you. Sometimes the worst tyrant finally gives in to face with determined resistance. And as paradoxical as it may seem, we thus force our respect.

What is gaslighting?

For Christel Petitcollin, communication and personal development trainer and author of numerous works on manipulation, gaslighting is extremely sneaky malice which aims to make the other pass for mad. The manipulator wrongly asserts things, denies facts. And then, sometimes, he compliments his victim, congratulates her. She then tells herself that she was wrong and that this person cannot want to hurt her. The manipulation also goes through the non-verbal. The aggressor can conceal or break objects to make it appear that the other is losing memory.

She remembers one of her patients who was harassed by her office manager. The latter had taken her glasses from her in her absence but claimed that it was not her and that it was ridiculous to accuse her. Difficult to go to complain to anyone. And then, why would she steal them? Her superior did not seem to have anything to envy her: she had a better job, a family life, a house... Something to make the employee doubt.

Victims gifted for happiness

According to Christel Petitcollin, these are high-end manipulators, completely aware of what they are doing. These people are "passive-aggressive," that is, they are full of anger, but they hide their hostility. They advance masked, using small vengeance, small aggressions. It is practiced in all environments with more or less finesse, explains the specialist. She describes these manipulators as immature people, like children in the playground, who enjoy mistreating others. And if they are exposed by their victim, far from stopping, they rejoice because they are untouchable.

Their favorite target? "Humanistic, open, kind people who do not see evil. They like to help others and flee conflicts. However, these manipulators hate optimistic people, gifted for happiness and joy because they are incapable of it", analyzes Christel Petitcollin. A profile that corresponded to the office worker harassed by her superior.

Gaslighting in a private setting with impunity

Gaslighting can also take place in the private sphere where the aggressor then has carte blanche, that is, a complete freedom to act as he wishes. Charlotte experienced this with her ex-boyfriend. "It was going well between us, Antoine was nice, and we loved each other. But soon after we moved in, I started to have doubts about myself, about my memory. I often lost things. As I am rather disorderly and head in the air, I thought that it came from me. I once waited for him in a cafe, but he never came. He told me that I had dreamed that we had an appointment. Sometimes Antoine told me that I had asked him to see such a film at the cinema when I didn't remember it. He said false things to our friends: that I was thinking of changing jobs, that I had seen such a girlfriend the other day... I was completely lost. By proof, I understood that he was the one who had a problem, and I left before going crazy," remembers the young woman.

Strong repercussions for victims

Depending on the situation, gaslighting can have significant repercussions. "Victims can develop post-traumatic stress symptoms that worsen over time. They can have sleep, eating, anxiety, tachycardia, or back pain disorders. It is destructive for the individual," warns Christel Petitcollin.

The solution to stop these manipulations, consists, according to the expert, in cutting the links. "The aggressor becomes intoxicated with his abuses, which become a drug for him. He feels almighty. This can only get worse," added the specialist. The victim may feel alone in the face of the actions of this manipulator. This one advancing generally masked, the victim does not notice the problem.

Also, Christel Petitcollin laments the lack of psychologists' training in dealing with this subject, which is rarely discussed at university. Professionals can then think that the victim is paranoid and make a wrong diagnosis if they do not know these behaviors.

To keep all your reason and protect yourself against these potential manipulators, it is better to flee.

CHAPTER 4

SUBLIMINAL PERSUASION

Using subliminal techniques to persuade a person to do or buy something they may not need is a way to contaminate the subconscious psychologically. This type of pollution can become much more dangerous than you can find in the world's big industrial cities.

These "hidden" messages have managed to manipulate human behavior at surprisingly high levels, and worse, people have no awareness of being manipulated by such messages.

Subliminal propaganda experts manage to connect with our most intimate needs, impulses and emotions and play with our prejudices. All our activities and fantasies can be manipulated through our eyes and ears, from the most secret thoughts to the most public behaviors, without us knowing anything.

These subliminal messages and techniques, according to popular belief, Gonzales confirms, become increasingly dangerous, have been used over the years to idealize people's lives, making them believe that buying a Coca Cola is synonymous with buying happiness, or that with a Mercedes Benz the problems you have in your life will end. They take care of beautifying the basic needs of people in everyday life, from love, security and family, to work and pleasure, from such simple things to something perfected.

431

They show life in an "ideal" way. Everyone expects to be the exception to this rule and find that perfection is shown on television, in movies, series, and publicity on public roads when reality has little or nothing to do with those fantasies shown in different advertisements.

Both in film, on television and the different platforms used by the advertising, showing, for example, the perfect family: the slender, brave and cunning father who comes home to find his perfect wife, make-up on, smiling from ear to ear and waiting for him with the kids and the ready food table, big delicacies, all impeccable. Real families are far from like that.

Advertising strives to make the illusion more real than reality, and it is deliberately contributing to creating a world of unhappy and crazy people. In the ads, they propose as real, illusions that are only fantasies. The dangerous thing is that a lot of people start by believing it and end up blaming their clumsiness for not getting it. Information, which helps confuse reality with fantasy, is endangering a trait of psychic health: the ability to distinguish the real and the imagined.

When you buy a Dove soap or a Nivea face cream, you don't buy it because you're going to remove dirt and bacteria from the body or because it will nourish the skin well, but because in their advertising they show you the incomparable beauty and perfection that you can come to have used these products, then, what people buy is the ideal brand, not the product itself.

All these messages manipulate our choice when buying a product or service. It uses a subliminal psychological stimulation that has great effects on our decisions by managing to change them to the point of preferring that "hidden" meaning they show in advertisements.

This resource that attacks the subconscious affects not only a specific audience but also everyone equally, from the child to the young person, to the adult, and the older man.

Advertising specialists are well aware that the widespread sexual arousal that comes from a magazine with strong erotic content contributes powerfully to ads for cars, food, beverages, or perfumes and products of all kinds that include camouflaged sexual stimuli. The same is true of impulses, artificially activated, such as the desire to eat, drink, dress or acquire, when they are reinforced by the presence of stimuli associated with such motivations.

The most common ways of presenting subliminal messages can be seen through images that pass very quickly (tenths of a second) or with mixed or low-volume sounds immersed within a melody, so people do not realize that their subconscious is being maneuvered as it is virtually invisible to the eye or ear that send signals to the conscious mind, but not so for the unconscious, which captures every image and every sound.

The area of emotions, motivations, and needs of each person is the main objective in most cases, where it points primarily to all kinds of advertising to be able to reach.

Likewise, it is important to clarify that an isolated subliminal message has almost no influence on a person's life, but if the person is repetitively subjected to these messages, they do have a great effect (as in the case of people addicted to television, movies, or series). Similarly, if you receive positive subliminal messages, they will ultimately influence your daily work by literally transforming your life for the better, but this is not a very common case.

Subliminal advertising

Subliminal advertising began to be implemented since the early 1950s. This technique affects people, whether presented in a hearing, visual or written way and portrayed as necessary to improve the lives of these people as they often believe. These often lead to the constant search for happiness and perfection through the purchase of products, and they have nothing to do with these concepts, but they get to the point of convincing you that it certainly is.

The first known case of this type of publicity happened when James Vicary (1957) conducted an experiment where he included two frames per second in which he showed a mark that was in the event of advertising, in these frames were the messages "Come popcorn" and "Drink Coca-Cola" during the footage of a movie. These images that, though they appeared printed on the frames and were displayed on the screen, were not perceived by the viewer consciously, made sales of Coca-Cola and popcorn increase by 18% and 58%, respectively.

As Gonzales asserts, there are several studies and experiments conducted by universities over the years that have shown that advertising can modify the subconscious mind to ensure that it wants whatever it proposes in the transmitted messages.

On the one hand, on television are news programs that constantly remind of the evil and suffering in the world today, which happens daily in all parts of the world. On the other hand, there is commercial advertising that promises an ideal world, the perfect family, the perfect life, the perfect friends, in conclusion, a paradise of opulence that does not necessarily always show them as something material. In that world of perfections everywhere, every problem or frustration has its solution within reach of purchase, and a product or service can satiate anything you want.

The media recalls all the consumer's dissatisfactions, preferences, and yearnings, notifying him that there are unsurpassed professionals who have taken the job of coming to his aid and selling him the proper invention for little money. Advertising has everything, knows everything, and loves you. Advertisers are the envoys of the new religion in the antipodes of asceticism, duty, humanism, or any ideal that is the most sybarite hedonism. Advertising has dogmas such as progress, happiness, abundance, and leisure. It holds the secret of eternal youth, in an innocent world, without tragedies, without disease, and standards.

Numerous companies and brands use these psychological

435

techniques to reach the target you want and influence your buying behavior without noticing. Some people consider this method unorthodox for causing stimuli in the person unconsciously and involuntarily.

Advertising is an incredibly lethal seduction, and it manages to realize all dreams and aspirations for a little money. However, this is not always virtuous, since it takes people away from reality by painting them a perfect world, a world that does not exist, an integrated utopia of pure brands.

Experts rely on studies where they analyze the yearnings and desires of individuals or societies to reach their unconscious and make them believe that they can offer them the perfect product to meet such needs, to the point of "training" recipients and instilling them with the acceptance and preference of certain brands.

Consumption is based mainly on the needs of each individual, which are considered as the engine of commercial activity, these can be innate needs, such as thirst, sleep, hunger, etc., or can be the needs learned or adapted throughout our lives, such as the value of money, the need for luxury, etc.

Subliminal advertising can become very subjective, that an image evokes something in someone does not mean that it also gets it in others; it depends a lot on the culture and teachings that each person has.

As unsold products accumulate, advertising needs to be more aggressive and use all of its resources. That's when subliminal advertising makes its appearance. An overly saturated market, if it wants to exit surpluses, ends up resorting to reinforcing traditional propaganda with subliminal techniques.

Being able to remember an ad is synonymous with the effectiveness of it; however, this relationship of effectiveness in being able to remember an advertisement does not necessarily lead to the acquisition of the product, it must be borne in mind that the important thing is to motivate the change attitudes and to incentivize the purchase of it, which can lead to investing not only money but also time.

Conscious or supraliminal advertising tries to ensure your memory to assess its effectiveness. However, subliminal advertising is intended for the opposite: not to be identified or remembered on a conscious level. All the power of messages lies in the unmeasured; otherwise, they would turn against the one who uses them. The cause-and-effect relationship between advertising and sales is currently difficult to find out. It is even more difficult to separate the part that corresponds to the supraliminal and subliminal propaganda since they almost always go together. Of course, advertising has its part in sales. The advertising message is at the exclusive service of sales, which is its sole objective.

However, transparency and honesty are characteristic concepts of advertising. As much as advertising is not subliminal, it always has a deeper meaning beyond the one it shows. They always adorn and embellish the marks, which makes the information transmitted in advertising not truthful, as its main reason for existing is selling, not reporting.

Investment in advertising

Today brands, rather than being identified as a logo on a product or service, go far beyond that. Not only are they recognized for allowing you to recognize a product, but are generally associated with added values, which is achieved through the investment, adding values such as prestige, happiness, elegance, popularity or admiration.

A brand that is equal to quality with another brand can succeed against its competitor for two reasons; either it has lower prices, or has very good values added through advertising.

While advertising is responsible, among other things, for the above, it generally does not create an image of the products or services themselves, but the image of consumers of the products they advertise. This creates a perfect prototype for the consumer to feel identified, or want to feel identified. For example, the reason why men buy AXE deodorant is very likely not much because it is the deodorant with better quality and longer duration, but because it represents the figure of a man who in any situation is longed for by all women, which makes said deodorant, be parallel longed for by all men, wanting to be that boy chased by beautiful girls shown in brand advertisements.

The same goes for example, with the advertisements of the most prestigious perfumes, showing you a life of absolute ostentatiousness, elegance and prestige that only that perfume can offer you. Or the case of Red Bull is not the best energizer on the market, the most expensive, nor the cheapest, however, it is so well positioned by its advertisements with the slogan "Red Bull gives you wings" that when you think of energizers, it is the first one that comes to mind.

Often the choice of brand of a product is not due to its taste, its quality, or by some particular characteristic of the product, but in many cases depends neatly on external elements that are added by advertising. The preferences between products, in most cases, are clearly due to advertising and brand image.

The position of a detergent brand of the many advertised on television depends primarily on advertising. In this regard, what Durán (1982) states, an expert in psychology of advertising and sales: It is proven that there is a position for each brand of products in the same class. The individual, if he is interested in the advertised object, can retain seven marks in his mind. In order of its importance, the leading brand will be located on the upper rung. The fact of positioning is basic in any advertisement and is used as a communication strategy, although ideally, the brand of the advertised product reaches the position of leader.

Advertising has been advancing over time, adapting to the needs of the market. Both brands and consumers do not focus solely on qualities of the product advertised and its many benefits, but places attention on the target of the product and its potential consumers, creating an image of the consumer, representing him through a character with whom he can identify quickly.

A portion of the expenses invested in advertising is intended to be fair, market research, and types of techniques that may become more effective in significantly influencing consumer behavior, making them want the product that's advertised.

This can lead a person to choose a brand from many existing products in the same type, and with the same characteristics. It is emotional engagement and positioning that creates that mark with the target. It's all about buying the people's emotions; emotions can be much more powerful and effective to make the consumer decide on your product instead of choosing the one from the competition. The creation of that brand-client link is made possible by advertising.

Brands need to know that when they decide to invest in advertising, not only are they paying for a spot on television, an ad in a magazine, a newspaper, a track on the radio, or the internet. Rather, they are investing in the establishment of this link, which once it is well-positioned in the consumer's mind, is very difficult to break overnight.

The financing of subliminal advertising is one of several methods that exist to lead to the success of a brand, everything is based on its effectiveness and the techniques used to reach the subconscious of the individual, which is not always very simple to achieve, so both large industries and advertising agencies, for the most part, have their research laboratories of these phenomena.

One of the inexcusable factors for the subliminal techniques chosen to fulfill their purpose well is that their true objectives are not revealed by "showing" themselves in a message.

In a brand-rich society, where new competitors are always emerging with products equal to each other, with better price, better presentation, or simply almost undifferentiated to each other, it is very important to know how to make a path to triumph in the market. For that, you have to know very well how the product is better and what to allocate money to that will place the campaign of a product that aims to be victorious in the Market.

The Basics of Persuasion

In general, persuasion can be understood as a form of strategic communication that aims to convince other people. Through persuasion, it is possible to induce someone to assume a certain position, perform a specific task, or accept an idea.

This communication includes an adequate posture, emotional appeals, and, mainly, a strong and logical argument. In this way, it is easy to see that the psychology of persuasion is associated with some basic topics such as knowledge, rhetoric, and image.

This competence is important for everyone, regardless of profession or industry, but it becomes even more essential for leadership positions, sales professionals, and those who work on projects. And, like most behavioral skills, it can be assimilated and improved.

Methods of Persuasion

The individual can develop this communication capacity to persuade the actions and decisions of others.

Based on his studies, Robert Cialdini created the persuasive communication theory, which is based on the concept of taking advantage of some patterns of conduct internalized collectively, to suggest behaviors. This theory lists the six principles of the psychology of persuasion, which can be taught, learned, and applied. They are:

Reciprocity

This principle defines that people are more willing to agree to a request when they have already received something in return. Social norms encourage us to respond positively to those who have done us a favor or helped us at some other time.

Consistency

The individual is also more likely to follow a pattern if he thinks that this model is consistent with his ideals and values.

Authority

According to this principle, the authority and seniority transmitted by the communicator determine factors for others to feel predisposed to approve or validate something. At this point, the communicator's argument and stance have a special emphasis.

Social Validation

According to Cialdini, the greater the common sense regarding a behavior, the greater the likelihood that someone will adopt attitudes that fit this pattern.

Scarcity

In this principle, the author reiterates that the charm generated by a product, service, or situation is inversely proportional to its availability. That is, the scarcer, the more relevant.

Friendship/friendliness

Finally, the sixth principle indicates that people are more inclined to collaborate or agree with others when there is an identification, a friendship relationship, or some attraction.

It is worth remembering that the principles of Robert Cialdini's influence should not be used autonomously, but combined, as part of more efficient and provocative communication.

The strength of the argument

The argument, in turn, is based on coherence and uses real facts to consolidate a thesis. A good argument is full of examples, data, technical studies, research, and comparisons, to prove the truth of a statement or the viability of a proposal.

Thus, the communicator can involve others, making everyone start following the same line of reasoning until they are persuaded.

This power of persuasion is significantly increased when the argument is joined with empathy. In this case, it is possible to create a communication that mixes reason and emotion, reaching the main centers of convincing.

Persuasion in the corporate universe

It is easy to see that relationships have become increasingly virtual and, often, less productive. This movement is caused not only by the advancement of technology but also by the underutilization of important skills.

Among these skills are empathy and the ability to argue, which together can ensure healthier and more collaborative relationships, especially in the corporate environment — where peaceful coexistence between professionals with the most diverse profiles is a basic need.

Individualism has become a major problem, hampering teamwork and collectivity. Therefore, care must be taken with the virtualization of communication and the almost exclusive use of e-mails, messaging applications, and social networks.

It is also important to consider that dialogue is an efficient way to perceive fears, motivations, and needs, normally hidden in fully digital communication. Personal contact creates ideal conditions for feedback, negotiation, guidance, advice, and convincing.

Also, the correct application of the psychology of persuasion is one of the main characteristics of true leaders, who manage to inspire and engage their teams.

444

Therefore, this issue must be present in the leadership preparation program. With a powerful argument, it is possible to induce critical thinking — a fundamental ingredient for the formation of high-performance teams. The results will be even better if the communicator is recognized for the positive reference that inspires others.

CHAPTER 5

WHAT IS NLP?
(NEURO-LINGUISTIC PROGRAMMING)

"A model of choice and therefore of freedom," "A philosophy of life," "A way of organizing and sequencing our thinking."

What is NLP?

NLP (Neuro-Linguistic Programming) is an approach in psychology. It is a pragmatic approach to communication and change. It focuses on "how to make it work." NLP can be articulated in three different aspects:

1. The essence of NLP is modeling what humans can do best. The process is to "learn from others."

2. The use of modeling gives rise to a large number of techniques.

3. NLP has also developed a certain way of looking at the world and life. It's a bit of a philosophy that advocates human development, autonomy, freedom of thought, ability to relate to others, openness to difference, tolerance.

NLP is a new approach to human functioning, the fruit of the mixing of ideas, and the confrontation of passionate researchers from various disciplines.

It offers an original synthesis leading to immediate use of the knowledge of psychology and neuroscience, anthropology, and artificial intelligence and management.

We are interested in "how it works when it works" rather than explaining "why it doesn't work." It makes it possible to decode the experience of people who are particularly gifted in a specific field (negotiation, communication, education, sport, health, therapy...) or who, placed in difficult situations, have discovered unusual and effective means of getting out of it (transform phobic or traumatic responses, get rid of unwanted behaviors like insomnia, bulimia, and parasitic emotions like jealousy, anxiety, lack of self-confidence).

When we have decoded all the how's of a behavior or a strategy of excellence, identified the components of someone's "talent," whether it is a way of being or a skill, NLP allows us to acquire this capacity for ourselves or to teach it to others.

Who is NLP for?

For all helping relationship professionals who want their clients to make faster, easier, and more predictable progress. For all professional communicators: managers, heads of personnel, executives, salespeople, etc. For all teachers and parents who want to give themselves the tools necessary for quality educational communication. For all humans concerned with the development and harmonization of their internal and external resources.

Discover the basics of NLP!

What can NLP do for you?

Modelization

Decode what specifically other people do to perform in a field: sport, business, education, therapy.

Education

Learn to use the skills decoded among experts, artists, or artisans in a field that interests you — having access to your resources when it matters most: before a meeting or an important presentation when an unforeseen event destabilizes you. Develop a real quality of relationship with your friends and colleagues.

Communication

Develop your communication skills and get better results, professionally and personally. Resolve conflicts between people, your internal contradictions, or those of others.

Transformation

Develop your value systems, belief systems, self-concept during life transitions, major changes in your environment (emotional, socio-professional, etc.). Help others to modify their behaviors, thinking strategies, beliefs, and the resulting emotions to facilitate their personal and professional development. Help companies, organizations, and social systems develop concrete tools to manage change and future challenges.

NLP Training

You might wonder what's going on in NLP school if you're one of those who aren't so familiar with NLP. If you are enrolled in NLP training, you will be in a program that can enhance the connection of extensive neurological processes, self-confidence, linguistics, and skills between the existing links. Some training programs say they will help you develop a new sense of self-awareness and self-esteem that will lead you, particularly in your profession, to new heights for your life. However, one point that has to be known is that NLP preparation is not meant to identify or cure psychological conditions; it merely reflects on the issues that the individual has and how to solve those "issues" to progress.

Most experts will say that realistic and hands-on teaching is the perfect form of studying Neuro-Linguistic Programming, much like any other study. Trainers or coaches most often use a unique training style, which includes humor and playfulness. The problem now is: What is NLP Teaching doing? One NLP Training Provider claims their programs provide their students with the skills, techniques, and knowledge to effectively create positive results that can transform their lives for the better. Just think if you're enrolling in one of these NLP Training programs, you're going to get a chance to become someone who's having amazing opportunities. You'll now have the chance to change your negative actions and turn it into something positive. Also, some NLP Training Programs teach you leadership skills and management preparation to take full responsibility for your life and learn to guide others to the improvements you want.

Even though there are many good and positive things one can get from joining an NLP Training, there are still some program critics. That, by the way, is natural and cannot be avoided; that is valid for any productive program. One major critic is that NLP therapists are only in fraud or that the NLP itself is a scam. I don't think NLP is a scam, but certain clinicians are highly doubtful and should be handled carefully. Also, there are so many untrained practitioners out there, so to prevent these things from happening, one needs to conduct research.

By joining NLP training courses, you'll be able to see the path you're on. You will be put in the right direction by fresh and creative thinking, and NLP Learning always helps you understand the broader horizons of life. Also, NLP is an effective way to assist you in interpersonal relations, including your job and education. It also lets you improve the way you teach business deals, among many more in your everyday life.

CHAPTER 6

BRAINWASHING & HYPNOTIC PROCESS

In 1962 the first version of The Messenger of Fear was released, a film directed by John Frankenheimer that had actors such as Frank Sinatra, Laurence Harvey, or Angela Landsbury. Released in the middle of the Cold War, at the same time as the missile crisis was taking place, the film tells how a Korean War soldier returns home to receive the highest award from the US Congress for his heroism. Little by little, he realizes that both he and his companions suffer nightmares and have strange behaviors. As a result of those nightmares, an investigation begins where little by little, it is discovered that the protagonist has been subjected to brainwashing, being the victim of an international conspiracy to commit a criminal act that may influence the politics of the United States. We are not going to reveal much more about the plot. In reality, it is too tangled, devoid of all logic and not without a certain conspiratorial paranoia, at least in its final twenty minutes. The film is valuable for its performances, for reflecting a theme that had its boom during the Cold War years, and for maintaining a plot very well carried out by actors and screenwriters until almost the end. [In 2004, Jonathan Demme made a worthy remake of this movie.]

Can you brainwash a person to commit all kinds of acts,

including murder?

Can hypnosis program a person's brain to commit any act unintentionally?

In the early 1950s, millions of Americans began to ask themselves these questions when they were able to see Hungarian Cardinal József Mindszenty, with a face that seemed hypnotized, confidently confess all the crimes he was accused of by the Stalinist government. The next thing was to see hundreds of American soldiers who had been captured by the North Korean army sign declarations in which they blamed themselves for all kinds of crimes, and requested the withdrawal of American troops from the war and denouncing the use of bacteriological weapons. Public opinion in the United States was not surprising, especially when many of these soldiers continued to hold the same opinions after returning home. What have they done to our boys? Many wondered.

In 1950, a CIA-linked journalist, Edward Hunter, began publishing a whole series of articles and books on the techniques used in Stalinist regimes to get a person's brainwashing. This expression began to be used for the first time then.

In 1951 the ARTICHOKE project was created that would become, under the command of Allen Dulles, director of the CIA, Operation MK Ultra, to obtain methods that would achieve control of the human mind. From the beginning, numerous investigations in different universities and research centers were financed to achieve, almost always through hypnosis, electric shocks, and the use of drugs such as LSD, purposes related to espionage in the Cold War. They had three objectives: to obtain all kinds of information from the captured spies, to create spies incapable of revealing secrets and, finally, to create programmed soldiers, capable of executing a murder at a certain moment and without knowing it consciously. The latter would be the 'Manchurian candidates'. Many millions of dollars were spent on this project to win the Cold War in the field of espionage. However, by the mid-1960s, many investigations had already been canceled due to the poor — and often counterproductive — results obtained.

At first, so much hope was put into hypnosis that even ARTICHOKE member Morse Allen himself attended a course taught by a famed New York hypnotist. Impressed by the enormous possibilities of hypnosis, he began practicing with his secretaries. The results were more than acceptable, by making one try to assassinate his partner following his orders. However, it was one thing to hypnotize a secretary, conditioned by his boss and the trust he placed in the institution where he worked, and quite another to hypnotize someone, program them to commit a crime, and get them to carry it out finally.

Not all subjects were good candidates for these techniques, and it was never clear if they would eventually be able to commit the act for which they were scheduled, bearing in mind that when executing it, they could be thousands of kilometers away from their hypnotized person. Who would be the person giving the order then? What if he acted by chance to hear the key phrase at the wrong time? It was one thing to hypnotize an individual so that they would then commit an act and quite another to be able to program it, leaving their faculties intact, to commit a crime at a precise moment. As John Gittinger, director of the MK Ultra, noted: "You cannot predict absolute control of a subject; any psychologist, or any psychiatrist, or any preacher, has relative control over certain individuals, but can never predict their reactions; there is the question. It looks like it was tried, but John Marks, author of In Search of the Manchurian candidate, where he documents all these investigations carried out by the CIA, does not confirm that nothing definitive of these projects was achieved. It even seemed like there were simpler methods for an assassin to kill someone without subsequently revealing any information if caught. The 638 attempts to assassinate Fidel Castro by the CIA demonstrate this. They tried everything, even if they were not successful.

The truth is that many of these investigations were carried out with unorthodox methods, even for the time. Doctors like Ewen Cameron did not hesitate to apply sensory deprivation to their patients for weeks, which, together with the stimulation with electroshocks and the administration of sedative drugs, ended up causing irreversible episodes of amnesia without, on the other hand, the disease to be treated (schizophrenia). These attempts at behavior modification through the deconstruction of the personality were very aggressive and with few results, but the CIA was very interested in its financing. The 'truth serum' and the application of the same Stalinist techniques to a Russian in the Nosenko case also failed. This ex-spy, who spent 1277 days under isolation and interrogation, did not reveal any conclusive evidence. As the CIA was not clear whether Nosenko was telling the truth, the Stalinist techniques did not work.

But then how did the Soviets get Cardinal Mindszenty to confess to any crime or get American soldiers caught in Korea to sign those statements? Harold Wolff, a neurologist and personal friend of Allen Dulles and his collaborator at Cornell University, Lawrence Hinkle, led a research group that collected all kinds of information, especially from former KGB members who knew the techniques perfectly well. That the detainees and the tortured themselves were subjected. In 1957, Wolff and Hinkle showed in their work that the Soviet techniques were based on a constant and overwhelming physical and psychological pressure, without further ado, which mainly affected the weakest aspects of the human structure.

In short, the method was as follows: the prisoner was subjected to rigorous isolation in his cell, without being able to communicate with anyone or anything. During this isolation, he was often forced to stand up, woke up in the middle of the night, and the guards beat him for no reason. After a few weeks, the interrogations began while a prisoner, totally exhausted, saw his interrogator as the only person who had spoken to him in a long time and, wishing to end everything, ended up signing anything.

According to former KGB members, the detainee was considered guilty; it was only a matter of time that he ended up signing his confession, which was achieved in a few weeks in most cases. The method was not trying to reveal the truth.

The Cold War encouraged many writers to write works that seemed almost science fiction. The idea of a programmed killer has been recurring in the cinema for decades. In 1965 Michael Caine was brainwashed by waves in Sidney J. Furie's Confidential Archive. In 1977, on Phone, an always tough Charles Bronson would have to discover the person activating the programmed assassins, that the Soviet Union had scattered throughout the United States. Pure paranoia of the Cold War? Undoubtedly, but the idea of a candidate from Manchuria gave a lot of play so that the film industry did not take advantage of it. However, the human mind is still much more complex, and its control seems less easy than many would like.

China and the Korean War

Initially, the Chinese term "brainwash" was used to describe the coercive persuasion used in China under the Maoist government to transform "reactionary" people into "well-thinking" members of China's new social system. The term made puns in the Taoist custom of "cleansing/washing of the heart/mind" (xǐxīn, 洗 心) before performing ceremonies or entering holy places.

The Oxford Dictionary of English documents the oldest recorded English use of the term "brainwashing" in an article published on September 24, 1950, by journalist Edward Hunter, in Miami News. Hunter was an ardent anti-communist and is believed to be an undercover CIA agent posing as a journalist. The Hunter and others used the Chinese term to describe some American prisoners of war (POWs) who cooperated during the Korean War with their Chinese captors (1950-1953), even crossing over to their side in some instances. British radio operator Robert W. Ford and British Army colonel James Carne also said the Chinese had brainwashed them during their imprisonment in wartime.

The United States Army and government put brainwashing charges to undermine confessions made by prisoners of war to war crimes, including biological warfare. After Chinese radio broadcasts asked Frank Schwable, Chief of Staff of the Air Wing First Navy, to participate in bacteriological warfare, United Nations Commander for General Mark W. Clark stated:

It is doubtful whether these statements passed those unfortunate lips each time they passed. However, if they did, all too familiar is the mind that annihilates these communist methods of extorting whatever word they want... The men are not to blame themselves and have my sincere remorse for being used in this abominable way.

Starting in 1953, Robert Jay Lifton interviewed American soldiers who had been war captives during the Korean War, as well as priests, professors, and teachers who had been held in China after 1951. Lifton interviewed 15 Chinese people who had left Chinese universities after being exposed to indoctrination, in addition to interviews with 25 Americans and European people. (Lifton 's 1961 book Reform of Thought and Totalism Psychology: An Analysis of "Brainwashing" in China, based on this research.) Lifton found that when the prisoners returned to the United States, their behavior gradually returned to normal, unlike the common image of "brainwashing."

In 1956, after re-examining the concept of brainwashing after the Korean War, the United States Army released a report titled Communist Interrogation, Indoctrination, and Exploitation of Prisoners of War, which demanded to brainwash. Brain "popular belief." The report states that "a thorough investigation by various government agencies did not reveal a conclusively documented case of 'brainwashing' of a US prisoner of war in Korea."

In George Orwell's 1949 dystopian novel Nine Hundred and Eighty-Four, the main character is subjected to prison, isolation, and torture to confirm his thoughts and emotions to the wishes of the future rulers of Orwell's fictional totalitarian society. The vision of Orwell inspired Hunter, and is now mirrored in the mainstream perception of the brainwashing idea. Written around the same time, JRR Tolkien's The Lord of the Rings also addressed brainwashing, albeit in a fantasy setting. Cordwainer Smith's science fiction stories (written from the 1940s until he died in 1966) depict brainwashing as a natural and benevolent aspect of potential medical procedure to erase the memory of stressful events.

In the 1950s, many American movies were filmed, which

included brainwashing of POWs, including the shelf, prison bamboo, Into the Unknown, and the Fearmakers. Forbidden told the story of Soviet secret agents who had been brainwashed through classical conditioning by their own government so that their identity would not be revealed. In 1962, The Messenger of Fear (1959 based on the Richard Condon novel) "put brainwashing ahead and center" by presenting a plot by the Soviet government to take over the United States by using a brainwashing presidential candidate. Brainwashing was popularly associated with research by Russian psychologist Ivan Pavlov, who mostly involved dogs, not humans, as subjects. In The Messenger of Fear, the head Brainwasher is Dr. Yen Lo of the Pavlov Institute.

In science fiction, mental regulation is still a big subject. Terry O'Brien said: "Mind control is such a strong concept that no hypnosis, then something similar ought to have been invented: the plot is too useful for any writer to ignore the fear of mind control, just as powerful an image." A subgenre is corporate mind control, where companies that rule society through advertisements are controlling a future society.

American government investigation

For twenty years since the 1950s, the United States Central Intelligence Agency (CIA) and the United States Department of Defense conducted a secret investigation, including Project MKUltra, to develop practical techniques for brainwash; outcomes are unknown. CIA studies using various psychedelic substances, such as LSD and mescaline, were based on Nazi human experimentation.

In 1974, a member of the affluent Hearst family, Patty Hearst, was abducted by a left-wing organization named the Symbionan Liberation Army. After several weeks in captivity, he agreed to join the group and participated in their activities. In 1975, he was arrested and charged with bank robbery and the use of a firearm in the commission of a serious crime. His attorney, F. Lee Bailey, argued at trial that he should not be held responsible for his actions since his captors' treatment was equivalent to the Korean War prisoners of war brainwashing. Hearst was found guilty, but his "brainwashing defense" brought the issue to the attention of the renewed public in the United States, like Charles Manson 's case of 1969-1971, who was alleged to have brainwashed his followers for murder and other crimes.

Bailey developed her case in conjunction with psychiatrist Louis Jolyon West and psychologist Margaret Singer. The two had studied the experiences of the Korean War prisoners of war. In 1996 Cantor published his theories in his biggest sale of books, Cults in Our Environment. In 2003, the brainwashing tactic was misused in favor of Lee Boyd Malvo, convicted of murder for his role in the DC sniper attacks. Several legal scholars argued that brainwashing security violates the fundamental principle of free will regulation.

Italy had a dispute about the definition of plagiarism, a crime consisting of an absolute physical-psychological environment, and eventually an individual. It is said that the consequence is the destruction of the problem of equality and self-determination and the consequent rejection of his identity. The plagiarism offense has been seldom charged in Italy, and only one person has ever been arrested. In 1981, an Italian court found the concept to be imprecise, lack coherence, and subject to arbitrary use. By the 21st century of child care and child sexual assault, the idea of brainwashing is being implemented "with considerable effectiveness." In some cases, "one parent is charged with brainwashing the child for refusing the other parent, and in child abuse cases where one parent is charged with brainwashing the child for making charges of sexual abuse against the other parent" (possibly resulting from or causing alienation of the parent).

In 2003, forensic psychologist Dick Anthony said, "No reasonable person doubts that there are situations in which people can be influenced against their interests, but those arguments are evaluated based on fact, not false testimony from an expert." In 2016, the Israeli anthropologist for religion and his companion at the Jerusalem Van Leer Institute Adam Klin-Oron said of the then proposed "anti-cult" legislation:

There was a surge of 'brainwashing' allegations in the 1980s. Then parliaments around the world looked into the issue, and courts around the world looked into the issue and came to a strong conclusion: No, there is such a thing as cults ... that the people who make these claims are often not adept at it. And in the final courts, including in Israel, rejected experts who affirmed that there is "brainwashing".

Lifton's eight criteria for thought reform

Milieu Management is a concept popularized by psychiatrist Robert Jay Lifton to describe strategies that regulate the environment and human speech by using social coercion and group language; these strategies can include ideology, advice, vocabulary, and pronunciation, allowing group members to recognize other members or facilitate cognitive improvements in individuals. Originally, Lifton used "milieu control" to describe brainwashing and mind control, but the term was already used in other contexts.

In his book, Dr. Lifton identified eight main themes or criteria for detecting, evaluating "ideological totalitarianism" and its implementation in groups, institutions, and others. These are not manipulation recipes but symptoms to judge its existence. Of course, things are never so clear in reality. It should also be borne in mind that this is not a theory but an attempt at classification made based on dozens of hours of interview with people just released from the totalitarian environment where they had been "reformed."

The more an environment presents these eight psychological themes, the more it resembles ideological totalitarianism ...

1. Control of the environment

... It is obvious, but this control is more or less visible: from physical confinement — prison — through "Revolutionary

University" to, sometimes, an entire country. This control is essentially that of communication, not only of each individual with the outside but also with himself. George Orwell, as a good Westerner, imagined the control using a device — a permanent, two-way television, each being recorded at the same time as it received the broadcasts. The Chinese, on the other hand, used human instruments.

As perfect as this control — material or psychological, or both — may be, it is never absolute. There can always be, from the outside world or from the subject itself, "parasitic" information interfering with the messages of the manipulators. For those who apply the system, if they cannot create an environment containing only their truth be told, they attribute these inadequacies to an imperfect application of the procedures and the total perversity of the refractory. For the latter, the ultimate consequence is his physical elimination; but this itself constitutes a personal failure for the manipulators. They have themselves been subjected to the impact of the "last truth": applying the same treatment to others, and successfully, is also the means to dispel their doubts, if they have any left.

For the individual, the main consequence is the disruption of the balance between the ego and the outside world. We normally operate a constant back and forth between an experience (what comes to us from the outside world and others) and our reflection: this is how we test the reality of the environment and maintain the sense of our own identity.

However, the pressure of the totalitarian environment tends to destroy this polarity, to replace it with another: between the "real" (the ideology and the behavior of the group with which each must identify) and the "non-real" (everything else). What comes from outside is "lie." Those who manage to achieve this identification experience an exhilarating feeling of omniscience shared with the group (the Party, the People, the Leader ...); they "see the world with the eyes of God." Others feel suffocated by those who control them and will try to escape them as soon as control is relaxed (not without having consequences).

2. "Mystical manipulation"

Once environmental control has been carried out, the next inevitable step is personal manipulation. Directed "from above," it aims to provoke a set of determined behaviors and emotions, but in such a way that they are felt as spontaneous. For the manipulated, this spontaneity led by an omniscient group assumes an almost mystical quality. "I reacted according to what I had been taught." Manipulators do not only seek power over others: they too are driven by a mysticism which not only justifies but demands these manipulations. They become the instrument of their mysticism, confer a divine "aura" to manipulative institutions — Party, Government, Organization, Church. They are the agents chosen by this higher force (History, Science, God, etc.). The realization of the "mystical imperative" takes precedence over any other consideration (including immediate human well-being). Any thought or action that questions the higher goal is

464

considered retrograde, selfish, petty. It is this mystical imperative that produces the seemingly opposite extremes of idealism and cynicism, the most cynical acts of which can be committed to serving the "supreme goal" ("the end sanctifies all means").

At the level of the individual, the answers revolve around the basic polarity between trust and distrust. He is asked to accept these manipulations based on ultimate trust — or faith — "like a child in his mother's arms," said a priest who had undergone reform in prison. Whoever experiences this degree of confidence comes to take pleasure in the suffering caused by the manipulations; he believes them necessary for the accomplishment of the "higher goal," which he has made his own. He then participates in the manipulation of others.

But such confidence is difficult to maintain permanently, and the higher goal does not always provide sufficient emotional support. The individual then responds with "pawn psychology": unable to escape from more powerful forces than him, he seeks to adapt to them above all. He develops the sense of the right answer, is sensitive to all kinds of signals, learns to anticipate the pressures of the environment, to let the wave carry himself; his psychic energies melt into the current, instead of turning against himself, which would be painful. He stops asking himself questions. For this, he must participate in the manipulation of others, bow to betrayals (towards others, and himself). His reaction can also be a mixture of the two attitudes. But anyway, he stripped himself of the ability to express himself and act independently.

3. The requirement of purity

In all situations of ideological totalitarianism, the world of experience is rigorously divided between the pure and the impure, absolute good and absolute evil. Pure and good: these are ideas, feelings, actions by the totalitarian ideology and line; everything else is relegated to the realm of the unclean and evil. Nothing human is immune to the island of moral judgments; all the "poisons," all the stains must be sought and eliminated.

The underlying assumption is that this absolute purity (the "good communist" for the Chinese ...) is possible. You can do anything in the name of this purity; it will be moral. This perfection is inaccessible, the "Reformation of thought" itself provides proof of its most malignant consequences: it creates a narrow world of guilt and shame. Ongoing reform requires everyone to strive for something that does not exist and is foreign to the human condition.

In this world, everyone should expect to be punished. As one never reaches total purity, one must expect humiliation and exclusion. The relationship with the community is a shame. Worse still: guilt and shame become values in themselves, privileged forms of communication, the subject of public competitions. Those who do not fully succeed may pretend these feelings for a while, but it's much safer to feel them.

Individuals are more or less prone to these feelings of guilt and shame, depending on their character and education, but these are universal human tendencies, and everyone is vulnerable. It is a matter of degree. The ideological totalitarianisms, setting themselves up as ultimate judges of good and evil in this world, use these tendencies as emotional levers to influence and manipulate, the individual internalizes absolute criteria and becomes his judge; but it also projects them outside: the "impurities" come from external influences. The best way to get rid of the burden of guilt is to expose these influences continually. The more guilty you feel, the greater the hatred. This leads to mass hatred, purges of heretics, to holy wars (political or religious). It is very difficult to find a more balanced sense of the complexities of human morality when one has experienced such a good-bad polarization.

4. The cult of confession

This obsession is closely linked to the requirement of absolute purity. We come to confessing imaginary crimes — this, in the hope of being healed of our sins. In the hands of totalitarians, confession becomes a means of exploiting vulnerabilities (feeling of guilt, shame) instead of relieving them.

Confession is, first of all, a means of personal purification. It is also a kind of symbolic surrender and finally, the means of maintaining total transparency vis-à-vis others, or at least the Organization, which must know all the past, the thoughts, the passions of each individual, and especially what is considered negative. This cult of confession can produce an orgiastic sense of unity between the co-confessors, a kind of ecstasy where the self merges into the great flow of the "Movement." For some, this can also satisfy a tendency to self-punishment, a desire to free oneself from repressed feelings of guilt (catharsis). Everyone becomes a penitent judge.

5. "Sacred Science"

The totalitarian environment maintains a sacred aura around its basic dogma, presented as the ultimate moral vision for ordering human existence. It is forbidden (or impossible) to question it and implies to revere the authors of this Word and its current holders. Although this "sacred science" is in the realm of revelation, it transcends (it is superior) the ordinary rules of logic, the totalitarian environment puts an exaggerated insistence on asserting its flawless logic, its absolute "scientific" precision. Daring to criticize it, or worse, have different ideas, even unspoken, becomes not only immoral and disrespectful but "anti-scientific." We exploit here the reverence which surrounds all that is "scientific" (Especially nowadays, with advanced imaging techniques and funding allocated to research in favor of disciplines which support contemporary scientific dogma).

Here the presumption isn't that man can be God, but that man's ideas can be God — that there is an absolute science of ideas (and therefore of man) — that it can be combined with an equally absolute body of moral principles, the resulting doctrine to be true for all men at all times.

This sacred science can offer comfort and security at the

level of the individual thanks to the apparent unification between the modes of mystical and logical experience. It brings together reasoning in the form of a syllogism (with a great deal of "consequently") and dazzling intuitions. The hold of this "sacred science" is so strong that the individual who feels attracted to ideas that ignore or contradict it will feel guilty and be afraid.

In a totalitarian environment, there is no distinction between the sacred and the profane. A counterfeit science mixes with a junk religion. The pressure to obtain personal closure is such that we prefer to avoid any knowledge or experience that could lead to authentic self-expression and creative evolution.

6. Coded language

In the language of the totalitarian environment, the cliché is king. The most complex human problems are reduced to a few short, peremptory sentences that are easy to remember and repeat. They are the beginning and the conclusion of all "ideological analysis." The cliché has the advantage of dispensing from any real discussion, from the exploration of various interpretations, from all personal reflection and expression.

Clichés are not only shortcuts, but they are polarized, with positive or negative emotional charges: some terms represent good, and those that represent evil, the devil. Maoist vocabulary, for example, repeated positive terms: progress, progressive, liberation, proletarian point of view, the debate of history, etc. Negative terms: capitalist, imperialist, bourgeois, exploitation... This very characteristic "language of non-thought" is frightfully boring for all those who do not share it. It also makes a member of a totalitarian group very recognizable.

Of course, every group has, to a certain extent, its jargon: family, school, profession, etc. Certain expressions are signs of recognition, but that does not prevent the members of these groups (an individual can also belong to several) from being equally at ease in general language. In the totalitarian group, the jargon becomes exclusive. It expresses the certainties of "sacred science," which strengthens them; the key expressions trigger the emotions, positive or negative, desired by the manipulators.

For the individual, this language has the effect of a narrowing ("constriction"), an impoverishment, a linguistic amputation. However, language and its richness are the very basis of human experience, and to amputate language is to remove whole swathes of the ability to think and feel, even if the individual does not realize it. Even if he takes pleasure in it, he thus feels his belonging to the group, outside of which he no longer wants to exist. It is also a very strong link with the group because the outside world becomes foreign to it. "Others don't think like we do." He even becomes a stranger to himself, to his past, to everything that made him become what he is: he can no longer even imagine his "old life" — and he does not want to: he realizes that this could constitute a danger for him.

This manipulation of language could be the subject of a

special study because it is fundamental: it is the most apparent wall between the adherents of totalitarian ideology and the rest of humanity. This is often what is first felt by "the others" (those outside the totalitarian system). For Westerners leaving Chinese prisons, it was all the more obvious that their "reform" was done in Chinese; but it was equally so for the Chinese themselves. One of them said: "When we have used the same patterns of expressions for so long ... we feel chained".

7. The doctrine above the person

This sterile language also reflects the subordination of human experience to the requirements of the doctrine: personal experience, feelings are continuously channeled, put in an abstract mold of interpretation, the feelings having to correspond to the official catalog.

This is obvious in the reinterpretation of history, rewritten in the form of black and white melodrama. There too, there were the bad guys: imperialists, capitalists, foreigners, feudal reactionaries inside — and the good ones — the resistance and the liberation of the People, salvation by the victory of communism. These reinterpretations also incorporate pieces of reality, without which they would not be accepted and would remain pure mythology. The myths themselves use and reinforce existing feelings, sometimes underlying, which can be justified. All mass revolutions rewrite history, by eliminating what does not fit with doctrine, or by reinterpreting it. The history of "historians" is never entirely objective or innocent.

But a serious historian strives to disregard his preferences and prejudices; at the very least, he will clarify his point of view. But when myth merges with totalitarian "sacred science," the resulting "logic" can purely and simply eliminate and replace reality: that of historical facts, even recent ones, and individual experience.

This is how the individual remakes his past to please his masters, reinterprets his whole life, and that of his family. Character and identity must be reshaped, not by the nature and potential of each, but to sink them into the rigid mold of doctrine. Camus says that "the executioners of philosophy and state terrorism ... place an abstract concept above human life, even though they call it history, to which they would agree, subject in advance, to apply certain ideas in complete arbitrariness ...."

The assumption is that doctrine, including its mythical elements, is more valid, truer, more real than any aspect of real human character, or human experience. And if the events contradict the doctrine, we will change the events rather than the doctrine — they will be downplayed, denied, or ignored. Likewise, individuals will go so far as to agree to reinterpret their acts and attitudes to coincide with the character they become if they ever fall out of favor (if they do not have the possibility, or the strength, to get out of the totalitarian system).

8. Absolute power over existence

The totalitarian environment establishes an absolute separation between those who have the right to exist and those who do not. The latter are "non-persons"; the reform of thought provides non-persons with the means to access existence.

This sovereign right to grant or refuse existence amounts to making God: this is what the Greeks called hubris. But under this hubris, there is the conviction that there is only one way leading to the true existence, only one valid mode of existing, the totalitarian ones feel obliged to destroy all the possibilities of "false" existences: it is the means of realizing the great project of true existence, to which they are devoted. And we can consider the whole reform of thought as the means to eradicate all these modes of existence deemed false not only among non-people, but also among legitimate people, but who could be contaminated.

For the individual, it is the ultimate conflict: "to be or not to be," being or nothingness. It is also the attraction of a conversion experience which offers the only possible path to the existence. The totalitarian environment — even in the absence of physical violence — encourages everyone to fear destruction. The person can overcome this fear and find confirmation of his existence in the source of all existence that is the Totalitarian Organization.

Existence then depends on faith ("I believe, therefore I am"), submission ("I obey, therefore I am"), and, ultimately, on the feeling of total fusion with the ideological movement. Of course, everyone operates compromises and combines this dependence with elements of their own identity. But everyone is constantly reminded that the room for maneuver is narrow and that one cannot deviate much from the single path without being deprived of the right to existence.

Lifton did not determine these themes as a priori. He released them from what he had learned by listening to subjects who had undergone "thought reform." We may find that other classifications would be possible, or that certain themes overlap, at least in part. Control of the environment, that of language, and therefore of communication, are intimately linked. Any ranking is an attempt, never entirely successful, to understand the experience as much as possible.

Lifton concludes by saying that the more an environment presents these eight psychological themes, the more it resembles ideological totalitarianism. But he adds that no milieu perfectly achieves totalitarianism. Some environments, rather moderate, can manifest some. Even an environment that seems dangerously close to totalitarianism, if one base oneself on these criteria, radically differs from it, insofar as it leaves different paths open.

Totalitarianism paroxysystic experience

Totalitarianism itself can offer a "paroxysmal" experience, which makes it possible to transcend all that is ordinary, banal, to free oneself from human ambivalences, to penetrate a sphere of truth, reality, confidence, and sincerity. Beyond anything, we have ever known or imagined. However, this experience is not spontaneous but directed and manipulated. Contrary to what the great mystics, the great spirituals have known, it has the effect of closing the mind and not of greater receptivity and openness.

In the absence of paroxysmal experience, ideological totalitarianism has even more negative consequences for human potential: destructive emotions, intellectual and psychological shrinking; it deprives man of all that is the most subtle, the most imaginative — by the false promise of eliminating the imperfections, the uncertainties, and ambivalences which help to define the human condition. This is what provokes the collective excesses so characteristic of totalitarianism in all its forms. In turn, these excesses mobilize extremist tendencies among those outside who are attacked, and we enter a vicious circle.

According to Lifton, the source of ideological totalitarianism, the origin of these extreme emotional reactions is not to be found in some external evil power, but in the very depths of man: the human quest for the all-powerful guide, for supernatural force (political party, religious ideas, great leader, Science ...) capable of bringing to all men perfect solidarity, will eliminate the anxiety of death and the terror of nothingness. This quest is at the heart of all mythologies, religions, the history of all nations, as in individual life. The potential for totalitarianism is different according to societies, their history, and their structure, as individuals, according to their character, their future (family, childhood, relationships with others...). It is never absent, and we cannot predict it: two people are never identical, no more than two companies at a given time. For totalitarianism to occur, many factors must be combined, which were not all apparent or predictable.

CHAPTER 7

WHAT IS HYPNOSIS?

"I'm afraid because you're going to put me to sleep and I won't know what happened."

First of all, hypnosis is not being asleep but a modified state of consciousness. The electroencephalogram confirms this without a doubt; the tracing of a person in a hypnotic state is different from that of the sleeper. The hypnotized subjects' plots show slight changes related to suggestions, but none of the electrical signs of REM sleep or deep sleep.

James Braid, an English surgeon, is the current namer of "hypnosis." In 1855, he introduced the concept of a modified state of consciousness, which he called "the theory of hypnosis and psych corporeal healing related to a given state."

This term "hypnosis" is derived from the Greek word "hupnos" which means "sleep." This etymology is the source of misunderstandings detrimental to the current practice of this technique. Indeed, hypnosis still often evokes a mysterious, magical or disturbing sleep and this conception generates either unrealistic expectations ("I want you to put me to sleep and solve all my problems during my hypnotic sleep") or an exaggerated distrust ("You will put me to sleep and subject me without my knowledge").

Far from inducing passivity, hypnosis is an active state in

477

which several phenomena occur through your collaboration. No practitioner can induce you into a hypnotic state if you don't want to. To make a comparison, you may be required to go to the cinema but not to watch the film. Indeed, to not see, you just close your eyes.

Hypnosis, therefore, requires your participation. You will remain present and witness what is happening inside you, even in a deep trance. While one part of you will be engaged in hypnotic work, another will remain in the observer position. For example, you can relive memories and the different sensations associated with it while remaining aware of the hypnotic context of reviviscency. The hypnotic trance can be compared to the viewer's state of attention fully captivated by a thriller. This one does not sleep, and the film absorbs him to the point of disinteresting the world around him (it is "in" the film, he is "in") but keeps in mind that he is in a movie theatre.

Also, be aware that you will only agree to respond to suggestions if they are consistent with your core values.

"If it's not sleeping, what is hypnosis?"

It is essentially a state of mental concentration during which the faculties of the person's mind are so overwhelmed by an idea, internal images, sensations, or emotions that he is momentarily indifferent to most aspects of external reality. If certain psychic functions are dormant, it is for the benefit of other processes, especially unconscious.

In hypnosis, our perceptions and understanding of reality

are altered, allowing us to function mentally in a different way and to be more open to ourselves. However, during the first sessions of hypnosis, it often happens that the patient does not feel like he is having a particular experience and will need some learning to access deeper states. However, it should be noted that the depth of the trance is not necessarily a criterion of quality. Surprising therapeutic results can be seen as a result of superficial hypnotic experiments. Psychological work can be compared to swimming. You can swim both in the small and in the great depth of a swimming pool. Similarly, quality work can be done both in a light trance and in a deep hypnotic state.

"Hypnosis is an unusual, abnormal, and artificial condition."

No, quite the opposite. Hypnosis is a common physiological condition that we all know.

If you are a motorist, you will have noticed that when you are focused on a subject of concern to you, you can drive automatically and not notice how far you have come. Similarly, you may have already experienced a second condition called "Highway hypnosis" when you drive alone in a silent atmosphere on a tree-lined road. If you're a film buff or a literature buff, you've probably been so "caught" in a story that you don't hear what a person is saying to you. You know how easy it is to forget the time that passes if you're passionate about computer science or video games. You also certainly "unhooked" from the outside reality in a waiting room or in a station hall to absorb you into yourself.

In all these situations, you have experienced an "ordinary daily trance." These states have, in common, a spontaneous shift of our attention to internal stimuli. We go through this type of hypnotic state, every day, every 90 to 100 minutes. These common trances are linked to the ultradian cycle, which also rhythms other physiological parameters. During these phases, some parts of our brain rest while others are activated, allowing a different functioning necessary for the mental organization of information and lived experiences.

In a schematic way, and with all the reservations imposed by this simplification, there would be, in a trance, a departmentalization of the left brain and activation of the right hemisphere.

According to neurophysiological theories, each of the cerebral hemispheres brings a different understanding of reality. The left brain would dominate the awakening activities, while the right brain would manifest itself mainly during dreaming, daydreaming, artistic activity, common trance, and hypnosis. With this in mind, it is accepted that the right hemisphere is responsible for unconscious phenomena and that it has greater activity when the usual consciousness is altered.

The state of hypnosis is, therefore, a natural and banal physiological phenomenon, and therapeutic hypnosis is only the amplification of this phenomenon with the help of another person.

"With me, it's not going to work because I have a strong character, or only the weak can be hypnotized."

Given what has just been mentioned, it seems obvious that each of us is capable of experiencing satisfying hypnotic states to varying degrees.

Hypnotism would be a relatively stable psychological data that would depend on the hypnotized and not the hypnotist. According to research, it is linked in particular to intelligence and the capacity of the imagination. So, you have all the more assets to start hypnotherapy as you have character!

You will have to learn not to do anything, to forget the outside world temporarily, and to let go. To the extent that we are used to being vigilant, learning a new type of behavior is a difficult matter.

"I don't want to lose control! I don't want to be under the power of the hypnotist!"

During the hypnosis sessions, the hypnotist tends to make it seem that he is the custodian of exceptional power to make a spectator do anything. This hypnotic power is a decoy. On the other hand, it is a real power of intellectual manipulation! In reality, no hypnotist can force you to execute or say things you don't want.

You will be the only one behind your altered states of consciousness. You will have control over your behaviour throughout the session. The therapist is only an instrument that, thanks to his know-how, will help you to emerge a process that you will keep in control of. You will learn to let go by immediately regaining control of operations. Therapeutic hypnosis is not intended to subject you, but rather to increase your control over yourself.

It may be surprising, at first glance, that this state of letting go is an opportunity for better personal control. Neurophysiological data can help to understand this phenomenon. Many psychological problems could be understood, such as the misapplication of rational approaches in the left hemisphere on situations that would be better understood by the right brain. Right brain stimulant hypnosis would, therefore, help the subject solve his difficulties through his solutions. Indeed, the latter already has the necessary resources in him, but he ignores them because they are outside his usual consciousness.

The hypnotherapist, it will be understood, is not intended to impose his solutions but to explore your unsuspected and unused potentialities with you. In this modified state of consciousness, you will start new solutions using the therapist's words and images that are relevant to you.

Here, if it were still needed, one last proof, by the absurd, of the inconsistency of this myth of the almighty hypnotist: it is possible to induce oneself a hypnotic state by resorting to his suggestions. This is called self-hypnosis. We have evoked the fact that we experience altered states of consciousness in our daily lives. These are of a self-hypnosis type. Therapeutic self-hypnosis is only the structured use of this phenomenon. We can, therefore, say that hypnosis is always in the essence of self-hypnosis and that even when a therapist is called upon, the therapist only guides the patient to trance.

"I'm afraid hypnosis is dangerous and harmful."

This widespread belief is false, with some reservations. Indeed, if hypnosis did not pose any danger, its beneficial action could be questioned. The risk of creating psychosomatic or psychiatric disorders exists, although these are rare and transient.

Negative self-hypnosis is used to describe a negative self-perception that causes pathogenic unconscious processes to start. Negative thoughts that the subject would have located himself outside his usual consciousness and beyond criticism would be powerful suggestions. According to the author, these self-suggestions are responsible for many disorders, including sexual disorders.

Moreover, psycho-neuro-immunology teaches us that the mind, through emotions and mental attitudes, can play a significant role in the genesis of bodily dysfunction or disease.

It cannot, therefore, be completely rejected, the assumption that a suggestion made by a hypnotist to a subject in modified consciousness cannot act negatively on him, either physically or psychologically. However, it is clear that the harmful consequences of hypnosis only appear in people with a long medical history and who have previously exhibited psychotic tendencies.

Hypnosis is, in fact, no more or less dangerous than any

other form of the psychotherapeutic relationship. After prior interviews, practiced by a qualified professional, who remains in his usual therapeutic framework, it is, on the contrary, an extraordinary tool. Indeed, the hypnotic state offers the patient an experience during which the usual limitations of his thoughts are temporarily suspended. Beliefs, habits, and preconceived ideas accepted since childhood can block opportunities for development or adaptation. However, these difficult borders to cross in the usual waking state are erased during trance, and returns in the apprehension of reality become possible. In other words, in hypnosis, the perception of what we are experiencing is changed, allowing us to be more open to ourselves and to change.

Let us define hypnosis proposed by the British Medical Association: "transient state of modified attention in the subject, a condition that can be produced by another person and in which various phenomena may appear spontaneously or in response to verbal or other stimuli. These phenomena include a change in consciousness and memory, increased susceptibility to suggestion, and the appearance in the subject of answers and ideas that are not familiar to him in his usual state of mind. Also, phenomena such as anaesthesia, paralysis, muscle rigidity, and vasomotor modifications can be, in the hypnotic state, produced and suppressed."

Sensory alterations are a usual phenomenon

The most common are heaviness or numbness in the body (especially the limbs), feelings of flutter or lightness, feelings of warmth or freshness, the feeling that the volume of the body changes (usually, the hands or feet), loss of sensation of limb positioning (for example, patients no longer feel / no longer know how their hands are placed), anesthesia and analgesia.

Time distortion. It is a change in the perception of the length of time that elapses. For example, the patient may feel that the session has been longer or, on the contrary, shorter than it has objectively been.

Post-hypnotic amnesia. Sometimes the patient forgets what happened during part or all of the hypnosis session.

Hypermnesia. It allows you to find memories, consciously forgotten. However, if hypnosis allows you to recover elements of the past, it can also create false memories. This ability to modify memory is also used therapeutically, in particular to create repairing scenarios.

Other frequent small signs include tearing and difficulty in speech.

Not everyone can realize all of these phenomena. Everyone can be gifted for some and not others, but hypnosis more often than not allows you to learn or cultivate them. Each of these signs can have therapeutic dimensions.

The actual induction of the hypnotic state

To enter a trance, you don't have to be fascinated by the look of a magician. The patient does not enter a trance because the hypnotist imposes it but because he wants it.

Induction is nothing more than a technique that helps the patient enter a state of inner focus.

The methods of induction of the hypnotic state are very numerous. They have in common to focus attention on an object (an object that the patient freely chooses in the room, across or a dot drawn on one of his hands, etc.), physical sensations (for example, the progressive heaviness of the body or breathing) or mental images (for example, a memory). One can practice an induction by relaxation with an awareness of bodily sensations or accompaniment in a pleasant memory. These are simple and often effective ways of doing things. The person is asked to concentrate as much as possible to make the memory more and more vivid. To do this, the hypnotist helps him to see, hear, and feel the different aspects of the situation. He absorbs himself so that he forgets what surrounds him. The usual conscious mind "picks up," and the unconscious emerges.

The inductions of the first hypnotic states are, on average, about fifteen minutes. However, this duration is most often significantly reduced as the sessions go on.

Therapeutic work in hypnosis

Since the hypnotic state is induced, therapeutic ideas will be presented to patients through suggestions and metaphors.

Suggestions are ways of proposing creative solutions to the patient's problem. In Ericksonian hypnosis, unlike traditional hypnosis, the suggestion is not an order but rather "an opportunity to make a new experience in an attitude of availability" (Godin). To suggest something to a person is not to condemn them to obey it. A suggestion is only a suggestion, and the unconscious of the subject is free to refuse or accept it, in part or totally. The therapist's goal is not to instill in the patient any well-made solutions, but to enable the patient to develop his internal skills.

Metaphors are stories, tales, anecdotes bearing an apparent meaning that captures conscious attention and a hidden meaning proposing solutions to the patient's problem.

The action of suggestions and metaphors is the result of a psychological process called ideodynamicism. This natural phenomenon activates ideas to turn into an act or sensation (as the evocation of a lemon in the mouth can cause salivation).

In some cases, the therapist may conduct interactive sessions in which the patient's unconscious will be "questioned" or directly mobilized to solve a specific problem. Without wanting to be exhaustive, we can mention the technique of the affect bridge, and that of the somatic bridge used respectively to know the origin of a psychological problem and an organic disease. Some painful memories can be the subject of a restorative scenario. The therapist will help the patient to relive the painful scenes in hypnosis and transform them so that he can experience them with the resources he then lacked. We should also mention the regression in age, useful to find problematic moments of the past and progression in the future that helps the patient to project himself into a future free of the problem. However, it should be noted that this session requires an experienced therapist and that the patient has access to good quality trance.

The termination phase and the exit from the hypnotic state.

The completion of hypnosis is gradual. The actual exit from the hypnotic state will be preceded by a latency during which the practitioner will make positive post-hypnotic suggestions for relaxation and well-being. The therapist will then accompany the "wake-up call" by counting and asking the patient to go back to each figure stated gradually.

Post-hypnotic interview

Care will be taken to allow the person to narrate his experience from the trance, and this for at least two reasons. The first is that the person will give information that will allow the therapist to adapt his techniques as best as possible during the later sessions. The second reason is that during these interviews, the patient gives crucial indications about his psychology. However, hypnosis is a therapy in its own right and, as such, cannot worry about the symptom without worrying about the rest.

CHAPTER 8

PSYCHOANALYSIS TECHNIQUES
OF SIGMUND FREUD

In this chapter, we are going to examine carefully some questions that interest the theory, several topics that affect the technique, and a few issues that concern the clinic around which psychoanalysis takes on its entity. But before starting this, it is necessary to place this particular therapeutic method in its conceptual dimension. Psychoanalysis is a treatment of a psychological nature that takes place between a specialist and a person who needs help due to their emotional problems. "It is carried out by a systematized methodology and based on certain theoretical foundations, and its purpose is to eliminate or diminish the suffering and behavioral disorders derived from such alterations, through the interpersonal relationship between the therapist and the patient."

Unfortunately, and despite such laudable ends, psychoanalysis has carried unwanted connotations throughout its history. Some of them have referred to their fundamentally mentalistic character, others to their excessive medical dependence, and, some more, to their marked unscientific condition. Mentalists, for being based conceptually on constructs about the psychic apparatus and intrapsychic conflict, little accessible to observation. Medical, for having been in its origins an almost exclusive professional domain of the medical professional. Unscientific in that the analysis process cannot be

489

described operationally and unrepeatable, almost irreplaceable experiences are managed. These and other peculiarities have contributed to psychoanalysis being considered more as a practice than as an applied scientific discipline.

Definition of Psychoanalysis

Before going on to point out the fundamental aspects that psychoanalysis contributes to modern psychotherapy, it is necessary to remember, even briefly, the beginnings of scientific psychotherapy and the current conceptions among S. Freud's contemporaries, to show more clearly the dimension and importance of psychoanalytic contributions. For this reason, we want to begin by outlining our way of understanding Freud's work and our particular point of view on psychoanalysis as a therapeutic method. Quoting Freud more or less extensively serves several causes. The most important of them is that, despite some excellent attempts at systematization, today, the statement is that "the best way to understand psychoanalysis is to follow the trajectory of its genesis and its evolution." The assimilation of classical texts remains a prerequisite to be able to understand the current problems of psychoanalysis and to be able to find more adequate solutions to modern times.

With this original intention, on the other hand, we want to meet the sources that have fed the therapeutic aspect of psychoanalysis. For this reason, too, we try to make the passages we quote serve as support and justification for our opinions in the process of argumentative interaction with Freud himself. Using quotes and examples that determine and demonstrate which have been the lines of development that have led us from the origins of psychoanalysis to current intervention strategies, we aim to achieve a systematic description of psychoanalysis historically oriented. Why do we proceed in this way? Because, undoubtedly, the divergences and contradictions that appear in Freud's work, as well as its variations over the decades, testify to the opening of psychoanalysis, which "scores without leaving the support of experienced, is always considered unfinished, and he is always ready to rectify or replace his theories."

Since his Psychology Project (1895), Freud cherished the idea of integrating all his discoveries into the general body of science, just as it was conceived in his time. For this reason, when I had to describe and explain what else was psychoanalysis, underlining once again the inseparable bond between cure and research, he did not hesitate to define it as follows:

Psychoanalysis is the name:

1) Of a procedure for the investigation of mental processes more or less inaccessible by another means.

2) Of a method based on this research for the treatment of neurotic disorders.

3) A series of psychological conceptions acquired by this means and that progressively converge to form a new discipline.

This definition, which appeared in his article

Psychoanalysis and Libido Theory, is frequently cited because it delimits what the great ones must be psychoanalysis problems. Let us analyze, then, each one of the sections of this definition:

a) For Freud, psychoanalysis is a research method that leads to the discovery and knowledge of new psychological facts that are hardly accessible by any other means. From this point of view, Freud was separated from philosophy and said so, and viewed its creation as a branch of psychology and as a part of science. He said that science consists of the formulation of hypotheses that lead to observation, which brings order and clarity to the phenomena studied. In love with his method and amazed at the importance of his discoveries, he felt the need for tight and precise definitions, but he had to accept, not without qualms, during the early stages of certain science, aspects of vagueness in concepts and a certain degree of speculation in theories.

"The true principle of scientific activity consists rather in the description of phenomena, which are then grouped, ordered, and related to each other ... Only after having further developed the research in the field in question will we be able to formulate scientific concepts that make it up more clearly. Thus, we can gradually modify these concepts until they become widely applicable and, at the same time, acquire logical consistency".

This is why the claim of experimental verification of psychoanalytic facts using techniques derived from other research methods is so problematic. It is not that there can be no verification but that it is very difficult to carry out with other methods. Therefore, Rosenzweig wrote to Freud to explain the experimental results of the validation tests to which he had submitted some psychoanalytic concepts. He replied that "the psychoanalytic concepts were based on reliable and abundant observations and therefore did not need independent experimental verification. Attitudes like this did not favor the understanding or acceptance of those who studied the same field, although with different perspectives.

b) In the second section of the definition, an implicit reference is made to the therapeutic nature of psychoanalysis and, therefore, to the clinic. Although for some psychoanalysis is an occupation of aesthetes and dilettants, the clinical spirit constitutes the best defense against analytical academicism that tends, in its theorizing zeal, to replace concrete drama with a conflict of abstract entities. The clinical observation of the patient's behaviors is what suggests the hypothesis and allows its verification. The behavioral clinic is the one that proposes the therapy, controls its progress, and diagnoses the cure.

Thus, defining psychoanalysis as "the exploration of the unconscious " is insufficient. As Lagache (1969) rightly points out, a definition of psychoanalysis cannot be attempted by excluding it from the framework of clinical psychology of human behavior, the more specific character of which would be the attention it gives to transference. However, there is no doubt that there are discrepancies among analysts themselves about the scope

493

and meaning of the term psychoanalysis, as well as controversies regarding the types of contracts and the different frameworks and rhythms of work. There is a discrepancy, for example, about disorders accessible to psychoanalysis. Some contemporary psychoanalysts have been interested in the extension or application of psychoanalysis outside the field of neuroses. But other psychoanalysts ridicule his performance since they are convinced that those who decide to delve into the indecipherable world of psychoses, unfortunately, have launched into a company that falls outside the analytical task: "to use the technique that Freud instituted outside of the experience to which it is applied is to row when the boat is in the sand" (J. Lacan, quoted by Laplanche, 1974). In any case, and without going into the legitimacy of these positions, in our opinion, this is not the case, as evidenced by the abundant current literature on the treatment of psychosis, perversions, psychosomatic disorders, etc.

c) The third point of the definition ensures that psychoanalysis is a science. Throughout all his work, the reasons and arguments that Freud uses to underline the scientific nature of his investigations multiply. Even with all the doubts and hesitations that may arise in someone who is only beginning to glimpse the vast possibilities offered by his research method, the creator of psychoanalysis was fully convinced of the suitability and truthfulness of his hypotheses that, in daily practice from the clinic, they were shown to him as undoubtedly plausible. So much so that, since his Psychology Project (1895), Freud always cherished the idea of integrating the set of his discoveries in the general body of science, at least, as they were conceived in his time. No doubt for Freud, the psychoanalytic method created a "New scientific discipline."

In his opinion, when analyzing a patient's psychoanalysis works scientifically, try to put your expectations aside and embrace patient data as it arises. He collects many disparate pieces of the patient's speech, pieces that seem not to match each other, and establishes laws to order and organize such disparate data. These laws or rules are contrasted with subsequent observations made during the analysis. Furthermore, the observations obtained from one patient are contrasted with those of another patient, and the observations of one analyst are contrasted with those of other analysts. As if this were not enough, the work's observations with the patients are in contrast with cultural documents, such as myths, legends, artistic material or folk customs, rituals, religious beliefs, etc. Even as Pervin (1979) points out, psychoanalytic hypotheses can be contrasted with observations extracted from psychological tests administered on a large scale.

It is clear, then, that this research method allows obtaining a large amount of data about a subject. There is possibly no other psychology procedure that does not even come close to the wealth of material obtained from a single person by the psychoanalyst. However, the analyst, unlike other scientists, does not carry out experiments — Freud himself pointed out. This is the great obstacle, the great pending subject, that psychoanalysis has to face. However, this great gap between experimentality and psychoanalysis has been narrowing to the extent that, in the last thirty years, some researchers have directed their interest towards psychoanalysis. Some analysts have tried to validate certain contents of the theory empirically.

Unfortunately, despite this approach of positions and these attempts at empirical validation, the claim that psychoanalysis is a natural science is not endorsed by all analysts. There is a current of thought within psychoanalysis, also supported by some non-psychoanalytic philosophers such as P. Ricoeur (1970) and J. Habermas (1971), who considers that psychoanalysis does not belong at all to the natural sciences, but is a science interpretive, in Ricoeur's words, a hermeneutic. In J. Blight's (1981) opinion, this renunciation of psychoanalysis as science has its origin in the publication of the proceedings of the symposium led by S. Hook, a symposium intended to discuss the place that corresponds to psychoanalysis within the world of science. (Hook 1959, Nagel 1959). From this event, a significant number of psychoanalysts decided that it was not worth the effort to find arguments that refute the criticisms that psychoanalysis was receiving and that it was unnecessary to seek new forms of research with which to validate or refute, psychoanalytic hypotheses, in order to accredit psychoanalysis as a scientific method.

To the question, Freud asks himself in Some Elementary Lessons on Psychoanalysis (1940) about what else psychoanalysis can be if it is not a science. They answered that psychoanalysis was something different from natural science; it was a hermeneutical science. These authors, and others with them, maintain that Freudian metapsychology, which tries to explain the causes of psychic processes, is like a foreign body in the psychoanalytic building that must be eliminated. Starting from the basis that two theories coexist in psychoanalysis, the clinical-psychological theory, which seeks to interpret the reasons and motives for human behavior — that is, to understand — and the metapsychological theory, which seeks to delimit and define the causes of This behavior — that is to say, explain — carried out what Blight calls an "atherectomy," an amputation of one of the theories, the metapsychological one, considering that it was nothing more than an erroneous sample of Freud's fidelity to the positivism of his time.

In summary, then, we can say that in psychoanalysis, despite these theoretical discrepancies, there has always been an inseparable union between healing and research, knowledge brought success, and it was not possible to try without finding something new, nor did you gain clarification without experiencing its therapeutic effect. "Our analytical procedure is the only one in which this precious conjunction remains assured. Only if we practice our analytical spiritual guide will we be able to deepen our developing conception of the human mind.

The Psychoanalysis Technique

For historians, López Piñero and Morales Meseguer (1970), psychotherapy in the strict sense did not appear until the middle years of the 19th century, when a series of British doctors, WB Carpenter and DH Tuke especially, began to think of new ideas about the relations between the body and the mind and regarding hypnotic techniques since hypnotism made possible the investigation of automatic, unconscious processes and the relation body-mind. However, it was James Braid (1795-1860), a prestigious Scottish surgeon, who took the decisive step from animal magnetism to "nervous sleep" or hypnosis. Despite all the criticism, Braid immediately grasped the healing possibilities of the hypnotic procedure, and in 1843 he risked publishing his seminal work, Neurypnology, where he exposes his method and the properties of the hypnotic state.

Hypnotism was welcomed by some British authors as a therapeutic hope, a progress that could generate changes in the patient's diseases, but the main thing is that these initial works were not isolated, but had a great influence on the evolution of French psychotherapy. Indeed, from 1860 the French became interested in the subject of "nervous sleep." This was the year in which Liébeault began the practice of hypnotism, and shortly afterward, Théodule Ribot (1839-1916) introduced texts on English and German positive psychology in France. This growing interest in hypnotism led to the emergence of two important schools in France that, at the same time that they studied the subject of hypnosis, advanced in the clinical care of neurotics.

Thus, as Horacio Etchegoyen (1986) suggests, it can be said

that psychoanalysis is undoubtedly a special form of psychotherapy. Psychotherapy begins to be considered scientific in nineteenth-century France. The two were founded and developed great schools on the suggestion that we have already mentioned in the previous chapter, one of them in Nancy, with Liébeault and Bernheim, and the other in Salpêtrière, with Jean-Martin Charcot. Precisely, the rivalry between the two schools — Charcot thought that hypnosis, far from being a method of curing diseases, was something related to hysterics, and at the same time, Liébeault argued that hypnosis was a normal phenomenon that could be induced in most people — mark the 1880s to 1890s. This statement can certainly be disputed, but there is no doubt that the climate of research on hysteria and hypnosis in France greatly influenced the young Sigmund Freud.

For what we have just said, and without wishing to review its history again, the birth of psychotherapy can be linked to France in the mid-nineteenth century. When Auguste Ambroise Liébeault turns his humble rural practice into the most important hypnotism research center in the world, this ancient technique, which twenty years before had received a name and endorsement from Braid, begins to be applied, at the same time, as an instrument of research and as a therapeutic technique. Liébeault uses it to show "the influence of morality on the body" and to "cure the sick"; the importance of their work is such that many authors do not hesitate to locate the beginning of psychotherapy in Nancy.

We will accept this statement with a single objection. The hypnotic treatment that Liébeault inaugurates is, without a doubt, personal and direct. Message and drug at the same time, are addressed to the psyche of the patient with the evident intention of curing him. Truthfully, there is still something missing to be psychotherapy: the patient receives the doctor's curative influence in a passive attitude. He does not actively and dynamically participate in the process. From a demanding point of view, the treatment used in Nancy's school is personal, but not interpersonal. Only when H. Bernheim, following the lines of Liébeault's research, places increasing emphasis on suggestion as to the source of the hypnotic and motor effect of human behavior, does the doctor-patient interaction emerge as one of the defining characteristics of the psychotherapy.

In his New Studies (1891), Bernheim reveals the amazing value of suggestion as a therapeutic agent in the treatment of hysteria, showing that the relationship between the hypnotized and the hypnotist is one of the cornerstones that support this particular type of intervention. Shortly afterward, the works of P. Janet in Paris and J. Breuer and S. Freud in Vienna, where the interpersonal relationship is increasingly evident and forced, partially give reason to these first intuitions of the School from Nancy. When Janet and Freud tried to cure the rich hysterical symptoms, they realized, each on their own, the enormous importance that some psychic aspects had in this pathology that went beyond the space of consciousness (unconscious) and that therefore, the therapist-patient relationship had to be necessarily one of the fundamental axes of any type of psychotherapy. From this moment, any treatment aimed at the patient's psyche will be considered as psychotherapy, in a framework of interpersonal relationship, and supported by a scientific theory of personality.

As Etchegoyen (1986) rightly points out, Freud psychotherapy has some characteristic features that stand out for its historical evolution. Through its method, psychotherapy addresses the psyche through the only practicable way: communication, whose instrument is the word (or rather verbal and pre-verbal language). Message and drug at the same time; its framework is the therapist-patient interpersonal relationship. And finally, its purpose is to heal, and any communication process that does not have that purpose (teaching, indoctrination, etc.) will never be psychotherapy.

However, as the scientific methods of suggestive and hypnotic psychotherapy reach their maximum development, a new line of research begins that must operate a Copernican turn in the theory and practice of psychotherapy. Towards 1880, Joseph Breuer (1842-1925), applying the hypnotic technique to a patient who, in the annals of our discipline, was named Anna O. (and whose real name was Bertha Pappenheim), found himself practicing a radically different form of psychotherapy.

Freud's new technique: Psychoanalysis

From what has been said so far, we can consider that the

therapeutic method practiced by Freud and known by the name of psychoanalysis has its point starting in the cathartic procedure, whose description has been detailed by J. Breuer and Freud himself in work published jointly by them under the title of Studies on hysteria (1895). Cathartic therapy was a discovery by Breuer, who had obtained, ten years before, the cure of a hysterical woman, in whose treatment she also came to glimpse the pathogenesis of the symptoms that the patient presented. The cathartic procedure had as its main premise that the patient was hypnotizable. Its effectiveness rested fundamentally on the expansion of the field of consciousness that took place during the hypnotic trance. The hypnotized memories, ideas, and impulses that had been absent until then in her consciousness emerged. Once the subject communicated to the doctor, between intense affective manifestations, such emotional processes, the symptoms were overcome, and their reappearance was avoided.

However, this simple therapeutic intervention scheme was complicated in almost all cases, as it turned out that a single traumatic impression was not usually involved in the genesis of the symptom, but rather that a good number of them were usually associated with the symptom. Furthermore, Freud always declared himself a bad hypnotist, perhaps because it was true or because, in reality, the cathartic method did not satisfy his scientific curiosity. And that was how he decided to abandon hypnosis and develop a new technique that would help him to get to the essence of trauma, a technique more in line with his idea of the psychological reason for wanting to forget the traumatic event. In any case, if the cathartic method had given up suggestions, Freud went one step further and gave up hypnosis.

He dared to take this bold step by recalling a famous experience of post-hypnotic suggestion, carried out by Bernheim, which he had to witness during his stay at the clinic in Nancy. When the experimenter gave a person a hypnotic trance to do something after awakening, the order was carried out exactly, and the author could not explain the reason for his actions and appealed to trivial explanations. However, if the investigator did not comply with these rationalizations (as E. Jones would call them many years later), the subject ended up remembering the order received when he was in a trance. And on this basis, he changed his technique: instead of hypnotizing his patients, he began to stimulate them, to invite them to remember.

This is how Freud operated with Miss Lucy and especially with Elisabeth von R., and this new technique, associative coercion, confronted him with new facts that would have to modify his theories again. Associative coercion confirmed to Freud that things are forgotten when you do not want to remember them. You do not want to remember them because they are painful, ugly, and unpleasant, contrary to ethics and aesthetics. This process of repression, this selective forgetfulness, was reproduced before his eyes in treatment, and then he found that his patients did not want to remember, that there was a force that opposed the memory. This is how Freud discovers resistance, the cornerstone of psychoanalysis. What at the moment of trauma conditioned forgetfulness is what at this moment, in treatment, conditions resistance: there is a play of forces, a conflict between the desire to remember and the desire to forget. And if this is so, then coercion is no longer justified, because you will always stumble upon resistance. Better to let the patient speak, to speak freely. In this curious way, a new theory, the theory of resistance, leads to a new technique: Free Association, typical of psychoanalysis, which is introduced as a technical precept, as a fundamental rule.

With this newly created technical instrument, new and surprising facts will be discovered, against which the theory of trauma and pathogenic memory gradually gives way to sexual theory. Conflict, for example, is no longer a matter that concerns only the will to remember and the desire to forget. On the contrary, there is now a tendency to interpret conflict as a problem between mechanical forces and repressive forces. From this moment on, the findings multiply infantile sexuality and the Oedipus complex, the unconscious with its laws and its contents, the theory of transfer, etc. It is a new context of great discoveries in which interpretation appears as the fundamental technical instrument. When it was just a matter of retrieving a memory, neither the cathartic method nor the associative coercion required interpretation. Now everything is different, and now the subject has to be given precise reports about himself and what is happening to him so that he can better understand his psychological reality, that is, that this revealing action must be carried out by force. In psychoanalysis, it is called interpreting.

In other words, in the first decade of the century, the theory of resistance expanded vigorously in two directions: on the one hand, the unconscious (the resisted) was discovered with its laws (condensation, displacement) and its contents (libido theory), and on the other hand, the theory of transfer emerges, a precise way of defining the doctor-patient relationship. Indeed, the first glimpses of the discovery of transference are found in the Studies on Hysteria (1895). In Dora's epilogue, written in January 1901 and published in 1905, the phenomenon of transference is already practically completely deciphered. It is precisely from that moment when the new theory begins to influence the technique and imprints its Councils to the doctor (1912) and on the initiation of treatment (1913), contemporary works on the dynamics of transfer.

The immediate repercussion of transfer theory on technique is a reformulation of the analytical relationship, which from now on, will be defined in precise and rigorous terms. The frame, we will see, is nothing more than the technical response to what Freud had understood in the clinic about the peculiar relationship of the analyst and his analysand. The belle époque of the technique in which the famous Man of Rats was invited to tea and herring has been definitively closed. For the transference to emerge clearly and the patient to be properly analyzed, Freud said in 1912, the analyst must take the place of a mirror that only reflects what is shown to him.

In any case, the coherence between theory and technique is understood at this point. The doctor must show nothing of himself: without letting himself be wrapped in the nets of the transfer, he will simply return to the patient what he has placed on the smooth mirror of his technique. For this reason, Freud (1915) says, study the love of transference, that the analysis must be developed in abstinence, which sanctions the substantial change of the technique in the second decade of the century. If there were no transference theory, there would be no reason for this advice to be entirely unnecessary in the cathartic method or the primitive psychoanalysis of associative coercion. Here again, we see this unique interaction between theory and technique that we point out as specific to psychoanalysis.

On the other hand, if we have discussed transfer theory in some detail here, it is because it clearly illustrates the thesis we are developing. As Freud becomes aware of the transference, its intensity, its complexity, and its spontaneity (although this is still being discussed today), a radical change in the frame is imposed on him. The lax framing of the Rat Man, which included tea, sandwiches, and herrings, is made more rigorous by the theory of transference, a fact that in turn allows greater precision in the appreciation of the transference phenomenon as long as that a stricter and more stable framing avoids the possible manipulations of the participants and makes it sharper, more transparent.

The Interpretation Of Dreams

"If I cannot reconcile the heavenly gods, I will move those of hell."

Already in the preface to the first edition of the Interpretation of Dreams (1900), Freud refers to the dream phenomenon as the first link in a series of abnormal psychic manifestations that interest the doctor for practical reasons, since for whoever fails to understand and explain the genesis of dream images, it will be difficult to understand the nature of phobias, obsessive ideas or delusions, and much less will they be able to exert a possible therapeutic influence on such pathologies. Furthermore, he is convinced that he can demonstrate the existence of a psychological technique that allows us to interpret dreams: psychoanalysis, a technique thanks to which each dream is revealed as "a psychic product full of meaning, to which it can be assigned a perfectly determined place in the soul activity of the awakened life."

Encouraged by this conviction, Freud carries out an exhaustive examination of the literature existing up to that time on dreams and the scientific status of dream problems, trying to clarify the processes on which the "singular and impenetrable appearance of dreams" depends — and trying to deduce from these processes a reliable conclusion about the nature of those psychic forces from whose joint or opposite action the dream phenomenon arises. The difficulty of writing a history of our scientific knowledge of dream phenomena is enormous, since, despite the efforts of many authors, it has not been possible to establish a firm base of indisputable results on which other researchers could continue building. Still, each author has started anew, and from the beginning, the study of the same phenomena.

The people of classical antiquity, for example, admitted that dreams were about the world of superhuman beings of their mythology and brought with them divine or demonic revelations, also possessing a certain intention regarding the subject: to announce the future. In the two studies that Aristotle dedicates to this matter, on the contrary, dreams appear as a much more human question: they are not divine, but demonic since Nature is demonic and not divine. To put it another way, dreams do not correspond to a supernatural revelation but obey the laws of our human spirit, although later, this spirit is closely related to divinity. Dreams are thus defined as "the mental activity of the sleeper during the resting state."

It would be wrong, however, to suppose that the theory of the supernatural origin of dreams already lacks supporters at present. On the contrary, we still find "men of subtle ingenuity," and inclined to everything extraordinary, who try to support the insolubility of dream enigma and religious faith in the existence and intervention of superhuman spiritual forces. For this reason, and since it has not been possible to analyze and master all the existing literature on this matter, Freud prefers to adapt his exposition on dreams to the themes and not to the authors, indicating in the study of each one of the dream enigmas the material that we can find for the solution of the same in previous works and authors. Let's discuss some of these puzzles below:

1. Relationship of sleep with awake life. Regarding this dream enigma, and in light of the literature that he has been able to handle, Freud raises the existence of two opposed positions. On the one hand, that defended by the old physiologist Burdach, to whom we owe a conscientious description of dreamlike phenomena, which states that "daytime life, with its works and pleasures, its joys and sorrows, is never repeated; on the contrary, the dream tends to free us from it. Even in those moments in which our whole soul is saturated by an object, in which a deep pain tears our inner life, or a work monopolizes all our spiritual forces, the dream gives us something alien to our situation; it only takes significant fragments of reality for its combinations, or it merely acquires the tone of our state of mind and symbolizes real circumstances" (OC p. 352). On the other hand, the one that gathers the widespread conviction that most dreams, despite their apparent singularity, lead us back to ordinary life instead of freeing ourselves from it. Jessen affirms in his Psychology (1855), "to a greater or lesser degree, the content of dreams is always determined by the individual personality, by age, sex, position, degree of culture and gender of the routine life of the subject, and by the events and teachings of his past. For his part, Freud openly declares himself in favor of this second option, resorting to the theories of FW Hildebrandt (1875) on the dream to justify his position:

"However unique their formations may be, they cannot become independent from the real world, and all their creations, both the most sublime and the most ridiculous, must always take their fundamental theme from what in the sensory world has appeared before our eyes or has found in any way a place of our waking thought; that it is, from what we have already lived before exterior or interior mind.

2. The dream material. Memory in the dream. There is no doubt that most of the material that makes up the content of the dream comes from what is lived and is, therefore, reproduced — remembered — in the dream. However, it would be a mistake to suppose that a mere comparison between the content of the dream and the events of awakened life is sufficient to show the relationship between them. On the contrary, only after painstaking and careful observation and analysis did we discover their links, and even, in some cases, managed to remain hidden for a long time. We observe, first of all, that in the content of the dream appears a material that later, in the awakened life, is not recognized as belonging to our knowledge or our experience. We remember, of course, that we have dreamed of this or that occurrence, but we do not remember ever having lived it. We are surprised and puzzled by the content of our dreams, being unable to explain from what source the dream has taken its components and in what subtle way they have become integrated. Despite this not very encouraging panorama, Freud seems to be very clear about things:

a) One of the sources from which the dream extracts the material it reproduces is the child's life, the childhood of the individual.

b) Elements can be discovered in dreams (people, objects, places, events, etc.) that correspond to experiences lived in the immediately preceding days, what Freud calls "day remains".

c) In the selection of the material that we reproduce in dreams, it is not always the most important thing that is taken into account, as happens in the awake life, but the most indifferent and trivial.

3. Stimuli and sources of dreams. The discussion about the provoking causes of dreams has always occupied a prominent place in dream literature. Whether the provocative stimulus of dreams was always the same or could vary, and parallel to whether the causal explanation of the dream phenomenon corresponds to Psychology or Physiology, has been present since an ancient theory was first proposed. Who considers dreams as a disturbance of rest: "we would not have dreamed if our rest had not been disturbed by a specific cause, the dream being, therefore, a reaction to such a disturbance? Regarding the sources of sleep, Freud recognizes the existence of four different types of dream sources, a differentiation that has also served as a basis for classifying dreams: external (objective) sensory stimuli, such as an intense light that reaches our eyes, a noise to our ears or a smell to our nose; the internal (subjective) sensory stimuli, in reference to those subjective, visual or auditory sensations, that hardly cross the threshold of perception and that in the waking state are known to us as luminous chaos of the dark visual field, ringing of ears, etc.; internal (organic) somatic stimuli, the result of the excitement or alteration of our internal organs, which in health state hardly give us any news of their existence, but which during states of excitement or illness become a source of sensations, mostly painful, equivalent to stimuli from outside; and, finally, the purely psychic sources of stimulation, a not insignificant oneiric source that supposes that the interests of the awakened life (occupations and daily worries) pass to the state of rest, justifying the presence of some of the contents of the dream.

4. Oneiric theories. Since sleep has become an important object of study for different disciplines (biology, physiology, psychology, etc.), a more than a considerable number of dream theories have emerged that try to reveal its enigmatic nature and its controversial function. Even though they are not the most rigorous and successful, among them Freud highlights:

a) Those theories that consider that during sleep, the psychic activity of wakefulness lasts. According to them, the soul does not sleep. Its processes remain intact but subject to the conditions of the state of rest, different from those of wakefulness, it produces, even when operating normally, different yields: dreams. Unfortunately, these theories do not explain why we dream or why the complicated mechanism of the psychic apparatus continues to function even after being placed in circumstances for which it is not prepared. The only appropriate reactions in this situation would be to sleep without dreams or to wake up when a disturbing stimulus occurs, but never to dream.

b) Those theories that accept that sleep is the result of a decrease in psychic activity and a weakening of coherence, theories, widely applauded by medical authors and, in general, by the scientific world, from which it follows that rest extends to the soul but fails to isolate it from the outside world completely, but penetrates its mechanism, making it temporarily unusable. Thus, the dream phenomenon must be considered as the result of an imperfect performance of the soul as a partial vigil, which allows us to explain the absurdity of some of its contents. Regarding the validity of this theory of partial wakefulness, numerous objections have been raised, most of them emphasizing its inability to explain: "Firstly, rest and wakefulness, and secondly, why some forces of the soul act in the dream while others rest" (Burdach, 1830).

c) In a third section, we can group those theories that ascribe to the dreaming soul the power to perform certain psychic functions that in the waking situation it cannot carry out or can only do very incompletely. The state of rest is, then, the time-lapse in which the soul recovers and accumulates new energies for daytime labor. To put it another way, dreams protect us against the monotony and vulgarity of existence, and they are a kind of psychic vacation. Therefore, we will have to see in them "a charming faculty and a friendly company in our pilgrimage towards the tomb."

5. Sleep function. Based on his extensive studies on dreams, Freud thought that dreaming fulfills two basic functions in psychic life: a) protecting the rest of the dreamer by converting the material and stimuli that could potentially disturb his rest into images and content type of dreaming; and b) satisfying during rest, even if virtually, those desires that the dreamer has not been able to satisfy in the waking state. To put it in other words, far from being foolish or absurd, dreams for Freud are the guardian of sleep, while representing a curious and very particular way of satisfying desires. Freud's theory seems supported by the fact that the small alterations that occur during rest are often incorporated in dreams, preventing them from waking us up at night. An intense nose, a change in temperature, hunger pangs, or strong pressure on the bladder can be incorporated into dream material (directly or symbolically), preventing the dreamer from finally waking up. Freud also proposes a second and more important function of dreaming: his famous theory of wish-fulfillment. Unmet needs, frustrated yearnings, contrary desires, are fully compensated during sleep, thanks to mysterious alchemy, in all its details, although, virtually, it is true. So much so that even the role of the guardian of sleep can be considered as a wish-fulfillment, since, after all, we dream because we want to stay asleep.

6. Structure of the dream. Thanks to the work of dream interpretation, Freud concludes that in the structure of dreams it is necessary to differentiate between the manifest content and the latent content — latent ideas — while proposing a new line of research for psychoanalysis: analyzing the relations between both contents and find out by which process the manifest content has emerged from the latest ideas. As for the manifest content, we must say what the dream develops before us, what we remember, and what we submit to interpretation. It is the dream as it is presented by the subject that carries out the narration, the difficult work of the dreamlike elaboration that, arbitrarily, presents it to us as if it were a hieroglyph, for whose solution we will have to translate each of its signs into the language of the latent ideas. Regarding the latent content, we will say that it is the experience (desires, experiences, memories, etc.) that motivates the dream and gives rise to the manifest content. It consists of daily remains, body impressions, childhood memories, and transference residues that give meaning to the manifest content. It constitutes the set of meanings to which the analysis leads and is, of course, before the manifest content and cause.

This being the case, we must now ask why it is necessary to make this distinction between latent content and manifest content, what are the reasons that justify such differentiation and, of course, why the contents of the dream are not identical. Freud, apparently, is very clear about the answer to these three questions: censorship, it is responsible for the deformation of the dream and, therefore, for the latent/manifest differentiation to which we have referred. Oneiric censorship is defined by Freud as that function that tends to prevent latent ideas from accessing consciousness, that is, the function that stops the transformation of latent ideas into manifest content, a function that acts by suppressing or merging elements of the dream, changing its hierarchy, substituting one element for another — or a symbol — displacing its center of gravity and/or its importance, etc. A task that he carries out against those deplorable ideas that we don't even want to think about.

7. The dream production. Freud describes dream-making as the work of the dreamer's psyche to transform latent dream ideas into manifest content. From this perspective, the dream that we awakened to remember would only be a summary of the dream-making process that, based on latent ideas, the dreamer has carried out while sleeping. As the subject cannot explicitly dream of everything he really wants, envies or ambitions without being assailed by an insufferable feeling of guilt (repression), in a Machiavellian display of adaptation, he masks those latent ideas that are rejectable from an ethical point of view, aesthetic, social or cultural so that they can find through the dream a way of expression and satisfaction, even if it is only virtual. We must say, therefore, that the dream-making work is completed with the presentation of a story (dream) that runs during the rest, a story that has been built from the latest ideas, which are those that reveal the true sense of sleep.

To carry out this arduous masking task, the dream-making basically uses five mechanisms: condensation, displacement, symbolization, dramatization, and the transformation of ideas into visual images.

a) Condensation. Condensation is considered by Freud as one of the most important mechanisms in the dream-making work. Specifically, he defines it as that oneiric elaboration mechanism by which various ideas or elements of the latent content come together in a single image or representation of the manifest content, a grouping that, in his opinion, is mainly due to economic causes. In fact, Freud considers that the manifest content is nothing more than the abbreviated translation of a group of latent ideas that have been grouped into a disharmonic unit in the manifest content (for example, a character made up of fragments or parts of others).

The manifesto is concise, poor, and laconic compared to the breadth and richness of latent ideas. In short, the condensation process makes the account of the manifest content much shorter than the description of the latent content.

b) Displacement. Displacement is an unconscious psychic process theorized by Freud in the framework of the analysis of dreams. Basically, it is an oneiric elaboration mechanism that, using an associative slip, transforms the essential elements of a latent content into secondary details of a manifest content. Although it can also act in other ways (for example, causing one element to be replaced by another), it is a mechanism that generally intervenes in the elaboration of dreams, causing the accent, interest, intensity and/or significance of a latent element is detached from it to go on to impregnate elements of the manifest content originally little or little intense, although linked by an associative chain to the first. In this way, the fundamental meaning of the dream can appear in the manifest content as an accessory or secondary element, and, conversely, the most important element of the manifest content can be presented as a secondary element of authentic meaning. Thus, the displacement causes the meaning to be transferred from the central part of the dream to its accessory places, thus hiding from the dreamer the true nature of his dreams.

c) **Symbolization.** It is, without a doubt, the most important dream elaboration mechanism. It consists of the indirect and figurative representation through symbols of a latent idea of a conflict or of an unconscious desire. This makes the analyst's task of understanding the dream essentially an interpretation task: the analyst has to move from the level of the symbol — located at the level of manifest content — to the level of meaning — located at the level of latent content. Religion, myths and fables, and art are also modes of symbolization that can be interpreted in the same terms as dreams. For Freud, the knowledge of symbols is not conscious, but neither is it arbitrary. Most of them are universal and require an interpretation of erotic or sexual nature, but must always be interpreted, taking into account the biography and personality of the subject.

d) **Dramatization.** Thanks to this oneiric elaboration mechanism, the dream presents, albeit covertly, distorted or surreptitiously, a latent idea, a conflict or a desire of the subject in a more or less complete story format; the dream turns a static reality, such as appetite, a need or past experience, into a dynamic reality in which various characters intervene and interact and develop an authentic drama.

e) Transformation of ideas into visual images. There is no doubt that the tasks of condensation, displacement, and symbolization are fundamental when it comes to an understanding and explaining the process of making dreams. However, we will still have to add another way, less intense but equally valid, of dreamlike deformation: the transformation of ideas into images. If, as it seems, we dream in the form of sensory images, there must be a psychic process that is responsible for transforming the latent ideas of the dream into images of this type. The argument is quite simple; if the manifest content of the dream is almost always made up of visual situations, the latent ideas must, above all, have to adopt a disposition that makes them suitable for this peculiar form of exposition.

8. Secondary elaboration. This action supposes a second time in the work of elaboration of the dream, affecting, consequently, the products already elaborated by the other oneiric elaboration mechanisms (condensation, displacement, symbolization, etc.). Ultimately, it is a dreamlike elaboration mechanism that aspires to give coherence to the dream through the selection and arrangement of the material, the insertion of associative links, and inclusion in an intelligible context. The most perceptible consequence of this action is that the dream loses its primitive aspect of delirium and approaches the context of a rational event. Subtracting the dream from its primitive appearance of absurdity and incoherence, filling its gaps, making a partial or total recomposition of its elements and recomposing it in such a way that it can be presented in the form of a relatively coherent and understandable script, is the aim of what Freud called secondary elaboration or also the consideration of representability.

Psychopathology Of Everyday Life

Psychopathology of everyday life (1901) is a work in which Freud, based on a subject as trivial as forgetfulness, errors, and mistakes, tries to delve into the unconscious mechanisms of the human psyche. In it, the creator of psychoanalysis expresses with great simplicity and no less insight the existence of a double functioning in psychic life: the conscious and the unconscious, a double functioning that, at times, ends up causing a real short circuit in saying and/or in the doing of the subject (forgetfulness, absent-mindedness, clumsiness, loss, etc.). In fact, the study detailed of phenomena of such anodyne appearance allow Freud to argue in an easily understandable way the endemic influence of unconscious material on the whole of conscious life. So much so that Peter Gay, in his biography of Freud (1988), goes so far as to affirm that the father of psychoanalysis deliberately chose the interpretation of these small facts of daily life as the starting point of his fruitful work.

Freud, apparently, was very clear that the goal of this work was to attract attention to things that everyone knows and experiences, to current everyday events, to subject them to rigorous scientific examination and to demonstrate, without any doubt, the accuracy of his proposals on the unconscious psyche. Furthermore, a tenacious defender of the thesis of an absolute psychic determinism that postulates that every physical event, including human thought and actions, is causally determined by the unshakable cause-consequence chain, Freud tries to demonstrate, as he recalls several times in the book, that the field of action of psychoanalysis should not be limited to the domain of pathology. On the contrary, to the wisdom acquired thanks to the conscientious analysis of the different clinical cases, we must add the wisdom derived from the experiences of everyday life, which, according to Freud, should never be denied a place in acquisitions, of the science.

Specifically, Psychopathology of everyday life is a work that is divided into twelve chapters dedicated to the different forms of forgetfulness, lapses, errors, awkwardness and other failed acts, a sensible division whose criteria is as arbitrary as descriptive, since as the author himself acknowledges, the phenomena studied have a logical internal coherence to which every book testifies. The first chapter, for example, deals with the forgetting of proper names, a period of memory that Freud tries to explain, arguing that human beings always try to forget what bothers, displeases or disturbs us, and which therefore has a lot to do with the repression mechanism.

The summary of the conditions for forgetting names is as follows: a) that there be a certain provision for forgetting the name in question; b) that a repressive process took place a short time before; c) an associative link is created between the name that is not remembered and the previously repressed element.

In the next two chapters, Freud uses several examples of forgetting names, foreign words and series of words in which he believes that this proposal is confirmed, a proposal that extends to all failed acts: the forgotten or deformed comes into connection, for any associative path, with an unconscious psychic content, from which that influence manifests itself in the form of forgetfulness, mistakes, errors and/or lapses. It should not be forgotten, he assures us, that the analysis of forgetting leads us, almost always, to intimate matters of the analyzed, sometimes even unpleasant and painful for him.

Failed act:

An act in which the explicitly pursued result is not obtained but manifests a different form of expression and still contrary to the original intention of the subject. It assumes the existence of two purposes: the disturbed and the disturbing. It can be in action, in verbal speech, or in gesture.

Features:

1. The subject is capable of performing the act correctly.

2. It is a momentary and temporary disturbance.

3. It is within the limits of normality.

4. The incorrectness of the act is immediately recognized.

5. It does not affect important areas of behavior.

6. There is an association between what is repressed and what is not remembered.

Childhood memories and cloaking memories are addressed, memories in which, apparently, the subject seems to have kept the most insignificant and secondary of his life, while the really important events do not seem to have left any mark in his memory. These indifferent childhood memories, Freud observes, owe their existence to a process of displacement, being nothing more than a substitute representation of other truly important impressions, the memory of which can be extracted from them through psychic analysis, but whose direct reproduction is hindered by a resistance (hence the expression "cover-up memory ").

As for the temporal relationship between this concealing memory and the transcendental fact that is hidden behind it, Freud believes it is necessary to differentiate three types of displacement: regressive, progressive, and simultaneous. Displacement is called regressive when the content of the covering memory belongs to the first years of childhood, and the life experiences replaced by it in memory — which remain unconscious — correspond to later years of the subject's life. On the contrary, in those cases in which an indifferent impression of early childhood is fixed in memory as a covering memory because of its association with previous experience, against whose reproduction a resistance rises (what is chronologically important is behind the covering memory), the displacement is called progressive.

Finally, the third type of displacement can be presented, the simultaneous one, in which the covering memory is associated with the impression that it conceals not only for its content but also for its continuity in time.

Freud analyzes oral mistakes (lapsus linguae), mistakes in reading and writing, forgetfulness of impressions and purposes, errors and misguided acts combined, giving them the same treatment as forgetfulness, since which considers that, like memory lapses, they are daily episodes that are accepted naturally without suspecting that they contain a covert-unconscious-intention, which cannot be brought to consciousness except through penetrating analysis. Now, to be included in the order of phenomena to which this explanation can be applied, a failed psychic functioning must meet the following requirements:

a) Not exceed to a certain extent what common sense considers as "Within the limits of normal."

b) Possess the character of momentary and temporary disturbance. The subject immediately recognizes the incorrectness of the act since he has been able to execute it correctly previously.

c) Be explained as a "lack of attention" or a "coincidence," since there is not the slightest hint of intent in carrying out the act.

Thus, and convinced that the failed acts "express something that the actor himself does not suspect," something that "escapes conscious intention," Freud tries to explain the presence of such acts in our daily life by enunciating the following principle: "Certain insufficiencies of our psychic functioning and certain apparently unintended acts are shown to be motivated and determined by unknown motives of conscience when subjected to the psychoanalytic investigation." In this way, the cases of forgetfulness, the mistakes made in the exposition of subjects that are perfectly known to us, the mistakes in reading and writing, the acts of erroneous term and the so-called accidental acts, all phenomena in which the main is the loss of intention, they become material for analysis, being able to refer to "an incompletely repressed psychic material, which is rejected by the conscience, but which has not been stripped of all capacity to externalize itself."

Finally, we will have to comment that Psychopathology of everyday life concludes with an exemplified chapter dedicated to the questions of determinism, beliefs and superstition, three original and controversial topics whose development forces Freud to confess that, unfortunately, "I belong to those Unworthy individuals in whose eyes the spirits hide their activity and from whom the supernatural departs so that nothing has ever happened to me that has brought about in me the faith in the wonderful. Like all men, I have had presentiments and misfortunes that have happened to me, but these have never corresponded to those. My presentiments have not been realized, and the misfortunes have come to me unannounced ... Nor have any of the presentiments that have been reported to me by my patients ever been able to achieve my recognition as a real phenomenon". It would be, therefore, correct to affirm that the failed act is, in synthesis, a kind of betrayal that our psyche does to us by revealing an unconscious desire or intention, a betrayal that finds its reason for being in the evidence that "in the psychic, there is nothing arbitrary or indeterminate."

Psychoanalytical Theory Of Neurosis

As is known, the theory and technique of psychoanalysis base their fundamental premises on clinical data from the study of neuroses. Understood as "psychogenic conditions whose symptoms are the symbolic expression of a psychic conflict that has its roots in the subject's childhood history and constitutes commitments between desire and defense" (Laplanche and Pontalis, 1987), neuroses still provide the original material more solid and reliable for the formulation of psychoanalytic theory. So much so that to understand the theory of psychoanalytic technique, Greenson assures in his Technique and Practice of Psychoanalysis (1976), it is necessary to have a broad practical knowledge of the psychoanalytic theory of neuroses.

Historical background

The Scottish physician first used the term neurosis and chemist William Cullen (1710-1790) in his Synopsis nosologiae exact (1769) to refer to sensory and motor disorders caused by diseases of the nervous system. In this ancient work, Cullen describes neuroses as "preternatural affections of sense and movement in which pyrexia — non-symptomatic fever — is in no way part of the primitive disease, and which does not depend on a local condition of the organs, but of a more general affection of the nervous system and of the powers that regulate the sense and the movement," a description that presents the neuroses as authentic physiological and general nervous ailments without fever or injury.

After Cullen's Synopsis nosologiae methodical burst onto the clinical stage, the definition of this "sense and movement " disorder confronts representatives of medicine. On the one hand, the defenders of the pathological approach to neurosis, with Philippe Pinel (1745-1826) at the head — which considers mental illnesses as a disorder of the cerebral faculties; on the other, the supporters of a more functionalist approach to neurosis, with Juan Martin Charcot (1825-1893) at the forefront — which maintains the existence of a supposed dynamic injury in neurotic manifestations. Somehow, however, both positions coincide in the supposed biological basis of the neuroses.

Meanwhile, various diseases are breaking away from the common trunk of neuroses when their strictly organic origin is discovered. We refer specifically to progressive general paralysis, dementia, catalepsy, tetanus, asthma, epilepsy, and neuralgia, a select and varied group of diseases that, according to a questioned differential diagnosis of exclusion, ended up falling in the domains of neurosis. Thus, the truth is that by the end of the 19th century, the body of neuroses had been reduced to psychasthenia or obsessive neurosis, hysteria, hypochondria, and neurasthenia, a few but very active ailments that brought neurologists upside down of the time. Among them, we will highlight Pierre Janet (1859-1947), a French psychologist and neurologist who, in addition to founding the *Journal de Psychologie normal et pathologique* (1904), made important contributions to the modern study of mental and emotional disorders. Specifically, Janet considers that neurosis is a mental disorder caused by a decrease in psychological tension, a decrease in tension due to chronic brain exhaustion that alters the subject's psychic reality.

Nevertheless, Freud (1856-1939) deserves credit for incorporating one of the most ingenious and revolutionary approaches in the argument on the subject of neuroses: the notion of psychic conflict. Indeed, already in the Studies on Hysteria (1895), Freud discovers to us how, as he approaches the pathogenic memories in the course of the cure, he finds an increasingly energetic resistance in the subject; a resistance that is nothing more than the current expression of an internal defense that stands up against the conflicting desires, the contradictory feelings and the incompatible representations that the analysis tries to reveal. Likewise, we must not forget that Freud, since 1893, has opted for a much more psychological — and, therefore, much less biological — interpretation of neuroses, especially hysteria, phobias and obsessive neuroses (psychoneurosis), having discovered that the cause of such conditions is in psychosexual traumas produced in early times of life.

Etiology of neurosis

As a result of diligent clinical work, Freud was able to develop a complex — and, at the same time, changing — theory about neuroses and mental illness. In his opinion, neuroses should originate from unconscious instinctual and emotional motivations, which would be tremendously active and would manifest themselves symbolically in the form of organic (paralysis, anesthesia, seizures, etc.) and psychological symptoms (anguish, fear, depression, melancholy, etc.), symptoms that, on the other hand, characterize the classic clinical pictures of the so-called "nervous diseases." But, let's go by parts. In 1889, Freud considered that hysteria, synonymous with neurosis at that time, was the result of the subject's fixation on an intensely emotional nonspecific experience. This experience played a primary role in the genesis of the disease and the father of psychoanalysis he referred to using the word trauma. Thus, any event in the life of the subject that exceeded his capacity for control and psychic elaboration of emotional excitement had to be considered traumatic. Therefore, it had to be interpreted as the immediate cause of neurosis (trauma theory).

On the other hand, Freud is convinced that there is a certain constitutional background in neuroses in which hereditary factors play a fundamental role, which undoubtedly points to a certain congenital predisposition towards such ailments. However, and despite this firm conviction, clinical experience shows him, case after case, that the etiology of neurosis is due, preferably, to intense emotional experiences related to the individual's biographical process, especially with his childhood. In fact, in his Fragmentary Analysis of a Hysteria (1901), Freud assures us that if we do not want to be forced to abandon traumatic theory definitively "we will have to go back to the childhood of the subject to look for influences and impressions that may have acted analogous to that of trauma, a setback all the more necessary since even in the investigation of cases whose first symptoms had not arisen in childhood, I have always found something that has prompted me to pursue the history of patients until that early period."

In any case, from 1900 Freud was forced to limit the scope of the trauma concept, affirming — and this had much to do with his patient Dora — that it was not an unspecific emotional experience that caused the neuroses, but that his nature was eminently sexual. From this moment on, and according to what he called seduction theory, he maintained that hysteria was produced by an early sexual experience, which occurred between the ages of four and five, in which the initiative corresponded to another person (generally an adult), an experience that could range from simple insinuations in the form of words or gestures, to a more or less defined sexual assault, that the subject suffered passively with fright (a state that occurs when you enter a dangerous situation without being prepared; the accent falls on the surprise factor). This early traumatic experience left an indelible mark on the subject's psyche, appearing later in the disease represented by the symptoms.

Constitutional factor Trauma

Now, as Freud went deeper into the study of clinical cases treated according to the technical principles of psychoanalysis, he was able to verify that, although most of the patients reported traumatic events of a sexual nature that occurred in their childhood, the investigations carried out among the relatives and friends of the patient showed that these events could never have occurred, and that, therefore, they should be considered as products of the subject's fantasy. Freud himself, in a letter sent to his friend Fliess on September 21, 1897, believes it necessary to reveal the great secret that has been slowly revealed to him in recent months: "I no longer believe in my neurotic," the seduction scenes that he relates are, at times, the fruit of his fantasy.

As a result of this discovery, Freud restricts the value of seduction in the genesis of neuroses, assigning, instead, greater etiological importance to fantasies, which he considers a nuclear factor in the appearance and persistence of such pathologies (theory of fantasies). The reasons for this drastic change, moreover, seem clear:

a) Not all neurotics have suffered early sexual trauma.

b) Not all people who have suffered real trauma have

subsequently developed a neurosis.

c) Traumatic experiences, while still being sexual, could very well not be genital, since, for psychoanalysis, sexual is everything that allows the rapid release of tension (everything genital is sexual, but not everything sexual is genital).

For these reasons, Freud is forced to acknowledge his errors: "My analytical research first fell into the error of overestimating sexual seduction or initiation as the source of infantile sexual manifestations and the germ of the production of neurotic symptoms. Overcoming this error was achieved by discovering the extraordinary role that fantasy played in the psychic life of neurotics, frankly more decisive for neurosis than external reality " in fact, and although until the end of his life Freud did not stop insisting on the existence and pathogenic value of the seduction scenes lived by the subject in childhood, from 1897 the etiological scope of the trauma diminished in favor of fantasies and fixations to the various libidinal phases.

It can be said, then, that the traumatic point of view, even when Freud does not abandon it, is integrated into a much broader conception of neurosis, a conception that involves other factors, such as the sexual constitution and child history. Furthermore, it is strikingly noteworthy that, in this scheme elaborated by Freud in the Introductory Lessons to Psychoanalysis (1917), the term traumatic is not used to refer to the childhood experiences that are at the origin of fixations, but that it is used to designate an event that comes to the subject in the second stage of their biographical history. Therefore, the importance and scope of the trauma are restricted and subordinated to the later history of the subject (accidental events of the adult), coming to be assimilated in this proposal to what Freud, in previous formulations, considered simply frustration.

In any case, the arguments collected by Freud in The New Introductory Lessons to Psychoanalysis (1932) and Inhibition, Symptoms, and Anguish (1925), allow us to complete this etiological equation of neurosis by adding the dynamic perspective. This perspective is facilitated by the fixation, regression, and sublimation concepts:

- Hereditary factor
- Fetal experiences
- Maternal experiences
- Children's experiences
- Predisposition
- Trigger event
- Reactivation
- Oral fixation

In this explanatory scheme, hereditary factors (together with maternal experiences — which would act on the fetus and fetal experiences that would act on the mother) represent what in psychoanalysis has been called the constitutional factor of neurosis, a factor that, as we have previously pointed out, points to a certain congenital predisposition of the individual towards such diseases.

However, we cannot forget that childhood experiences,

especially if they have been emotionally intense, play a fundamental role in the etiology of neuroses first, because they leave an indelible mark on the life of every human being. Second, because they determine the fixation points linked to childhood to which the regression mechanism — a psychodynamic process that involves the return to archaic evolutionary stages of the libidinal organization — drags the subject when, after having faced a traumatic event that has occurred and having unsuccessful in the attempt, frustration and disillusionment arise.

Freud himself, in lesson XXIII of his Introductory Lessons to Psychoanalysis (1917), does not hesitate to affirm that it is a mistake to "undermine the importance of the events that occurred during the subject's childhood and to emphasize, instead, that of those corresponding to the life of their ancestors or their maturity," an error that could be avoided if child events were given " a very special meaning since by taking place at a time when the development of the subject is still unfinished, they bring more serious consequences and are susceptible to traumatic action."

In this sense, and returning to the scheme that concerns us, it is worth remembering that when an unexpected traumatic event generates frustration and, due to this, the libido — psychic energy of the sexual drives that your regime finds in terms of desire and aspirations amorous — stops flowing freely and stagnates, the events of infantile sexual life act as true centers of attraction for the immobilized libido, to which it returns every time that its satisfaction, in reality, is impeded.

When libido cannot flow freely, it is inhibited and stagnant in the first place. If also, it finds difficulties redirecting the tension that the traumatic event (sublimation) entails, it returns to earlier positions and tries to discharge again to that level. If also at that level the satisfaction of the libido is impeded, and the sublimation is still insufficient to mitigate the tension generated by the traumatic event that occurred, the anxiety is triggered, the anguish that the subject perceives as an alarm signal, proceeding to activate their defense mechanisms. If the defense mechanisms that the subject activates are sufficient, timely, and successful, the anxiety is reduced or neutralized; if, on the contrary, they are insufficient, inconvenient, or objectionable, the anguish remains, increases and becomes a symptom.

Defense mechanisms

In his 1894 essay Defense Neuropsychosis, Freud introduces the concept of defense and places it at the origin of hysterical phenomena, since, after analyzing several cases of acquired hysteria, various phobias and obsessive representations, and certain hallucinatory psychoses, he concludes that an experience, representation or sensation, when it is intolerable for the subject, can generate an affection so painful that, if it is not elaborated mentally and is excluded from consciousness, can give rise to various pathological manifestations. Well, the different mental operations that the subject uses to free himself from these intolerable representations, which almost always settle in the field of experience or sexual sensitivity, is what begins to be considered "defenses" in these first moments of psychoanalysis.

Until the appearance of The Interpretation of Dreams (1900), the term "defense" continues to appear in Freud's work as an indisputable reference to the set of operations with which the ego (region of the personality in charge of protecting us from all disturbance) defends against intolerable representations. However, it must also be said that, from 1900, Freud preferred to use the term "repression" to refer to the defensive process aimed at subjugating the intolerable experience: "repression" as I have begun to say instead of defense.

In any case, from this arbitrary Freudian preference, it should not be inferred that repression equals defense, on the contrary, the mechanism of repression constitutes for the psychoanalytic plot the paradigm of defensive operations, while the defense is a generic concept that designates a general tendency to the reduction or suppression of all excitement likely to endanger the integrity of the individual.

Subsequently, in Inhibition, Symptom, and Anguish (1926), Freud returns to the investigation of defense mechanisms, striving to clarify the convoluted question of its equivalence with the term "repression," a question he intends to conclude with what he calls the "restoration of the old concept of defense," that is, invoking the need for a global concept that includes, in addition to repression, other defense methods such as displacement, isolation, conversion or sublimation. Let us not forget that Freud himself, when he had already included repression among the defense mechanisms when commenting on Endless and endless analysis (1937) the book by his daughter Anna, The Self and Defense Mechanisms (1936), writes:

"It was from one of these mechanisms, that of repression, that the study of neurotic processes had its beginning. He never doubted that it was not the only procedure that the self could use for its purposes. But repression is something very peculiar and is now more clearly differentiated from the other mechanisms than these among them."

Defense neuro psychosis (1894)

It can be said, then, that defense mechanisms are the "different types of operations in which defense can be specified" (Laplanche and Pontalis, 1987), or, if you prefer, those unconscious psychodynamic processes through which the subject it tries to harmoniously integrate the demands of its internal world with the demands of the external world. Namely:

Repression- It is the operation which the subject tries to reject or maintain in the unconscious representations (thoughts, images, memories, etc.) linked to a drive to be considered unpleasant, threatening, or destructive from the ethical point of view, aesthetic, social or cultural. Repression is particularly manifest in hysteria, although it also plays an important role in other mental disorders and normal psychology. It can be considered a universal psychic process since it is at the origin of the unconscious constitution as an autonomous domain separated from the rest of the psyche. Let's say of it:

a) What is the earliest-onset defense mechanism?

b) That tries to prevent the direct satisfaction of the drive.

c) That at some point, the repressed has had to be conscious.

Regression - The unconscious psychodynamic process involves the return to forms of behavior and satisfaction typical of previous stages of development that were believed to have been overcome. In a formal sense, regression designates the transition to modes of expression and behavior at a lower level, from complexity, structuring, and differentiation. It is a kind of return, back in the evolutionary process, towards more satisfactory forms of behavior and relationship in the face of the frustrating nature of current living conditions. In any case, if we listen to Freud in the passage added in 1914 to The Interpretation of Dreams, we will have to distinguish three kinds of regressions:

a) Topical, in the sense of the scheme of the psychic apparatus (cons - icons).

b) Temporary, since the oldest psychic formations are reactivated.

c) Formal, since it goes from the usual modes of expression and representation to more primitive ones.

Isolation - Defense mechanism, typical above all in obsessive neurosis, which consists in isolating a thought or behavior so that its connections with other thoughts or with the rest of the subject's existence are broken. Among the isolation processes, we can mention pauses in the course of thought, ritual formulas, and, in general, all the measures that allow us to establish a hiatus in the temporal succession of thoughts or acts.

Reactive training - Attitude or psychological habit of opposite sense to a repressed desire and that has been constituted as a reaction against it (for example, the modesty that opposes exhibitionist tendencies). It is a defense mechanism that involves reinforcing the dam of repression to such an extent that the subject carries out the opposite behavior that made him drive his drive.

Projection - Operation through which the subject expels from himself and locates in the other (person or thing) qualities, feelings, and desires that moral censure repudiates in oneself. It is a defense of very archaic origin that is seen to act particularly in paranoia, but also in some normal forms of thought, such as superstition. It supposes, in any case, the failure of the repression.

Introjection - Unconscious psychological process evidenced by psychoanalytic research through which the subject makes fantasized pass, from "outside" to "inside", characteristics, qualities or traits of other people or objects, this way, they become their characteristics.

Fantasy - An imaginary scenario in which the subject is present and represents, in more or less distorted by defensive processes, the realization of a desire that otherwise could not be satisfied. It can be presented under different appearances: conscious fantasies — daydreams, unconscious fantasies —subliminal dream — and original fantasies — linked to unconscious desire. Frequent in adolescence, fantasy can become pathological if used by adults with great frustrations.

Sublimation - The unconscious psychological process postulated by Freud explains certain human activities that have no relation to sexuality, but that would find their energy in the force of the sexual drive. In general, sublimation is spoken of as a process by which the subject derives part – or all – of the energy from the sexual drive towards the achievement of socially recognized purposes. It has ideal values and does not involve pathology at all.

Rationalization - The procedure by which the subject tries to give a coherent explanation, from the logical point of view, or acceptable from the moral point of view to an attitude, an act, an idea, a feeling, etc., whose true motives do not perceive. It involves the search for logical and ethical reasons that justify an action that is motivated by unconscious factors.

Conversion - Defense mechanism thanks to which the subject transforms the repudiated desire into a bodily manifestation. It consists of the transposition of psychic conflict and an attempt to resolve it in somatic symptoms (phonation disorders, allergies, dizziness), motor (paralysis) or sensitive (anesthesia or localized pain).

Denial - The unconscious psychological process, by which the subject, despite formulating one of his previously repressed wishes, thoughts, or feelings, continues to defend himself by denying that it belongs to him. Annoying representation is excluded by rejecting the perception linked to that representation. Reality itself is denied; it is as if the event had not taken place.

Punishment - The defense mechanism by which the subject tends to carry out certain behaviors tending to compensate the feelings of guilt originated by the existence of certain behaviors, desires, and feelings that the moral conscience repudiates.

Cancellation - Psychological mechanism by which the subject performs an act or carries out a certain activity to cancel the meaning of another previously carried out.

Displacement - A defense mechanism that consists of separating the affective charge from the painful representation, passing it to catheterize (load with psychic energy) other more or less related mental content symbolically with annoying representation. The accent, interest, and intensity of the representation come off to impregnate other representations that were originally not very intense, although linked to the first by an associative chain.

Neurosis classification

According to Enrique Freijo (1987), the term neurosis has two meanings in psychoanalysis that must be differentiated, the descriptive and the etiological. From the descriptive point of view, the word "neurosis" refers to a certain group of disorders that are characterized by peculiar conjunction of signs and symptoms, both psychic and somatic.

From the etiological point of view, it is a word that tells us of the existence of a psychic conflict of an unconscious nature, of a private conflict between one or more impulses that tend to discharge them and the psychic forces within the subject that oppose to the person, in short, of a hidden conflict that, to a greater or lesser extent, is symbolically expressed through different combinations of signs and symptoms.

It can be said, then, that neurotic reaction is a pathology of interpersonal relationships. This pathology manifests itself in somatic dysfunctions, psychic disorders and behavioral disturbances, a pathology whose main cause is the existence of a psychic conflict which, given its unconscious nature, causes symptoms to be experienced subjectively as inexplicable and irrational.

In summary, psychoanalysis has come to demonstrate that neurosis is the result of the subject's inability to adequately resolve the unconscious conflicts that exist in the psyche, conflicts that have their roots in childhood history, and are expressed symbolically in the form of symptoms.

By this, we mean that no matter where you look, neurotic conflict is nothing but the dramatic consequence of the failure of the ego in trying to carry out its work of synthesis and integration on the three different fronts on which it must be carried out: that of instinctual impulses, that of moral demands and that of external reality. This unfortunate failure gives priority to neurotic symptoms.

Adapted from E. Freijo (1987)

Current Neuroses - This group of neuroses' origin should not be sought in childhood conflicts but present experiences, normally related to disorders in sexual life. The symptoms do not constitute a symbolic and overdetermined expression, but rather result directly from the lack or inadequacy of sexual satisfaction.

Neurasthenia - Condition described by the American doctor George Beard (1839-1883), whose clinical picture revolves around physical fatigue of nervous origin. It includes symptoms from the most diverse registers: headaches, spinal paresthesias, vague pain, boredom, lack of interest, and impoverishment of sexual activity. Its origin points to an inadequate satisfaction of the sexual drive in adults, specifically masturbation.

The neurosis of Anxiety - Psychogenic condition in which anguish (anxious expectation, attacks of anguish, or somatic equivalents of it) appears as the main symptom. It is specifically characterized by the accumulation of sexual arousal, the arousal that is directly transformed into a symptom without psychic mediation. It is associated with situations of forced abstinence, sexual overexertion, and continued practice of coitus interruptus, situations, and experiences, all of which lead to strong frustration in sexual satisfaction. There is no harmony between the physical and the psychological response in terms of satisfaction: there can be sexual intercourse, and yet there can be no satisfaction.

Psychoneurosis - In contrast to current neuroses, this is the name given to the group of psychogenic disorders whose symptoms constitute the symbolic expression of childhood conflicts. Also called transference neuroses, they differ from narcissistic neuroses in that the libido is generally displaced on objects rather than on the self. They are the only ones capable of psychoanalytic treatment.

Hysterical Neurosis - Psychic affection of very varied clinical pictures whose two best isolated symptomatic forms are conversion hysteria, in which the psychic conflict is symbolized in the most diverse bodily symptoms (cyanosis, urticarias, hemorrhages, lethargy, etc.), paroxysmal (attacks of hiccups, tremors, tics, an emotional crisis with theatricality, etc.) or long-lasting (anesthesia, paralysis, pharyngeal <bolo> feeling, etc.), and the hysteria of anguish, in which the anguish is fixed more or less stable to a certain external object (phobias). The regression of libido is a pathology linked to the phallic phase of libidinal evolution since it correlates with the Castration complex and imposes the approach and resolution of the Oedipus Complex.

Obsessive-compulsive neurosis - A form of neurosis isolated by Freud in the years 1894-1895 that constitutes one of the great pictures of the psychoanalytic clinic. In its most typical form, the latent psychic conflict is expressed by the so-called compulsive symptoms:

a) Parasitic ideas of an obsessive nature, which are recognized as their own despite accepting their absurdity.

b) Compulsion to perform undesirable acts.

c) Constant struggle to escape these thoughts and tendencies.

d) Performance of certain ceremonies tending to conjure obsessive ideas.

e) A type of thought characterized by doubts, misgivings, and scruples; symptoms that inevitably lead to inhibitions of thought and action. The regression of libido is a pathology linked to the sadistic-anal phase (secondary anal) of libidinal evolution, a phase in which the triad order, greed, and stubbornness appear to us as a paradigm of anal eroticism.

Narcissistic Neuroses - In contrast to the transference neuroses (psychoneurosis), Freud thus names the group of mental illnesses characterized by the withdrawal of libido from the ego. It is a term that currently tends to disappear from psychiatric and psychoanalytic language, but which is found in Freud's writings as an expression equivalent to "psychosis", conditions to which Freud, at least in the early days of psychoanalysis, prefers to call "paraphrenias" — a term proposed by Kraepelin to designate chronic delusional psychoses that, like paranoia, are not accompanied by intellectual weakness or evolve into dementia, but resemble schizophrenia in their delusional constructions based on hallucinations and fables.

Manic-depressive psychosis - A term coined by Kraepelin

to refer to recurrent manic and depressive disorders that, having common features — both are affective disorders — followed one another (cyclical evolution) and had a very similar prognosis and evolution (periodic episodes). In the manic phase — a state of exhilaration and excitement disproportionate to the circumstances the subject is experiencing — the most frequent symptoms are a distraction, the flight of ideas, the alteration of judgment, anger, and aggressiveness, and the ideas of greatness. In the depressive phase, the mood is markedly depressed by sadness and unhappiness, with some degree of anxiety. Activity is usually decreased, but there may be restlessness and agitation. Also, there is a marked propensity for recurrence that, in some cases, can occur at regular intervals. As far as the regression of libido is concerned, it is a pathology linked to the oral-sadistic stage — second time of the oral phase, according to a subdivision introduced by K. Abraham in 1924, which coincides with the appearance of the teeth and bite activity — of the evolution of libido.

Schizophrenic psychosis - Term created by E. Bleuler (1911) to designate a group of psychoses, whose affinity had already been indicated by Kraepelin grouping them under the heading "early dementia", which in psychiatry, over time, have become classic: hebephrenic schizophrenia - the subject gradually loses the ability to plan and foresee the future, leading a wandering life without any purpose (they consider themselves great inventors and/or benefactors of humanity) ; catatonic schizophrenia - the subject falls into an alarming state of stupor without responding to the environment, a state that is intertwined with outbreaks of senseless excitement and hyperactivity; and paranoid schizophrenia - the subject develops a true delusional system in which everything revolves around himself: first, he feels observed, watched and controlled by one or more people; later, he becomes convinced that they persecute and harass him to kill him or make him suffer; Lastly, he folds back on himself and isolates himself from objective reality to live in a world of fantastic representations.

In general, we can say that schizophrenia is a mental illness characterized by the loss of the sense of reality, the predominance of the inner life and the presence of hallucinations, a disease that refers us to the oral phase of the evolution of libido — a phase in which sexual pleasure is linked to the excitation of the oral cavity and lips.

CHAPTER 9

CHALLENGE AND IMPROVE YOUR MIND

The most powerful faculty in our mind is its ability to stay focused. Improving our mental focus will allow us to benefit more.

Maintaining a higher mental focus minimizes the power of distractions and improves our performance. The good news is that each of us, with a little practice and insight, can improve our ability to focus.

With the mind, a maxim resembling that which works with our muscles may apply. The more you work on its abilities, the more strength you will gain. Improving mental focus is perfectly possible. But that does not mean that it is a simple and fast process. To achieve this, you will have to make conscious efforts to eliminate, change, or introduce new habits.

Assess your mental focus

Assessing your present condition is the first step to strengthening your mental concentration. It would help if you asked yourself some questions about that. Does your imagination stretch out to other horizons while doing an essential task? Do you ever get off track of what you've been doing? Need to start all over again? Will you have problems getting away from distractions? If you answer those questions in the affirmative, your mental concentration will need to be dramatically increased.

You also need to ask yourself about the level of

concentration you achieve when you perform tasks that test your abilities. Do you like setting goals and dividing tasks into more manageable segments? If you catch your mind wandering, will you take a break and go back to what you've been doing? During the time zones where you are most involved, do you appear to overcome the most difficult challenges?

Keep distractions away

Even if it seems obvious, eliminating distractions is fundamental to improving mental focus. The problem is that very often, we are not aware of the immense amount of distractions around us.

To do this, start by locating and minimizing sources of distraction. It sounds simple, but it isn't. Studies tell us that over the long term, this habit will become very profitable.

One thing to notice here is that the disturbances are not permanent at all. From outside, sounds and interruptions are always harder to handle than the things that circle in our ears. Especially disturbing and persistent can be exhaustion, worry, anxiety, lack of motivation, and other internal disorders.

To minimize internal distractions, it is important to make a list of everything we need to "let go" so as not to drag this fatigue behind us. Building on positive thoughts and affirmations is also a good strategy, especially when dealing with anxiety and concern.

Focus on one thing at a time

Multitasking is not effective, even if it might seem fantastic for our mental focus. It reduces productivity, and targeting the details to separate the most important from the superfluous becomes much more difficult because our attention has a limited capacity.

Part of enhancing your mental concentration is to take full advantage of the opportunities you have. So, you have to give up multitasking and pay attention to one thing (or one problem) in full.

Take breaks

After a while, your mental focus may start to "fill up with vices," becoming less and less effective. Ultimately, your performance is affected.

Traditional explanations of psychology have suggested that this is due to the depletion of attention resources. However, some researchers believe that this point is more related to the brain's tendency to change sources of stimulation.

It was discovered that with very brief pauses and by diverting attention to another point, the mental focus could improve. Thus, introducing "breathing moments " during activities that require a lot of concentration will help you considerably. In our agenda, it is essential to see moments of work and moments of diversion.

Train to strengthen your mental focus

There are two things to keep in mind: mental focus takes time; we will always have room to improve it. One of the first steps is to recognize the impact of distraction as a source of exhaustion. By changing your mental focus and following the strategies we have listed, you will discover that you can maintain a high level of attention. And this for longer.

Other things affect our mental focus. We think for example of our food or the quality of our sleep. By taking care of the influencing factors, direct and indirect, we will see how agile our mind can be.

CHAPTER 10

Why do people say YES

They don't want to do it and still do it. People who say yes when they mean no have a particular fear.

People who keep saying yes when they mean no want to keep the peace at all costs in the world and not be noticed negatively.

You prefer not to attract attention. Because if you stand out — in whatever form — it can always provoke conflicts of all kinds. So, it is not that some find the behavior useful, and others do not. That's why they just say "yes" as often as possible.

Notorious yes-man

"Can you still quickly ..." "Would you please ..." or "I still need you today for ..." The question is, it is simply an invitation for notorious yes-sayers to say yes? They adapt to any situation that may appear spontaneously and thus always serve others well. One could almost forget that these people still have their own lives — they always work perfectly and are available without any complaints.

However, their own needs are the very last place. And with that, unfortunately, that of their favorite people too. Does someone have to stay back and work overtime again? You don't have to think long about who to ask. Does anyone have to change their vacation schedule because of an urgent order? The name is programmed.

552

But why are they doing this? Because they're afraid of others' reactions. And this is immediately followed by the fear of rejection, which — like so many things — already arises in childhood.

A behavioral pattern in which you always say yes to others is, unfortunately, often the first step in burnout.

Relationships are chronically stressed

Anyone who thinks they have to say yes always and everywhere has another problem in addition to the organizational stress: They live in constant tension. Because it is never predictable when, where, and what they will be used for, and they will have to say yes again. And because it means that they always have difficulties in explaining to their loved ones.

So, if you take a close look at relationships, there is something very unhealthy about them. Because if you don't allow yourself to speak about your own needs in one relationship, but always orientate yourself towards the other, this relationship is very difficult.

Who feels addressed now: Set clear boundaries to the people who make demands on you that they cannot or do not want to meet now.

A healthy relationship is not characterized by constantly saying yes, but by the fact that a dialogue is possible.

So, if you are asked again whether you can stay longer today or do this or that service, you can say that it won't work. It is the most natural thing in the world to refuse a request — for whatever reason. You can, but don't have to explain why. Sometimes a conversation is easier if you substantiate statements with reasons; for example, "Unfortunately, today it is not possible, I have to pick up my children from kindergarten" or "I have agreed to eat with my husband/wife for 6:00 p.m." etc. The "why" is none of their business, so you shouldn't justify reasons. It is also essential that you only say such reasons once and not always repeat them. The other one has already heard it.

Prepare for resistance

And to come back to the fear of the reaction of others — and thus the fear of rejection – mentioned above: Yes, the reaction of others will probably not be very pleasant because it has always worked wonderfully so far – you have always worked wonderfully, for others. If you are aware of this in advance, you can better deal with it if your counterpart may rebel and want to blame you or even feel guilty. You know that can happen, and therefore you can develop resistance to it.

Over time, however, you will notice that the more certain and confident you appear, the more other people will also accept and respect your rejections. And the quality of your relationships will improve because you meet other people at eye level.

Important: See every little "no" — however you put it – as your success, which will motivate you to say "yes" again next time – namely yes to yourself and your own needs.

Anyone who always wants to please everyone ensures that everyone is fine but they themselves are miserable. Start today by standing by your own needs and standing up for them. If you are aware that a "no" can offend others and may surprise or even annoy them, you will know what is coming, and you can better deal with it.

Why we should say less, "yes, but."

Does this situation seem familiar to you? You are in the middle of intensive communication. Because you have a lot of ideas on the subject, you respond promptly with "Yes, but we also have to consider ..." "Yes, but shouldn't we ..." or " Yes, but that also includes ... "?

We all do this from time to time. And like to place this "yes but" between the execution of our interlocutor without letting him or her say it. We may then be surprised if our counterpart gets louder, discusses more heatedly and somehow seems very dissatisfied. There was no result, the ideas were really good, and the interest from both sides was honest.

What could have happened? Here's an idea: Even if you did not want it, you have signaled to your counterpart that you do not agree. A "yes but" may seem like an affirmative addition to an argument; every "yes but" is a sign to your conversation partners that they are wrong and have not considered certain things. Instead of "Yes" = confirmation and "but" = supplement, your counterpart hears "Yes" = "I heard you," "but" = "You are wrong." The "yes" opens the door so that you can kick your shin even better with the "but." Doesn't sound good, does it? By doing so, you force your counterpart into justification pressure. Instead of a solution-oriented discussion, an exchange of blows perceived as unpleasant develops.

Yes, I know you don't mean that. But it matters. "Yes, but"...

- ... are like a wall against which ideas bounce off.
- ... immediately redirect the dialog: "Stop, you can't get any further here."
- ... interrupt the flow of thought, and you always start over.
- ... do not continue an idea but oppose it.

It is like cooking - "Yes, but" pours the recipe into the sink because it has not yet been completed. On the other hand, if you added spice or another ingredient, you could enjoy a delicious meal. Such a perfection creates a "yes exactly" or "yes and" in conversation.

"Yes, exactly," or "Yes and" enrich the communication

These two formulations are invitations to think ahead. An almost revolutionary approach to positively receiving and spinning every impulse that is indispensable. If we replace "but" with "and," we achieve something big with a small change. The "and" connects, it places two viewpoints side by side, so that they can exist in parallel. The "but" is very different — it evaluates and contrasts your point of view with the other or even above the other.

We can achieve with a "yes and": We listen to each other and constructively pursue a common goal. New ideas will continue. You get the space that you deserve. A situation can relax; creativity grows. Beautiful right? Give it a try: Discuss a topic with colleagues or friends, to solve a problem. For example, think about what you could do tonight. While you start each paragraph with "Yes but" in the first round, in the second round, you start your writings with "Yes and" or "Yes exactly." How does that feel?

Typically, the "yes exactly" round is much faster. The resulting common idea is much richer than the occasional split of ideas from the first round.

The decisive difference between "yes but" and "yes and": While "yes but" starts a new train of thought, "yes and" or "yes exactly" will always continue or supplement a train of thought. That is why in the end, a whole is created – regardless of whether it was a professional conversation or just the question of what you cook in the evening.

Let's take a look at this question in practice:

B: What are we eating tonight?

A: Do we want to make pizza?

B: Yes, but we already had it yesterday.

A: What do we want to do then, suggest something.

B: I don't know, suggest something.

A: ...

Scene change - same question again:

B: What are we eating tonight?

A: Do we want to make pizza?

B: Yes, exactly, and today we make them with tomatoes and mozzarella, not like yesterday with ham and Edam, then it is lighter and tastes completely different.

Do you notice what happens? "Yes and" answers get to the goal faster, but they need a little more brainpower for the respondent. Perhaps it is because so often a "yes but" is used. There are other reasons for this.

Why we say "yes but" so often

- We have been brought up to be problem thinkers.

It is almost a good thing first to analyze, think through, organize and structure everything. If we have identified all potential gaps and eliminated all sources of error, we could come to a solution. For us, things are broken. First, glasses are usually half empty. The deficiency is omnipresent, and it needs to be remedied. In other words, we see problems as opportunities.

- We are security and preservation oriented

If you say "yes but," you can stay in your comfort zone, you have to move (mentally) less. It is not about problem-solving, but (unconsciously) about keeping the current state. The "yes but" practically blocks further development that creates security. It is good for everyone who is anxious and likes to have the situation under control. (And there are many, I would like to include myself in it!) Whoever does not want to dare is against it on principle and will feel more comfortable in "Yes but" than in "Yes and."

- We are trained to place our own opinion in the best possible way.

With the "yes," yes-sayers initially agree to speak. And because they are better informed, they always have an objection, have legitimate doubts and can argue against something. In doing so, they manifest their expert status as "know-it-all," drawing everyone's attention. They are the focus and enjoy their special position, however, at the expense of the result.

What do we say about ourselves when we say "yes but"?

Language is more than the transmission of information. You have heard of the factual level and the relationship level. If you have followed the explanations so far, you will have realized that a "yes but" transports little on the factual level and a lot on the relationship level. If you want to eradicate it, with yourself and with others, you can work on the relationship. And also on yourself. I dare to guess: Those who are at peace with themselves say less "yes but" and more often dare to say "yes and" to a situation or the other person.

CHAPTER 11

HOW TO GAIN AN ADVANTAGE OVER ANYONE'S MIND

You wanted to know what someone was doing hundreds of times. To know what a person thinks is an advantage for a better understanding, attracting, selling, revealing criminals, and many other benefits, both positive and not so positive.

To know how to benefit from people's, men's, or women's minds is not something magical, but one must be careful about the conclusions reached. In general, the more observant and interested you are, the more effective you are in reading others' thoughts.

On the other hand, one does not know exactly what someone feels that takes advantage of the mind. You won't hear a sound in your mind if you don't have a sixth sense — telepathy.

The aim is to analyze people's behavior and deduce their feelings, state of mind, and thinking. Also, the meaning would be essential as well. Many solutions will be more probable than others, depending on the situation.

Although you know it, you already take advantage of the mind

We would not be able to handle social situations or develop personal relationships with others without knowing other people's feelings or ideas.

The theory of mind is an ability that arises from 3 to 4 years of age and relates to other people's ability to relate thoughts and intentions.

If a person has developed this capability, he can understand and think about his personal and other mental conditions.

According to the University of Texas researcher, William Ickes, foreigners can "scan" each other with 20% accuracy and friends and partners with 35% accuracy. Those who have built this capacity are as high as 60%.

How to learn to take advantage of the mind:

-Begin by knowing yourself

How do you know what other people are if you don't know yourself? It is not a single, but a dynamic process that we know what others think or feel.

To begin with, you should know how you are feeling at any moment — your inner state.

The more you are conscious of yourself, the more you recognize your mental state. And you or your interlocutor can contribute to this state of mind.

Negative emotions are more communicated than positive, so that's a way to know how you feel with whom you speak.

Have you spoken to a person with "good vibes" transmitted to you? And did you speak to someone who expressed stresses or negative emotions to you?

It's mentally tainted. The more you know your mental

condition, the happier you are.

Anything that can assist you is mindfulness or meditation, strategies that let you learn about the "inner world."

Remember that you won't realize what the other person thinks without interacting.

You would, therefore, need to communicate with yourself. There are more positive ways in this case than others:

Good: it seems that you feel a bit sad. Am I wrong? Am I right?

Bad: I know what you think / you sound like me.

-Read lips

This part is due to the experience of FBI agent Jack Shafer.

Pucker your lips slightly

A gesture that shows you disagree a little with the clearing of your lips. The more it is, the more the discord.

Pursed lips indicate that the person produced a thought that was contradictory to what was said or done.

If, for example, you want to convince someone, it's a trick to "change your mind" before you can convey your opposition verbally.

Once a person expresses their opinions publicly, the psychological concept known as consistency makes it very difficult to change his views.

It causes much less psychological stress to retain a position than to make continuous decisions, regardless of the arguments.

Lip biting

A common way of "reading the mind" is to see as the speaker mugs his mouth. It consists of the lower or the upper lip with a soft bite.

This gesture means, though he doesn't dare, that someone wants to say something; usually, people don't say what they think because they believe they offend others.

You can communicate more effectively if you know what your partner or friends do not dare to say. One way is to state with empathy what you believe causes fear.

For example:

You: Do you agree that we should spend more time together

He/she: No, I want you to help me in my house.

Press the lips

This happens if you combine the upper and lower lip, pinch the mouth, and darken the lips. This compression is a sense of biting the lips, although it has a more negative significance.

This happens anytime someone needs to say something but twists their lips not to say it. In clear empathic comments, you can persuade a suspect to bear witness:

"You've got to say something, but you don't want to think about it."

Here are some tricks:

If you see pickled lips, "change the person's mind" before he expresses his objections.

Use a compassionate statement to learn why the person is anxious about what you are saying when you see bitten and pressed lips.

-Work empathy

You don't have a link to other people's emotions if you use your brain to think about the future, the past, or your problems.

It is how the subconscious senses the thoughts of other people. And even if you're not looking after it, you have the potential.

Today students at college exhibit 40 percent less empathy than those from the 1980s and 1990s, according to Sara Konrath of the University of Michigan.

However, while empathy can be overlooked, everyone can grow it and apply it.

Your brain is empathetic; when someone you are watching is acting, you have neurons called "mirror nerves."

These neurons play an important role in linking the emotions and thoughts of other people besides socializing.

Have you happened to walk down the road, meet someone, and decide to go in the same direction and block you were coming from?

This is because your mirror neurons imitate the other

person's behavior until the information is processed, and the opposite movement is carried out by your mind.

Christian Keysers from the University of Groningen says that you feel fear or disgust when you see a spider creeping up your leg.

Likewise, you feel your emotions as if you're there when you watch your soccer and basketball team lose or win.

When you watch others, you will experience social emotions such as shame, anger, pride, or lust.

To increase your empathy follow these steps:

Live now: The more your brain is, the more you can sense your thoughts and those of the other person, the more you worry about the past or future. Therapy is a good practice. Practice watching people and the environment without considering anything else.

You can watch movies that tell plays or humorous people's stories. Watch and listen. The links in the emotional brain are enhanced by being interested in someone else's life. It's still better in a theatre. However, the best way to meet friends or relatives is to listen to one another face to face and pay full attention without interruption.

Ask yourself what you feel: Your self-awareness will strengthen your understanding of other people. You will ask yourself what you expect. Stand three to four times a day, wondering: How do I feel? Right now, what's my emotion? Also, find out where you feel your emotions in the body. For starters, where do you feel anxiety or fear? In the chest? Arms?   The neck?

Check the intuition. Tell them the feeling that you feel or try to find out what you feel if you talk to someone. If you see, for example, your boyfriend looks animated, say to him: 'Is something good happening to you? You look very animated.'

-Eye contact

Vision is a human being's most essential feeling.

According to a study by the University of Miami, the importance of the eyes in communicating with others is so important that 43.4% of our attention towards someone else is focused on their eyes.

You can deduce what a person feels or schemes from a person's eyes. You will find out more about this topic in this chapter.

To blink

The frequency of blinking can alter emotions toward another human.

It can indicate that you are drawn to your speaker when you blink more than 6-10 times per minute.

Blinking more can also show the person's nervousness.

Since 1980, the person who blinked the most lost in presidential debates.

Raise eyebrows

People lift their eyes when they want a better understanding of themselves.

It also shows compassion, empathy, and a willingness to get along.

Squint

Squinting means distrust or unbelief and is an often-involuntary expression.

Gaze direction

After the NLP was first identified, several people have written about the direction that the eyes look to.

The contact model helps you recall everything looking to the left.

In comparison, looking to the right means that thoughts or images are produced, which some people interpret as lying.

Note: it's the other way around for lefties.

Pupils

In 1975 Eckhard Hess found that when an individual is interested in others, the pupils dilate.

The pupils contract when we see situations that disgust us. Dilation: the pupil's size increases. Contraction: the pupil is reduced in size.

-Mind activity is more difficult; the pupils dilate more. Nevertheless, pupils are limited when mental activity is too high.

-As we experience pain, they dilate.

Seduction

There appears to be a consensus in flirtation and seduction that:

-When the other party does not respond to you and initiates contact, they might not be involved.

You leave him/her uncomfortable if you continue to look at him/her after he or she turns away or fails to look around.

-The other person is probably going to feel comfortable and react positively if you start eye contact.

Boys may take account of the following:

1) When a girl looks you in the eye, looking away and then going back to your eyes; surely she's interested.

2) When she breaks eye contact and looks out, nothing is certain.

3) If you take care to make eye contact, you're probably not interesting.

For girls who want to seduce with their eyes: For a man to start knowing that she is interested, he requires an average of three glances from a girl.

Dominance

Rich, high-ranking individuals or others who choose to show dominance tend to have less eye contact.

To look elsewhere is another way of showing dominance.

Avoid eye contact

Avoiding looking into other people's eyes may indicate that they are ashamed for some reason.

Therefore, avoiding interaction with anyone else also means being frustrated.

You must also bear in mind that the contact time is culturally important. In New York, for example, 1.68 seconds is acceptable.

The 'Reading The Mind in the Eyes Test,' is a psychologic test created by the University of Cambridge's Simon Baron-Cohen that enhances your ability to read thoughts.

-Other keys of non-verbal language

Are you aware that non-verbal language dictates 93 percent of the strength of human communication?

The influence and impact of our communication are determined by:

- Non-verbal: 55%
- Paralinguistic elements: 38%
- Oral content: 7%

There are certain aspects that you should consider in this subject:

Touch the nose and cover the mouth: People tend to cover the mouth and touch the nose when they are lying. The adrenaline in the capillaries of the nose could be increased. On the other hand, it would be the aim to bring the hands close to the mouth.

Unrest: When a person searches out something or his body is still moving around. It is presumed that anxieties that are released from physical movements that affect part of the body compulsively are generated by telling a lie. The issue is whether the behavior, as a person normally does, is different.

Speak slowly: The person can pause to find something to say by telling a lie.

Throat: A lying person can constantly swallow.

The expression is confined to the mouth: When someone forges emotions (happiness, shock, sorrow ...), the face only shifts at the mouth: the chin, the eyes, and the front.

Microexpressions are facial expressions that are almost invisible and shown by people as they occur in a split second. Some can detect them, but most of them can't. The microexpression of an individual lies in a stress emotion characterized by raised eyebrows that create expression lines on the front.

Knowing all the signs of non-verbal language is very extensive.

CHAPTER 12

HOW QUICKY CAN I LEARN NLP?

While respecting the person as he is (both cognitive, emotional, and behavioral), NLP gives us the keys to "being at best with yourself," associating things that happen with positive, taking a step back to avoid feeling the negative emotional impact.

This can help in many situations where one may encounter difficulties: to be comfortable during a presentation of an important issue at work, be quiet and available for the children's homework, be full of energy in the morning upon waking, or remain attentive and kind to a client or an angry person.

- **Exercise 1: anchoring**

The objective of this Exercise

Anchoring is a natural process that unconsciously and automatically associates an internal reaction with an external stimulus: a hello, a wink, a "top there" during an agreement reached. We memorize these links and thus create what are called "anchors." As soon as an anchor is stimulated, the feeling experienced in the past returns instantly.

The anchors can be visual (a seashell in your bathroom reminds you of holidays in Mauritius), auditory (this piece of music, a romantic moment), kinesthetic (this ball in the stomach, this moment of panic during of an examination), olfactory (this delicious smell of chocolate, your childhood in your grandmother's house) or gustatory (the most famous description of a gustatory anchor is, of course, Proust's madeleine!).

Instructions for use

Think of a situation where you feel an unpleasant internal state and ask yourself which positive internal state (a memory, a place that calms you ...) do you want to be in this situation?

Stressed out — you want to be relaxed, anxious — you want to be serene or full of self-confidence.

Once you have chosen your desired internal state, follow this procedure:

- Sit in a quiet place, close your eyes, and find a memory where you experienced this positive internal state. Relive the scene by being fully associated with it, until you feel it completely in your body.

- Anchor the positive internal state. In this situation, the kinesthetic anchor is the most effective. For example, you can clench your fist or stimulate a point on the body (wrist, knee, ear, etc.) for at least 20 seconds. Repeat this operation 2 to 3 times to reinforce the anchor in place.

- Test the impact of the anchor. Forget the previous steps for a moment and think of something else. Then once in a neutral internal state, stimulate the anchor in place and let the positive internal state return.

- While stimulating the anchor, project yourself into the future in a difficult context. And let yourself experience what this positive internal state now allows you to do and your new behaviors ...

This magic button is now at your disposal to help you in difficult situations. But an anchor wears out if you don't use it! Remember to activate it regularly and strengthen it by stimulating it in new situations where you experience this positive internal state.

- Exercise 2: Submodalities

The objective of this Exercise

The "submodalities" represent how the brain sorts and codifies experience. By modifying the structure of our experience, it is possible to modify the experience itself and our emotional and behavioral reactions.

The sensory representations are all different: a mental image can be pale or dark, large or small, in color or black and white. In the same way, an auditory representation has a certain volume or rhythm.

How to use

Now learn to juggle submodalities. Take an unpleasant task and a pleasant task. For example, you hate ironing or filing your tax return but love to garden. Make a representation of these two experiences. Now go through your submodality checklist and fill in your table.

Look at your two columns and identify the differences. This is called doing contrast analysis.

573

You will now transform your unpleasant task and make it pleasant by playing with your submodalities: give your negative representation the pleasant task's components!

Among your parameters, there are undoubtedly 1 or 2, which will have a dominant impact: it is the critical submodality (often it is a question of size or distance). Now look at this "redesigned" representation: your motivation and your feelings are likely very different.

- Exercise 3: Swish

The objective of this Exercise

The word swish means "whistling" or "rustling," like the noise of an image which would quickly cover another.

This technique makes it possible to modify a person's internal representations and transform a negative feeling into a positive feeling. This is to short-circuit the trigger of the anxiety-provoking situation.

It is appropriate whenever an internal image triggers an unpleasant feeling: stage fright, malaise, anxiety, lack of confidence, demotivation ... It can also be used in addictive behaviors.

Instructions

- Identify the problematic situation: In which situation do you want to react differently?

- Identify the image linked to the problem: Locate the internal image that you see in this situation just before having the attitude you want to change. Identify the internal manifestations that this negative image triggers in you.

- Create a positive image: Let a second image come, an image of you having full self-confidence. To serve in all circumstances, this image must be dissociated (you can see yourself as if we had taken a photo of you) and not contextualized. Modify this image so that it is really attractive and gives you positive bodily reactions, a feeling of well-being, and fulfillment.

- The swish: Close your eyes and view the first image. It must be large and clear. Then place a small dark image at the bottom left, your 2nd positive image. Grow this little image that lights up as it covers the other, while the first image shrinks and becomes dark. Start again by repositioning your two images and do these 5 or 6 times in succession faster and faster. At the end of this process, visualize a white screen and open your eyes.

- Test the result: Turn the screen back on and look at the image before you. Can you find the first image? What difference does it make?

- Project into the future: Imagine yourself in a few weeks in a situation similar to the one you mentioned at the start... How does this new person you have become behaves? What do you feel? What can you now do in different contexts of your life?

Manipulate the mind through Dark NLP

NLP's bad reputation is well known. It can be used to manipulate people and influence them against their will.

Others think that it is valuable to help and has made them happier both professionally and personally. So what is really behind these three letters?

Neuro-linguistic programming – the explanation of the abbreviation. Translated, it means "the new formation of the connections between nerves and language." There is a complex idea behind it. It is about recognizing old patterns of thought, both for myself and my counterpart, to break them down and transform them into new ones that are more suitable for me or others.

NLP was developed by the then math student and later psychologist Richard Bandler and the linguist John Grinder in the early 1970s at the University of California in Santa Cruz. They wanted to use it to design new short-term psychotherapy.

The method is based on observing people who are particularly successful in different areas and filtering out commonalities. These successful behaviors can be learned separately from others.

To achieve this, there are various basic assumptions and techniques in the NLP:

Although basic assumptions cannot be directly proven, they serve as the basis for a thought model. Every community has such so-called postulates. In the NLP, this would be, for example, "Behind every behavior, there is a positive intention." What may seem surprising at first glance makes sense on closer inspection. Imagine a teenage boy stealing from someone. If you ask for the reason, he will first say that he wanted this item. Upon closer inquiry, however, it soon becomes clear that he wanted to impress his friends and thus belong to the group. These basic needs for recognition, security, and belonging are our strongest drives. This idea is not to excuse any action, but it should enable positive behavior that meets the same basic needs.

Further postulates would then be:

- "Every behavior is useful in a certain context."
- "There is no failure, only feedback."
- "People always make the best decision available to them."

To expand this available choice of decision options, NLP now has different techniques, but they all have the same basic structure.

Pacing - Outing - Leading

To be able to communicate successfully with a person, rapport must be established. If we want to communicate with someone, we create a subconscious rapport . If you want to design this process consciously, you have to consider the following stages:

Pacing, also called mirroring, is the first stage. You try to adapt yourself as well as possible to your counterpart, i.e., imitate posture, language style, etc. This happens automatically when we meet up with good friends.

Outing describes the conscious perception of one's sensations that have arisen through pacing. This is also a good tool for a quick check of your counterpart's situation in everyday life. Try it! Sit up straight, shoulders back, head raised – how do you feel? So, you can see that our posture already says a lot about how we are doing.

Leading - Once we have established a good connection with our counterpart, we can try to help them, because only if we have won their trust will they be ready to accept our help.

The subsequent change work can now be done in different ways. It is impossible to give a complete treatise since NLP has always been based on a wide variety of therapy concepts. The Gestalt therapist Fritz Perls was particularly influenced by the family therapist Virginia Satir and the hypnotherapist Milton H. Erickson.

The problem with NLP is that there is no clear theoretical framework. We therefore often find a mixture, especially with various esoteric teachings.

NLP was not designed to manipulate people. The goal was to help them faster and more efficiently than ever before. It opens up countless new opportunities and is a great tool. But just because a tool could be dangerous, we don't throw all knives out of the kitchen. And just because a doctor could kill us, we don't refuse to go back to the doctor when we are in pain.

As with any tool, it depends on which hands it comes in, and we should never stop thinking critically about the things we encounter. It can then advance each individual in their personal development and help us significantly improve communication with our fellow human beings!

CHAPTER 13

THE TRUE STORY OF BRAINWASHING
& HOW IT SHAPED THE WORLD

One of the "classics" in the History of "Brainwashing" is to believe that it does not exist. Architects of this "classic" officiate as preachers willing to proclaim to the four winds that no one is brainwashed.

One of the main detergents of this "washing" system is the fear that, whether with biblical genesis or with nuclear warheads, it presses our lives, minute by minute, to make us happy and obedient to everything that exploits us, humiliates and neutralizes us. It is about erasing all critical, organizing, and mobilizing thinking and methods ready to transform the monstrous reality perpetrated by capitalism. They show it on TV.

Today, all intimidation operations (always invented) seem like child's play alongside the images perpetrated by Gaza's bombings, the ISIS paraphernalia, and the macabre deployment amplified by the alliance between "organized crime" and the bourgeois mass media. The seven deadly sins and Orson Wells seem like fairy tales. At the end of the discourse, reigns — unpunished — the moral that shows the power of harm to subject us to deception. Isn't that why the crucified Christ is exposed to the dead?

The "acute" phase is when the victim becomes wilful and takes the initiative to wash her brain alone and wash it promptly to her "loved ones." She learns to brainwash

579

meticulously, with determination and good humour, making it a moralizing exhibition among her own and others. The collaborative and sustainable attitude that saves the bourgeoisie many expenses. The acute phase is expressed at ease when the victims are grateful (intimately and in the public square) for being victimized and recognize that the victimizer was always right and continues to be right. Mission accomplished.

Brainwashing has taken modern forms and has been institutionalized according to the specialties demanded by the imperialism market. The laundries of brains concentrated in the plunder of natural resources and particularly plunder of oil. "It is for your good," they say, "it is because you do not know how to take advantage of it," "you do not have the technology or understand it," "it is progress," "it is modern," "it is transparent" ... "it is inevitable." There are jewels of cynicism and self-confidence enshrined in contracts, agreements, alliances, and decrees with many clappers with or without wages.

At the top of the brainwashes are the recently visible "vulture funds" that have made the verb "pay" a dogma with unprecedented fanaticism chained to ancient traditions. No matter the caliber of the aberrations it implies, you have to pay because the "judges" say so. Not only the "judges" subservient to capitalism but the hierarchical "judges" of bourgeois morality who regulate the quality of honesty with the amount of what is paid and brainwash us to "honor the debt." It does not matter if we walk into the abyss of the worst crisis of misery and dispossession that we could have imagined... they want us to pay with a brainwashed mind ready to meet the next payments set for eternity.

We will not say that they did not warn us. We have centuries of inventions and havoc in the art of brainwashing. There are schools, debates, and diverse tendencies that, to which more, dispute the paternity of one or another "technique" better to stop an efficient and thorough washing. There are specialized universities, and there are awards with planetary prestige for those who, in whole or part, perfect brainwashing in their individual or mass versions. Churches and sects have, in this notable circle, their "number seats" even though it is increasingly difficult to distinguish them from bourgeois television channels, some political parties, and some scientific research and teaching centers.

The Battle of Ideas is the class struggle expressed in thought for revolutionary action. Our anti-capitalist and world struggle must understand that the transformation of the world lies in modifying the relations of production and the ideas about the reality for the egalitarian and just life in collective. Thus, it is necessary to identify and deactivate all the weapons of ideological warfare that the bourgeoisie has invented and prepare ourselves to develop antidotes as strategies with revolutionary methods of simultaneous thought and action.

Living as mourners will be useless to us, no matter how effective our analyzes and claims are. It is time to move forward and not stay in the complaint, in the observation, or the diagnosis because it is urgent to integrate all our best strengths into a creative unity and struggle program that gives the production of ideas its forced and indissoluble place in the production of actions.

CHAPTER 14

IS HYPNOSIS REAL?

We have all heard of hypnosis. But the image that has usually been given to this technique is something mystical that drives you to do strange things, or something typical of quacks who want to deceive us. What is hypnosis? Does it work? Why is it not effective for everyone? Here we reveal it to you.

It is not true that you are at the mercy of the hypnotist, and that, for example, you are capable of killing a person in a trance. First of all, your rational capacity continues to function, although in a different way.

Not all people can be hypnotized equally. And this is because they have different brain structures. Also, hypnosis has effects at the brain level, causing changes in its functioning.

Hypnosis can be defined as a state of consciousness during which a person has intensified attention and concentration, allowing him to explore his thoughts, talents, and experiences that are not normally accessible to us. Many professionals in psychology and psychiatry consider it a useful, scientifically supported technique with the ability to treat medical and psychological conditions.

Why can't all people be hypnotized?

Not all people are susceptible to being hypnotized since some are more suggestible than others. Therefore, it is essential to know if a person can be hypnotized before starting hypnotherapy since this technique may not work.

According to a study, people who cannot be put into a hypnotic trance have less connectivity in the areas associated with executive control (planning, organization, short-term memory) and attention than highly hypnotizable people. These people may be less able to allow themselves to be absorbed by day-to-day experiences, in which attention, action planning is coupled.

However, it has recently been seen that it is possible to improve people's hypnotic capacity by stimulating certain areas of the brain.

What happens in the brain during hypnosis?

Less activity in the brain area related to rationality:

According to a study, during the hypnotic process, activity in the brain area related to rational cognitive functions decreases. During hypnosis, we make less use of rationality, planning, we get carried away, and we stop worrying.

Greater mind-body connection

Also, in this study, an increase in the connections between two brain areas (dorsolateral cortex and the insula) was observed, which allows the brain to process and control what is happening in the body. Hypnosis gives us more control over our bodies.

Fewer connections between actions and action consciousness:

Another finding was the decrease in the connections between two areas involved in action consciousness and the action itself. When we are committed and involved with something, we don't think about doing it or how, we just carry it out. That is, during hypnosis, we are less aware of our actions. We are allowed to be more involved in the activities that are suggested to us or that we suggest to ourselves, saving us the mental resources that are put in place when we are fully aware of the activity.

However, it is not that you lose control; on the contrary, people feel much more control over their sensory, motor, and body functions. What happens is that they do it in an involuntary sense, as if they were simply observed doing it but without participating.

Facilitates deep sleep

According to a study, listening to audios before bedtime hypnotics significantly increases the amount of produced slow waves during deep sleep. This indicates that hypnosis also provides great levels of relaxation, improving the quality of sleep.

What can hypnosis be used for?

In easily hypnotizable patients, this technique effectively relieves chronic pain, labour pain, treating tobacco addiction, post-traumatic stress disorder, and improving symptoms of anxiety, phobias, and sleep disorders. It has also been seen as effective in treating dementia symptoms.

History of Hypnosis

The first manifestations of hypnosis already occurred, in the form of self-hypnosis, among the primitive men, who, with their mysterious songs, their ritual dances, enigmatic passes, and words, made spells regarding magical powers. Thus, they became collectively desensitized to pain, had visions and overcame tiredness, cured functional disorders, and reached cataleptic states. This was the beginning of magic, the appearance of healers and healing sorcerers who exerted great influence on the tribe.

There is evidence that hypnosis was already used in ancient Egypt, specifically in Ebers. In a papyrus of more than 3,000 years old, studied by Bordeaux, it is indicated that hypnosis was used, with induction techniques very different from those we currently use, to lead subjects to deep states of drowsiness. In the bas-relief of a tomb of Thebes, we see an Egyptian priest hypnotizing a person. Hypnosis spread to everyone.

In Greece, these suggestion techniques were so effective that special temples called "sleep temples" began to be erected, in which Asclepios (Aesculapius), God of Medicine, was worshiped.

In India, it became completely dominated. Through the repetition of mantras and the techniques of suggestion, the yogis managed to dominate the state of self-hypnosis.

Mesmer (born in 1734 in Germany, Ph.D. in Philosophy and Medicine) very influenced by the theories of Paracelsus, who claimed that there was etheric energy creating matter (later called "magnetic force") that penetrated everything and exerted great influence on men began using magnets, was advised by the Jesuit Father Hell, to control the magnetic force and use its healing powers. After his first important cure in 1773 of a young woman named Francisca Oesterling, who suffered from fainting, urine retention, melancholy and temporary paralysis, among other symptoms, Mesmer soon filled her with magnets (she even had one on her neck) with which she achieved cures (surely due to suggestion).

During the treatment, Mesmer turns a vat (he built his famous bucket or health vat, a large wooden container, inside which he puts bottles with water magnetized by him. From the bottles come large rods that patients apply to the different parts of the body) observing the healing of the sick, from the infinitely poor to the richest. The more successful he was, the greater the Faculty of Medicine's complaints, which accused him of departing from traditional teachings.

In 1777, he cured Maria Teresa Paradis, daughter of the Ambassador of Vienna's secretary and goddaughter of the Empress, of blindness started at four years of age. Mesmer put her under treatment, providing a full recovery, but the blindness manifested again (suggesting hysterical blindness). A great scandal arose, joined by his medical rivals, and he had to leave for Paris.

In Paris, the success was not small, and Mesmer began to earn a lot of money. As planned, the doctors rejected his proposals. The first protests were not long in coming, which ended in a great scandal. Individuals, societies, and sects (including Freemasonry) unconditionally sided with him: "War on the Academy."

Upon verifying Mesmer's great prestige and his "miraculous cures," Louis XIV asked the Academy of Sciences for an official magnetism report. A report that declared the absence of any magnetic fluid and that "magnetism without imagination produces absolutely nothing."

An outstanding disciple of Mesmer, Puységur, magnetized a tree (an elm), and the sick who came to him fell asleep quickly.

In 1813, a priest from Portuguese India appeared, Father Faria. Faria denied the magnetic fluid existence and demonstrated it in public exhibitions in which he stared at a subject and shouted "Fall asleep!" His fascination called this induction system. From Faria, things began to clear up, and scientific hypnosis appeared, and it is based on the fact that everything consists of a psychophysiological state. However, the above trajectory should not be underestimated as it reveals the power of suggestion.

In 1819, a Catalan dentist surnamed Martorell, and a resident in Paris, was the first to remove a tooth without pain.

Scottish surgeon James Braid (1795-1861), after some experiences with his wife and assistant, formulated the following theory: "The sustained fixation on a person's gaze paralyzes the nervous centers of the eyes, destroying the balance of the nervous system and producing the dream state." Braid gave the name of hypnotism to this state.

Liebault, a young doctor at the French Academy of Sciences, after reading Braid's works, began working with hypnosis. His colleagues soon called him a charlatan, and even Bernheim went looking for him to humiliate him. But he was so surprised by what he saw that he joined him and together they formed Nancy's first school of hypnotism, where Bernheim published The Suggestion. These two doctors claimed that hypnosis is as effective as it is harmless.

Meanwhile, in Paris, Charcot experimented with Salpêtriere's hysterics, although he did not hypnotize but one of his students. Charcot sent a report to the Paris Academy of Medicine in 1882, in which he divided hypnosis into three states: lethargic, cataleptic, and sleepwalking. After being systematically rejected, hypnosis was finally recognized in the official scientific world. However, Charcot defined hypnosis as a symptom of hysteria. Hypnosis entered a moment of confusion.

In Spain, Ramón y Cajal proved to have a remarkable personal influence on his patients' imagination, and the success of hysteria and neurosis was so great that he had to close the office for lack of time to attend to people.

Already occupying the chair in Barcelona, his wife becomes pregnant with her sixth child. Silveria, who trusted him fully, allowed herself to be prepared and hypnotized when the time came, and in this way, her last two children were born.

Sigmund Freud at a conference in 1910 declared: "The history of psychoanalysis's genesis will never weigh the importance of hypnotism. In both the theoretical and therapeutic sense, psychoanalysis administers an inheritance that hypnotism transmitted to it."

After attending a hypnotist session during his student years, he became interested in the therapeutic possibilities of hypnosis when Breuer informs him about his hypnotic experiences in Anna "O.."

His stay in Paris and his relationship with Charcot and Bernheim made him aware of these possibilities. From 1886 he became a strong advocate of hypnotism in the German-speaking medical world. By 1887 he began to use the hypnotic suggestion, initially with the Bernheim procedure and later with Breuer's so-called "cathartic technique."

Between 1892 and 1896, he developed the method of free association, taking advantage of hypnosis experiences and technical aspects, especially Berheim's demonstrations of the possibilities of recovering memories of the hypnotic state during the waking state through voluntary concentration.

At the age of twenty-nine Freud had spent six months at Charcot's office where he was impressed by the reality of the hypnotic phenomenon, later he continued to train Nancy where he wrote: "I witnessed extraordinary experiences regarding the possibilities opened up by the powerful psychic procedures that, they were hidden from the conscience of man."

Later, together with Breuer, he established the ideas of hypnotic regression and dynamic psychotherapy. Psychoanalytic theory suggests that hypnosis is a regression state in which the patient does not have the controls present in normal waking consciousness, and therefore acts impulsively and engages in fantasy production.

Freud abandons hypnotic ritual methods, surely because he was a bad hypnotist, very abrupt, simple, and authoritarian, but also because he was afraid of transference phenomena that he could not control.

From his hypnosis experience, the conviction that the patient has all the necessary elements for his healing, was important to get him to express himself freely to help him free his unconscious.

After Freud, the study and use of hypnosis go through a dark stage except for a few words. The appearance of psychoanalysis and pharmacological anesthesia contribute to this fact.

An honorable exception is the work of Clark Hull (1933), this neo-behaviorist author takes up Berheim's ideas and postulates the absence of qualitative differences between suggestion and hypnosis. In "Hypnosis and Suggestionability," he explains how there are only quantitative differences between suggestibility in the hypnotic state and the waking state. For him, we must speak of suggestion and hypnosis from a perspective based on Pavlov's inherited experimental psychology (who had explained hypnosis as a phenomenon of cortical inhibition), placing special emphasis on the subject's responses to certain demands of the ambient.

Numerous authors throughout the 20th century have attached importance to the role of suggestion and suggestibility in psychology such as Binet (1900), Eysenck and Funrneaux (1945), Benton, and Bandura (1953), Stuark (1958), among others.

During World War II, the need for rapid and effective interventions revived interest in hypnosis. As a consequence, in the late 1940s, professional societies were founded with their respective publications: The Society for Clinical and Experimental Hypnosis (SCEH 1949) with the "The Journal of Clinical and Experimental Hypnosis," the International Society for Clinical and Experimental Hypnosis (ISH 1958) with the "International Journal of Clinical and Experimental Hypnosis," and the American Society of Clinical Hypnosis (ASCH, 1958) with the "American Journal of Clinical Hypnosis."

From the 1950s onwards, there was a revival, this time in the USA. Authors such as TX Barber, Martin Orne, William Kroger, Herbert Spiegel, ER Hilgard, TR Sarbin, Spanos, Chavez, Etzel Cardeña, Ph.D., among others, have been responsible for the increase in interest and the use of hypnosis, especially as a result of the influence of Dr. Milton H. Erickson and his work, which deserves a separate chapter in the historical evolution of Clinical Hypnosis.

Currently, the study and research in these areas are in a good moment. Over the past decades, prominent international groups of health professionals have publicly expressed their appreciation of hypnosis's therapeutic utility, including the American Medical Association, the British Medical Association, and the American Psychological Association.

The creation of the American Society of Clinical Hypnosis under division 30 of the APA (created in 1973) and the European Society of Hypnosis in Psychotherapy and Psychosomatic Medicine reinforce and incorporate numerous professionals' therapeutic and experimental scientific activity. The definitive entry of hypnosis into experimental psychology laboratories begins the period of the so-called Scientific Hypnosis based on the work of, especially three laboratories that will defend their perspectives, that of Hilgard founded in 1957 at Stanford University, which studies the hypnosis relationships with variables such as age, sex, personality characteristics, etc. Barber's (1959) at the Medfield Foundation of the Massachusetts Hospital studied the role and effects of imagination, expectations, beliefs, motivations, and emotions on the ability to be hypnotized and the psychophysiological reactions produced by hypnotic suggestions. Finally, Orne's founded in 1960 at Harvard University, later transferred to the Hospital of the University of Pennsylvania, dedicated to studying the motivational factors of hypnosis and different hypnotic phenomena such as hypnotic regression production of amnesia and hypermnesia.

All three groups have developed scales to measure suggestibility (e.g., Weizenhoffer and Hilgard 1959, 1962; Shor and Orne 1962; Barber and Wilson, 1978).

This state of the situation has brought the consolidation of the so-called Experimental Hypnosis, which studies the phenomena of hypnosis in a laboratory situation and will frequently qualify and criticize the results obtained in the clinical or applied field so-called Clinical Hypnosis.

CONCLUSION

Are you afraid of having a conflict with your friend or another significant one? Do you make bad choices to please him? Will you tell little white lies to avoid problems? Can you blame him for his unhappiness? Rush to pamper him when he's getting irritated? Do you suffer and give, give, give, and feel sad and lonely, anyway?

You might be under an expert's thumb at emotional manipulation.

An emotional manipulator (EM) unconsciously and often subconsciously regulates and manipulates others' emotions for his gain. He wants to take control and have power over you. He employs understated methods, often without you knowing it, to change your perceptions. Qualified emotional manipulators will get you to give up your emotional self-esteem. Once you put your well being into an EM's hands, he will try to get control over you, methodically chipping away until there's very little left of the original.

How can that happen to you, and what kind of person becomes a manipulator of emotions? He makes use of underhanded methods.

Many EM's are narcissistic and feel a sense of entitlement because of their upbringing or genetics or a combination of both. As children, they may have been subjected to similar emotional abuse by their parents. Or, oddly enough, those kids could have been over-indulged or neglected. Extremes of either can in later life push a child into narcissism.

The entitlement of a narcissist makes them feel they should have what they wish without earning it. They don't need to take responsibility for themselves or their behavior. They don't have to be honest or treat other people fairly. It all has to do with them and what the world has done to them.

So how can a pretty person like you fall under an emotional manipulator 's spell?

You might be co-dependent and attracted to an emotional manipulator. You don't like to be alone either. If you are co-dependent, you'll need people to be helped. You feel the need to take care of anybody. And the emotional manipulator needs somebody to look after him.

It is so easy to fall for the EM who instantly develops trust with you. He shares with you deep emotions, and you perceive him to be delightfully sensitive, open, and perhaps a little vulnerable. You want to help him. And slowly you're getting engaged.

You are hooked after that, and you don't even notice that you are being manipulated emotionally.